T0083190

From Blue Mills to Columbia

Cedar Falls and the Civil War

From Blue Mills to Columbia

Cedar Falls and the Civil War

Kenneth L. Lyftogt

University of Iowa Press, Iowa City

University of Iowa Press, Iowa City 52242
www.uiowapress.org
Copyright © 1993 by the Iowa State University Press
University of Iowa Press paperback edition, 2007
Printed in the United States of America

No part of this book may be reproduced or used in any form or by any
means without permission in writing from the publisher. All reasonable
steps have been taken to contact copyright holders of material
used in this book. The publisher would be pleased to make suitable
arrangements with any whom it has not been possible to reach.

The University of Iowa Press is a member of Green Press Initiative and
is committed to preserving natural resources.

Printed on acid-free paper

Library of Congress Cataloging-in-Publication Data
Lyftogt, Kenneth.
From Blue Mills to Columbia: Cedar Falls and the Civil War /
by Kenneth L. Lyftogt.—University of Iowa Press pbk. ed.
p.   cm.
Originally published: Ames: Iowa State University Press, c1993.
Includes bibliographical references and index.
ISBN-13: 978-1-58729-611-6 (pbk.)
ISBN-10: 1-58729-611-X (pbk.)
1. Cedar Falls (Iowa)—History—19th century.   2. Cedar Falls (Iowa)—
History, Military—19th century.   3. Cedar Falls (Iowa)—Social
conditions—19th century.   4. Iowa—History—Civil War, 1861–1865.
5. Iowa—History—Civil War, 1861–1865—Social aspects.   6. United
States—History—Civil War, 1861–1865—Social aspects.   I. Title.
F629.C28l94   2007   2007009471
977.7'02—dc22

07 08 09 10 11 P 5 4 3 2 1

CONTENTS

ACKNOWLEDGMENTS *vii*

1 A Town on the Cedar *3*

2 The Pioneer Greys *12*

3 Missouri *25*

4 Home in Cedar Falls *39*

5 Shiloh *46*

6 The Cedar Falls Reserves *60*

7 Vicksburg *79*

8 A Third Summer *90*

9 Chattanooga *103*

10 Atlanta *115*

11 Marching through Georgia *134*

12 Triumph and Tragedy *145*

EPILOGUE *162*

NOTES *167*

REFERENCES *179*

INDEX *183*

ACKNOWLEDGMENTS

This book began as my M.A. thesis in history at the University of Northern Iowa. The thesis was the 1989 recipient of the university's Outstanding Thesis Award. I am very much indebted to the members of my thesis committee, Alvin Sunseri, Robert Martin, and Theodore Hovet. Dr. Sunseri was the university's authority on the Civil War as well as a friend. Many aspects of the book were the result of casual conversations with him. All three members served as more than just committee people; they provided much of the needed quality control.

Many individuals aided in the many stages of the work. Michael Prahl has been a friend, confidant, and tireless advisor for over 20 years. This book is a tribute to his skill and patience. Rosie Peterson of the Cedar Falls Historical Society was an invaluable help with much of the research. She and Rosemary Beach served as proofreaders, as did Jeff Piper of the Northeast Iowa Civil War Association.

Many citizens of the area were kind enough to share their personal collections of letters and diaries. Among these are the Robert Klein family and Jean Parker of Waterloo. Andrew J. Karl drew the original maps. Mike Hudson and Gary Voss of *Ireland Publishing and Design* created the original manuscript. Mary Russell Curran did the copyediting.

I would also like to express my appreciation to some of the individuals who aided the work in ways that they may never know. William Graves first suggested that a book like this would make a dandy thesis, and his idea took me into graduate school. John Johnson, head of the university's Department of History, has been a friend and supporter. Robert Gish, Glenda Riley, Charles Quirk, Leland Sage, David Walker, Harold Wohl, Cal Wolfe, and Steve Moravec are but a few of the friends and colleagues who served as inspiration throughout the project.

The last note of thanks goes to the Grateful Dead and the Quicksilver Messenger Service for providing typing music.

From Blue Mills to Columbia

Cedar Falls and the Civil War

1

A Town on the Cedar

Ayoung army explorer named Albert Lea led a troop of cavalry through the valley of the Cedar River in 1835. The Cedar, known originally as the Red Cedar, was the key waterway in northeast Iowa, and Lea was much impressed at what he saw. He wrote that

> the river is perennially supplied with pure and limpid water, and as it meanders its way for 300 miles to the Father of Waters, receiving large tributary streams, as it moves along through rich meadows, deep forests, projecting cliffs and sloping landscapes, it presents to the imagination the finest picture on earth of a country prepared by Providence for the habitation of man.[1]

At the time of Lea's journey, Iowa was a part of the Wisconsin Territory, which had been acquired from France in 1803 as a part of the Louisiana Purchase. Land-hungry settlers could see the beauty of the territory just west of the Mississippi. They could also see its potential, and by 1846, when Iowa was admitted as a state, major communities had been established along the principal rivers. Independent farmers were claiming land, breaking the tough prairie topsoil, planting crops, and building homes. It was an ideal place for pioneers.

The first white people to set up their camps in the Cedar Valley were traders and trappers, people who had no intention of settling there permanently. They sought convenient sites where they could trap near the streams and rivers, hunt in the forests, and trade with the few remaining Native Americans. Since the defeat of Chief Black Hawk in 1832, most were being driven from the territory.

The first settler to look beyond a traders' camp was a Canadian-born farmer named William Sturgis. Sturgis was living in Iowa City with his wife, Dorothy Kidder Sturgis, when he heard of good land near a small waterfall a few miles from where the Cedar joined the Shell Rock River. Sturgis and Dorothy, accompanied by his sister, Catherine, and her

3

husband, Erasmus Adams, packed their covered wagons and moved there in the spring of 1845. The men filed land claims: Sturgis chose an area on the south bank of the river near the falls, and Adams selected a spot a little farther south.[2]

Both couples built cabins, cleared about five acres of ground for crops, and began their new lives. Both women had babies in their new homes, and soon other families settled near them. A real community was beginning: by 1847, ten families were living near the falls, and they began to call their little town Sturgis Falls.[3]

William Sturgis had selected the site near the falls with a larger purpose in mind. He could imagine the near future when the valley would be filled with farms. The farmers would need to have their grain milled and transported downriver to the eastern markets. The future of the town lay with the river, and he had plans for both a dam and a mill.

Sturgis's plans would indeed come to fruition but not through his efforts. Such ambitious plans required money, and though he was able to construct a rough dam, he could not afford to do the job properly. The job was completed by the Overman brothers, John and Dempsey, along with their partner, John T. Barrick. The partnership of Overman and Barrick purchased the Sturgis claim in the fall of 1847, and Sturgis returned to Iowa City.

Work on the mill began in earnest the next spring. Many of the growing number of settlers were employed on the project. They hollowed out the ground just south of the river and created a millrace 70 feet wide and six feet deep, which would carry water to the mill's wheels.[4] They soon had the first sawmill in what was by then Black Hawk County. The rough board mill was torn down in 1850 and replaced by a large, five-story stone building. The new building housed both the sawmill operation and the first gristmill in the county. The gristmill was a crude affair—the burrs had been carved from granite boulders found along the banks of the river—but it worked. Soon farmers from the length of the upper Cedar Valley and from as far away as Fort Dodge, 100 miles to the west, were driving their grain-filled wagons to the falls. As the town grew and changed, the name also changed. The first name, Sturgis Falls, had honored the first settler family; the new name—Cedar Falls—honored the river and the forests along its banks.[5]

Frontier life carried with it intrinsic physical hardships and the possibility of violence. Despite rough times and setbacks, the town grew rapidly in its first years. By 1855, nine waterwheels on the river supplied power not only to the large Overman mill but also to three other sawmills and a furniture factory. The four-block downtown area, near the millrace and stretching southwest of the river, was a busy place.

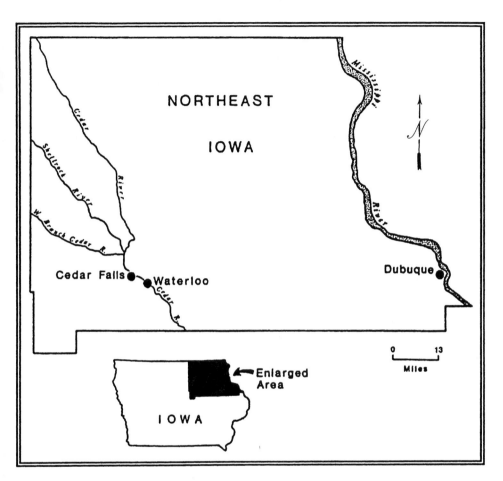

NORTHEAST IOWA
Map by Andrew J. Karl

It boasted a general store run by an Irish-born merchant, Andrew Mullarky, and a newspaper, the *Cedar Falls Banner,* as well as other stores and businesses. There was a full block of multistoried brick buildings—the Overman Block. The largest of these buildings, the Overman Building, had several halls large enough to seat hundreds of people. A school on the corner of Fifth and Main streets was crowned with a belfry. The citizens of Cedar Falls had been so proud of their new frame schoolhouse that they had raised funds and sent to New York for a 150-pound bell, the first tower bell in the state. A brick factory just south of town turned out more than 75,000 fired bricks in 1855.[6]

Cedar Falls was named the county seat of Black Hawk County in 1853, and John Overman donated 50 town lots as the site of the proposed courthouse. Andrew Mullarky's store served as the unofficial seat of county government in the meantime.

Cedar Falls was not, however, the only prospering young community in the county. Waterloo, also located on the Cedar and closer to the center of the county, was another contender for the honor of being the county seat. A sometimes bitter rivalry grew between the people of the two communities. A mob from Waterloo invaded Cedar Falls on one occasion and tried to storm Mullarky's store and carry off the official records. Local legend has the battle ending with the determined citizens of Cedar Falls driving the Waterloo bunch out of town by pelting them with rotten eggs. The incident did not settle the issue, however, and in 1855 Iowa's General Assembly called for a new election. Cedar Falls lost the county seat by a 260-to-388 vote, but many people in Cedar Falls complained that outsiders had been brought to Waterloo to cast illegal ballots.[7]

When the town lost the battle for the county seat, Overman's donated land was used as a downtown park. In spite of the loss, however, Cedar Falls continued to grow. It was a Yankee town, settled for the most part by people from New England, New York, and the states of the old Northwest Territory—hard-working people who took a great deal of pride in their new home.[8] Two of the most important of these early community builders were Peter Melendy and Zimri Streeter.

Melendy had been born in 1823, the son of a successful Cincinnati businessman. He grew up as Cincinnati changed from a small town to a modern city, and its progress showed the young man just what ambitious people could accomplish. From an early age, he had developed a keen interest in all aspects of agriculture and stock breeding and had become well known throughout Ohio for both his knowledge of farming techniques and his business expertise. Melendy and several other Ohio businessmen had become interested in Iowa as a possible place to set up a large-scale farming and stock-raising operation. The venture failed; for while such an operation could work on a limited basis, a truly large operation required better means of transport than Iowa's rivers and dirt roads. It needed a railroad, and no line was anywhere near. The Ohio Company had ceased operations by 1859.[9]

Although the company lost money, the project had fired Melendy's enthusiasm for Iowa. While in Iowa, Melendy had started a correspondence with the *Cedar Falls Banner* editors, who persuaded him to visit the town. He did visit and was very impressed by the apparent progress and future potential of the place. Melendy purchased land at the edge of town, on the corner of Washington and Tenth streets, and built a fine house for himself, his wife, Martha, and their two small children. He formed a partnership with A. J. Graves in early 1860, selling farm machinery and tools. Once established as a citizen of Cedar Falls, he became one of its staunchest supporters, freely giving his aid to all social, educational, business, and political activities.[10]

Zimri Streeter was one of the original settlers in Black Hawk County. He was born in 1801 and was more than 50 years old when he brought his wife, Lucinda Dean Streeter, and their 10 children from Illinois to Iowa. The large Streeter cabin was situated halfway between Cedar Falls and Waterloo, and Zimri Streeter tried to serve the interests of both communities. For example, he worked to calm the tensions that had arisen during the battles for the county seat. Elected to the Seventh General Assembly of Iowa, the first to meet in the new capitol in Des Moines, he quickly became known as a practical, commonsense politician and was nicknamed "Old Black Hawk" by his fellow legislators. In an age of fiery oratory, Streeter defied convention with his short, often humorous but still pertinent speeches.

There were many more such pioneers, all doing their part to build the town, people like Samuel and James Q. Rownd, Henry and George Perkins, George H. Boehmler, and the Massachusetts colonel, William Sessions.

Samuel and James Rownd were born and raised in Ohio. Samuel became a successful land speculator, and in 1850 he and his wife, Eliza, and her brother, George Philpot, drove a horse and buggy to Sturgis Falls. Rownd purchased more than 4,000 acres of land just southeast of town. He used old land grants given to Mexican War veterans in lieu of their pay, purchased at less than half their worth, as payment. Rownd and Philpot continued to live in Ohio until 1859, when both men pulled up stakes and moved their families to the Falls.[11]

James Q. Rownd had been a tanner, a potter, and a schoolteacher in Ohio. His first wife, the mother of their eight children, Ann Lawvey Rownd, died in 1840. The widower married Caroline Brown 18 months later. The family lived in Summerfield, Ohio, until 1856 when, after hearing descriptions of Cedar Falls, he decided to move his family there too, settling on a 240-acre farm just outside of town.[12]

The owners of the *Cedar Falls Banner* moved their operation to Waterloo in 1858, leaving Cedar Falls without a newspaper. Henry and George Perkins arrived in 1860 and set up another paper, the *Cedar Falls Gazette*. The brothers were from New York, where they had learned the printer's trade. Once in Cedar Falls, they quickly established themselves as leading boosters of the town. They found a friend and fellow community builder in Peter Melendy. They asked Melendy to write a regular column for their weekly paper that would keep the area's farmers informed of the latest farming techniques and innovations. Melendy's column was an example of the Perkins's personal approach to journalism.

Mexican War veteran Colonel William Sessions, his wife, Elmira, and their three sons and two daughters came to Cedar Falls from Massachusetts in 1859. The colonel was an experienced organizer and quickly found himself involved in many community activities. His eldest son, Fitzroy, 29 years old, was appointed constable of Cedar Falls.[13]

George H. Boehmler, who operated a large shoemaker's shop on Main Street, came from the Alsace region of France in 1803 and settled in New York, where he and his wife had four children. His first wife, whose name is not recorded, died when their eldest child was 14. George remarried a few years later. His new wife, Barbara Schoffner Boehmler, was also an immigrant from Alsace, and in 1858 the family, now numbering 10 boys and two girls, drove a covered wagon to Iowa.[14]

Samuel and James Rownd and George Boehmler were middle-aged men, family men seeking new homes and opportunities. Other Cedar Falls residents were younger people just beginning to make their way. George and John Rath were two examples. The Rath brothers were born in Germany and had come to the United States in 1855, when George was 18 and John 15. They first lived with relatives in Dubuque, where they worked, went to school, and learned English. They moved to Cedar Falls in early 1861. George was employed as a cabinetmaker and John worked in the town's second flour mill, a large, six-story stone building that had recently been opened by Edwin Brown.[15]

Brown's new mill was another example of how rapidly Cedar Falls was growing. By 1860, there were more than 1,500 people living there and hundreds more living on nearby farms. There was regular communication with Cedar Rapids, Des Moines, and Dubuque by stagecoach.

Peter Melendy's farming and stock-raising project had failed because there was no railroad, so he became one of the leading figures behind efforts to bring a line to Cedar Falls. In 1858, an agreement was reached with the Dubuque and Pacific Railroad. The citizens of Black Hawk County subscribed a total of $300,000 in land and cash to ensure its completion. Cedar Falls businessmen such as Peter Melendy, the Overmans, and Edwin Brown put much of their personal fortunes into the project. All totaled, the people of Cedar Falls put up one-third of the county's money. This was done with the understanding that Cedar Falls would be the end of the division and that the roundhouse and machine shops would be located there. Although the Dubuque and Pacific Railroad failed in 1860, it was taken over by the Dubuque and Sioux City line, which honored the old agreement.[16]

The new railroad grade was on the northeast side of the Cedar, and by March 1861, anyone downtown could look across the water and see men working and the huge locomotives puffing their way along the tracks. The new railroad company was hard-pressed for money, and while the line could get to Cedar Falls, it could go no farther. There was not enough money to build a railroad bridge across the river, so the new depot had to be built on the northeast side, opposite the downtown area. Access was over the town's Millrace Bridge, a 16-foot-wide, five-pier, wooden bridge built in 1857. When it was obvious that the line was nearing completion, plans were made to host the biggest celebration in the town's history.[17]

The spring of 1861 had been very wet; it seemed that it rained every day. The streets of Cedar Falls, which still had hundreds of tree stumps in them, became thick with mud and all but impassable for wagons and teams. On 11 April 1861, several thousand people from the surrounding farms and nearby towns ignored the mud and came to join in the festival.

At 4:00 in the afternoon, a procession of citizens was formed by the appointed parade marshals. Mill owner John M. Overman proudly led the march. Music was supplied by the town's brass band, which had been organized by Dempsey Overman a year earlier. The band was making its first public appearance seated in a new, brightly painted wagon drawn by a full four-horse hitch. The procession marched across the Millrace Bridge to the new buildings of the depot, where the marchers stopped, each person in the crowd looking down the tracks for the train. At 4:45 they heard a train whistle, and in a few moments they could see the smoke from the locomotive. As the huge engine approached, the people began to cheer and shout, and in a moment the first train into town stopped at the depot.[18]

The women of Cedar Falls had organized a women's association designed to improve the town, and their group had helped plan the celebration. The women had fashioned a large wreath from evergreen boughs in honor of the occasion. Jennie Powers, wife of lawyer Joseph P. Powers, and Mary Cameron, wife of businessman John R. Cameron, were chosen to represent the ladies of Cedar Falls by placing the wreath over the engine's smokestack. Attached to the wreath were a number of cards from individuals, local organizations, and businesses. Each card bore a message, such as

Dubuque editors—We thank you for your efforts in behalf of Cedar Falls.

Iron Horse—The best blood of modern stock.

Ladies of Dubuque—We hope to meet you and greet you at a future time in large numbers.

Ladies—the true moral conductors on the great railroad of life may they never grow less.

Ladies of Dubuque—Second to none, but the bright eyes and warm hearts of the ladies of this wide awake village.

We greet you one and all. W. H. Sessions, H. H. Carpenter, G. B. Van Saun, George Secord, A. F. Brown, Edwin Brown, J. B. Powers, P. Melendy.[19]

A speakers' stand and stage had been constructed at the depot, and there were 128 local dignitaries on hand to formally greet the passengers, many of whom were from Dubuque. One passenger was Herman Gelpeke, president of the Dubuque and Sioux City Railroad, and accompanying him were several other officials of the line. The keynote speaker for the day was Cedar Falls lawyer Alfred E. Brown. Brown had been the first notary in Cedar Falls in 1853 and was now the first state senator elected from the young town. Directing his attention to the railroad executives, he said,

We contemplate this event gentlemen with feelings of the most unlimited satisfaction: a satisfaction which arises not merely from the fact that we have secured a railroad connection with Dubuque and the entire eastern States, but more because in its completion the people find the substantial guarantee of permanent and increasing prosperity.[20]

President Gelpeke then took the stand. After thanking the people of Cedar Falls for their past support and the day's celebration, he gave a short speech, in which he expressed an equal optimism for a very prosperous future. There were more speeches, and in the evening the crowd went to the Overman Building for an evening of toasts and speeches. The celebration was followed by a dance, which lasted until well after midnight. The next day the train left town, carrying as passengers some leading Cedar Falls businessmen, the first people to ride the cars to Dubuque.

The next day, 12 April 1861, while the farmers stayed home and tended to their crops and stock and local citizens went back to their daily jobs, Henry and George Perkins hurried to put out a very important edition of the *Gazette*. It contained a detailed account of the great railroad celebration, the most important news in the valley. But while the paper's newsboys carried their copies to subscribers or hawked them on the streets, a more important story was taking place more than 1,200 miles away. A gun crew, sworn in allegiance to a new government, the Confederate States of America, was taking aim at the U.S. flag flying over Fort Sumter in the harbor of Charleston, South Carolina.

2

The Pioneer Greys

The enthusiastic speeches made at the Cedar Falls railroad celebration had emphasized the grains, wools, and other goods that would soon be carried out of the valley. Those who made the speeches could not know that the guns at faraway Fort Sumter had created a new demand. There would soon be another more immediate and more precious cargo shipped out on the rails—volunteer soldiers for the Union armies.

The guns fired from Charleston were the first shots of a bloody, four-year tragedy in which the Southern states tried to tear themselves loose from the rest of the country. There were many reasons for the war, for the United States had never been a simple, homogeneous society. Each of its sections had its own origins, traditions, and values. The differences were most clearly exemplified by the Southern institution of race—slavery. Most Northern states, including Iowa, had harsh laws on their books that discriminated against black people and served to discourage any but whites from settling there. But while such laws represented racial bigotry, they also forbade the practice of enslavement.

The ongoing conflict between slave and free states was brought to a head by the United States victory in the war with Mexico. Mexico's defeat in 1848 had cost it most of its land claims north of the Rio Grande. That area included California and most of the present-day southwestern states. The new lands belonged to the nation as a whole, and slaveholders took the position that they could take their slaves along when they settled there. Free-soil advocates disagreed and said that the national Congress had a responsibility to protect free labor by restricting the spread of slavery.

Iowa had come into the Union as a free state, the first created from the Louisiana Purchase, as a result of congressional action. Statehood had come under the terms of the Missouri Compromise of 1820, which forbade slavery north of Missouri's northern border. Iowans often agreed with their southern neighbor's racial views, but they drew the line at slavery. The pioneer dream was of success achieved through one's own ambition and drive. John and Dempsey Overman had not needed slave labor to build the Cedar Falls millrace and grain mill: they had hired free labor. Their employees were men like Edwin Brown, people with their own dreams and ambitions beyond laboring for the Overmans. Most Cedar Falls people, like most Iowans, agreed that Congress should regulate the spread of slavery. As far as they were concerned, the Missouri Compromise line should be extended clear to the Pacific Ocean. Let the Southerners keep their slaves, but don't let the hated institution spread north.

By 1859, only 1,069 black people were living in Iowa. Most were in the east along the Mississippi, where they were often employed on the waterfronts or in the lead mines. The 1860 census showed only five blacks in Cedar Falls. Two—a man named Hilary W. Bauk and a woman, Minerva Dutton—resided with local families and were presumably employed by them. Another man, William Dutton, lived with his eight-year-old son and a four-year-old girl dependent. Dutton earned his living as a barber, and his business was as much in the spirit of pioneer free labor as was Boehmler's shoe shop or Mullarky's general store.[1]

Political parties that might have served to unify the country tore themselves apart over the issue of slavery. The Democratic Party split into Northern and Southern wings. The old Whig Party fell apart, and numerous smaller parties, such as the Free Soil Party, emerged. Stephen Douglas, a Democratic senator from Illinois, tried to repair the split in his party by introducing what he called the principle of "popular sovereignty." In its simplest form, popular sovereignty held that when the territories were organized as states, it would be up to the people in those territories to vote whether or not to allow slavery.

Douglas's position did not heal the split in his party, but it drove home the last few nails in the coffin of the Whig Party. It also shoved the Kansas Territory into its own civil war, as advocates of both slave- and free-state status fought for control. The bloodshed in Kansas and the threat of new slave states in the West gave life to a new party, the Republican Party.

The central core of the new party was made up of old antislavery Whigs and Democrats. The party also attracted former members of the American Party, the Free Soil Party, a few true abolitionists, and many reform-minded young people just coming of voting age.[2] While the slavery issue served as a powerful catalyst, the combination of elements gave the party a diversity and depth beyond any single issue.

The Republican Party, formed in 1854, was able to field candidates for both state and national offices in the 1856 elections. The Republican presidential nominee, John C. Fremont, did very well, though he lost to

"DEPARTURE OF VOLUNTEERS FROM DUBUQUE, IOWA, APRIL 22, 1861"
From Harper's Weekly

James Buchanan in the national race. Republicans on the local level won many key offices. Iowa Republicans won control of both houses of the General Assembly and sent two of their members to Congress. Iowa's governor, James W. Grimes, elected as a Whig, was within a year calling himself a Republican. Fremont's strong showing and the numerous local victories showed that the party had a good shot at victory in the 1860 election.[3]

The party's candidate for the 1860 race was a former Whig congressman named Abraham Lincoln. Lincoln had earned a national reputation as an able spokesman for the free-soil position when, in 1858, he engaged Stephen Douglas in a series of debates on popular sovereignty. While the Republicans closed ranks and supported Lincoln and his running mate, Hannibal Hamlin, the Democrats fell apart. The Northern wing of the party nominated Stephen Douglas, while the Southern wing nominated former Vice-President John C. Breckinridge of Kentucky.

There were few moderates left. Southern leaders had made it clear that a Republican victory would mean an end to the Union. They would pull their states out and form their own nation.

The passions of the 1850s were felt strongly in Cedar Falls. Many of the town's leading citizens joined the Republican Party and made Cedar Falls one of Iowa's Republican strongholds. One of the best examples was Peter Melendy. Melendy's family had been firmly antislavery. In fact, his uncle, John Melendy, was an outspoken, active abolitionist.[4] Melendy's organizational skills and personal energy were well suited to politics. When the Republican Party was formed, Melendy joined it and in 1856 voted for John C. Fremont.[5]

Melendy was not alone in making Cedar Falls a Republican town. Henry and George Perkins had founded the *Cedar Falls Gazette* as a Republican paper in open opposition to the Democratic papers in the state, the *Dubuque Herald* in particular. The Perkins brothers stated their politics in their first issue:

> Firmly and conscientiously believing that the principles of the Republican Party . . . are above all others, best calculated to promote the vital interests of this country, and secure to the "greatest number the greatest good" we shall unflinchingly advocate its doctrines and labor earnestly for its success.[6]

State representative Zimri Streeter, "Old Black Hawk," was another leading Republican voice, as was Colonel William Sessions and his son, Fitzroy Sessions. State senator A. F. Brown claimed Republican credentials, as did the early settlers Erasmus Adams and Edwin Brown. Early in 1860, the members formed the Republican Club as a way to advance their ideas. They met in a large room of the Overman Building, and they hung a banner outside the Main Street window which read "Republican Headquarters."[7] After the party selected Lincoln at its national convention, the Cedar Falls Republican Club was renamed the Lincoln and Hamlin Club. Colonel Sessions had attended the national convention and was elected as the new club's first president.[8]

That fall, club members began to organize a pro-Lincoln rally, one they hoped would be the largest political event ever seen in the county. Invitations were sent to officials across the state and to other Republican clubs in the nearby towns asking them to come to Cedar Falls on 6 September and join in.

It was a pleasant autumn day, a bit cloudy and not too warm. The first of the up-country delegations to arrive was the one from Charles City, 50 miles to the north. Its members had prepared several large banners, which read "We Maul Black Democracy," "Lincoln and Hamlin the People's Choice," and "A Free Press and Free Homes For Free Men."

About 10:00 on the morning of the sixth, the next delegation arrived, this one from Bremer County. The Bremer County people arrived with 20 wagons and teams. Most of them were four-horse hitches, and one had six horses. The delegation from Butler County was next to arrive. The long column included people from New Hartford, Willoughby, and Butler Center and was led by a large wagon drawn by six horses. The wagon was followed by an 18-by-20-foot flatboat that had been put up on wheels and was drawn by six horses. The Butler County banners read "Protection To Industry, Improvements of Rivers and Harbors" and "Free Homes and Free Territories are Farmers' Mechanics' and Sailors' Rights." The Butler Center delegation carried a banner which read "We Are For Lands For the Landless, Not Niggers For the Niggerless."

The Waterloo Republicans sent more than 100 people to the rally. Many rode in a large platform wagon, and others rode in carriages or came on horseback. The delegation from the small town of Vinton brought their brass band along; they arrived riding in a colorful wagon drawn by four horses. At about 10:30 in the morning, the parade marshal, Dempsey Overman, assisted by Constable Fitzroy Sessions, formed the different delegations into a column, and the great parade began.

First in line were the carriages carrying Zimri Streeter, honorary president of the day, and the other guest speakers: Tom Drummond of Vinton, S. P. Adams of Dubuque, and John A. Kasson of Des Moines. The carriages were followed by the Cedar Falls Brass Band in their brightly painted wagon, and then came the long procession of teams, wagons, and carriages of the other delegations. The Cedar Falls Lincoln and Hamlin Club was last, and its display was striking. Members carried a large portrait of Lincoln at the head of their part of the parade. Those carrying the portrait were followed by a "Liberty Car," which contained 33 young girls, each dressed in white and carrying a small U.S. flag. Hanging from the top of the float was a banner which read "Our Fathers Are For Lincoln."

At the rear of the Liberty Car, outside of its box, rode another little girl, strikingly dressed in black and wearing a red sash. She represented the bloody state of Kansas, which was still kept out of the Union. A 20-foot flatboat that had been put on wheels and drawn by three oxen followed the Liberty Car. One hundred flag-waving women rode inside the boat. Banners on the side of the boat read "Old Abe Is Going To Be President" and "Hurrah For 'Old Abe' Who Is For National and Constitutional Rights."

The Liberty Car flatboat was followed by another flatboat. The second ox-drawn boat contained a 22-year-old laborer named Dave Stitler. Stitler was a tall, lanky man, and many said he was a dead ringer for Lincoln. This day he was dressed like Lincoln and was busy swinging a maul as he split several Lincoln-type rails while riding in the boat. Next was a wagon that contained an arrangement designed to ridicule Stephen Douglas: a Douglas effigy was perched on a log cart, and the cart was drawn by two mules. The rest of the parade was made up of citizens from Cedar Falls and the surrounding countryside. They carried more banners, which read "God Made the Territories Free and Pronounced Them Good," "No More Slave Territory," and "The Union Shall and Must Be Preserved."

After enthusiastic speeches by Tom Drummond, John A. Kasson, and other well-known Republicans, the rally was adjourned. In the evening, it reconvened in the largest hall of the Overman Building, Overman Hall. The large room was filled, and the Cedar Falls Brass Band played a variety of martial tunes. There were more speeches and more cheering. Large transparencies in the windows of Overman Hall and the windows of other downtown buildings glowed out into the darkness: "By the Law of Nature and of God All Men Are Free—Abraham Lincoln," "Abe Is the Choice of Free Men of the West," "Republicanism—Protection To Freedom In the Territories," "Mudsills and Greasy Mechanics Are For Lincoln," and "Free Labor the Hope of the World."

The Ladies of Cedar Falls had prepared a large meal, which they served after the speeches were finished. The meal was followed by a grand ball, which lasted through the night. The first Republican rally in Cedar Falls had been a success.[9]

On 6 November 1860, the Cedar Falls Republicans joined the rest of the nation at the polls. The result was a Republican victory, with Lincoln receiving 1,866,000 votes to Douglas's 1,383,000. John Breckinridge received 848,000 votes, and John Bell of the Constitutional Union Party received 593,000. The votes in the Electoral College reflected the sectional nature of the contest. Lincoln carried 18 states, all of them Northern free states. Breckinridge carried 11 slave states, Douglas carried one slave and one free state, and Bell carried three slave states.[10]

The voters of Iowa supported Lincoln by 70,118 votes to Douglas's 55,639 and Bell's 1,763. The Republicans also scored well in local contests; the most important were the two seats in Congress won by Samuel R. Curtis of Keokuk and William Vandever of Dubuque. The party won in Black Hawk County by 1,122 votes to 557. Abraham Lincoln received 218 votes in Cedar Falls, and Douglas received 115. After the votes had been carefully recounted, the victorious Cedar Falls Republicans threw a celebration on Main Street on the night of 10 November. There were fireworks and a large bonfire. Men fired their muskets into the air and cheered themselves hoarse. Some rowdies in the crowd even went so far as to throw rocks and fireballs at the homes of well-known Democrats, breaking a few of their windows in the process.[11]

Lincoln's election was unacceptable to the South. A Republican victory meant a war for Southern independence, a civil war.

Iowa was not ready for war; there were no military forts, no organized state militia, and few arms for volunteers.[12] Iowa's governor, Samuel J. Kirkwood, was advised by the national government to organize Iowa's militia in case it was needed. The governor's task was simplified because communities across the state had already begun to organize their own volunteer companies, which they offered to the government.

The first meeting of men who wanted to start a military company in Cedar Falls was held on the evening of 19 January 1861. Henry and George Perkins supported the effort and used their paper to encourage enlistment. After the first steps had been taken, the *Gazette* carried this editorial statement:

> We have the material here from which to form a "crack corps," which, if properly organized and equipped, would be of great advantage to us on our gala days and public occasions,—and who knows but in these troublesome times might be the means of preserving the country from ruin and give some of the members an opportunity to cover themselves with immortal glory. Let us have the "sogers" by all means.[13]

The Cedar Falls company numbered 40 men by February and was under the command of their elected captain, John B. Smith. Smith was a former resident of Dubuque who, in October 1860, had moved to Cedar

Falls, where he managed the Carter House Hotel. The men of Smith's company were proud of their frontier heritage and chose to call their company the Pioneer Greys. The Greys, named after the traditional uniform color of the day, leased a large hall on the third floor of the Overman Building and used it as their arsenal and meeting place. They were serious about their duty and appearance as soldiers. Their first public statement proclaimed that "We intend by gentlemanly and soldierly deportment, and strict drill and discipline, to earn a name which shall neither discredit ourselves or the town in which we live."[14]

The Greys were fortunate in that there were several members, and other men in Cedar Falls, with military experience. Smith had been a member of one of Iowa's first militia units, the Governor's Greys.[15] Fitzroy Sessions, orderly sergeant of the Greys, had learned military matters from his father, the colonel, and while they lived in Massachusetts, he had been a member of a local militia company.[16] Peter Melendy was not a member of the company, but for five years he had been a member of Cincinatti's Harrison Guards and had achieved the rank of first lieutenant.[17]

The Pioneer Greys were an established part of Cedar Falls by early spring. The *Gazette* continued to publish glowing descriptions of the company, such as the following:

> We now have a real live "Infantry Corps," numbering 60 rank and file, and is composed of men whose motto is "Excelsior," and who are determined to do their whole duty under any and all circumstances; men who respect and revere the names and memories of those who suffered and sacrificed so much that we their descendants might enjoy the blessings of a government, free and based upon equality and intelligence, as contrasted with aristocracy and ignorance.[18]

Governor Kirkwood was relaxing at his home in Iowa City when a telegram arrived from U.S. Secretary of War Simon Cameron. It specified Iowa's share of troops to put down the rebellion, and had come over the wire at Davenport. The telegraph lines had not yet gone beyond Davenport, and to avoid any delays, Congressman William Vandever volunteered to carry the message to the governor by train. He found Kirkwood working near his barn and gave him the message. When Kirkwood read it, he exclaimed: "The President wants a *whole regiment of men*! Do you suppose, Mr. Vandever, I can raise that many?"[19] The governor had no reason to fear, for across the state the hometown companies all seemed eager to volunteer. The hometown company from Cedar Falls was no exception.

The war mood in Cedar Falls was expressed in the *Gazette*, which, after the surrender of federal troops in Fort Sumter, carried this message:

Sumter has fallen, treason is triumphant, and the rattlesnake bunting flaunts in defiance of the Federal Government. To the question "How will this matter end?" there can now be but one answer. It must end in war—terrible, devastating war, all the more terrible because waged between those but lately bound together by the ties of a common country. . . . But terrible as the results appear; horrible and sickening as is the idea of civil war, in the present case we do not see how it can now be avoided.[20]

Three days after Lincoln's call to arms on 18 April 1861, the Pioneer Greys received a communication from Iowa's adjutant general, Jessie Bowen, asking that the company be brought up to wartime strength and stand ready to be called into active service. Two days later the company members met in their armory and Captain Smith called his men to order. Once formed in double file, they marched down the two flights of stairs and onto Main Street. A large banner had been stretched across the street from Smith's Carter House to the Overman Building. The banner was emblazoned with the words "Our Flag: We Will Defend It!" At their captain's command, the company stopped and then wheeled into an open square beneath the banner and gave three loud cheers. The Cedar Falls Brass Band was on hand and marched forward playing patriotic, martial music. Passersby downtown on this Saturday evening gathered around and cheered their volunteer soldiers: "Now one for the Greys! One for Old Glory! One for our country, our whole country!"[21]

The response to Governor Kirkwood's call for 10 companies was so strong that he had no trouble raising Iowa's first regiment. The state had so many volunteer companies that most, including the Pioneer Greys, had to be turned down.

Cedar Falls became a hotbed of patriotism in the weeks that followed. War news became the primary preoccupation of most people. Flags seemed to be everywhere, on fences and hanging from windows and porches. In the four-block downtown business district, 27 flags were counted. The *Gazette* proclaimed the prevailing sentiment: "War! War! is all the talk—everybody is for war! Most assuredly this is no place for traitors."[22] Many citizens paid a quarter for silver pins in the shape of a star and engraved with the words "Constitution and Union." A young bride even had her wedding cake decorated with colored sugar spelling out the words "The Union Forever."[23]

The company roll, as of 21 April, listed 82 names, but the list included some disabled men and others with responsibilities which prevented them from enlisting in the regular army. Captain Smith and his men wanted to recruit more men than just the required minimum, so they sought recruits from nearby communities. Charles Mullarky and Thomas Salisbury were sent by horseback to Waverly, Charles City, and other towns in search of volunteers. Three days later they galloped their mounts up Main Street to the Carter House Hotel. Mullarky and Salisbury were accompanied by 15 more riders, and they carried pledges from more than 20 other volunteers. The arrival of the horsemen prompted another large, energetic demonstration and an impromptu parade.[24]

The War Department ordered the organization of two more Iowa regiments on 16 May 1861. Governor Kirkwood immediately ordered enough volunteer companies to make up a second regiment to rendezvous at Keokuk on 25 May and a third to meet at the same place by 3 June. The last call included the Pioneer Greys.[25]

Peter Melendy, the Perkins brothers, and other leading citizens called a mass meeting for Monday night, 27 May, to make plans for a proper send-off for the men and to consider ways to aid their families while they were at war. More than 600 people crowded Overman Hall that night. The meeting was chaired by Colonel Sessions, who, upon motion, appointed a committee of five to decide the particulars of how the town could support the men and their families. While the committee met downstairs, the crowd in the hall listened to speeches declaring that the time for compromise had passed and that war was now necessary to preserve the nation. At one point the crowd called upon a local merchant to speak. Remarking that he had no gift for words the merchant pointed to the flag draped over the speaker's stand and declared, "There's Old Glory! That's my flag!" and the crowd cheered their approval.[26]

The committee members then returned with their report. The committee suggested that the present body pledge funds for uniforms for the soldiers and aid to support their families. Though it was late, past 11:00 P.M., the crowd gave nearly $600 in pledges ranging from gifts of $5 up to $150. The next day another committee working on the streets of Cedar Falls came up with $350 more in pledges.[27]

Two days later, Wednesday, nearly 60 women gathered in the Horticultural Room of Overman Hall to begin the work of making uniforms for their men. The uniforms were to be grey wool trousers and navy blue cotton shirts. Several local tailors, J. J. Ball, Rob Roy, and Samuel Berry, set up sadirons, pressing boards, and a half-dozen sewing machines. The tailors also offered their services and those of their apprentice tailors. They cut the woolen cloth into pants, belts, and caps. They measured the men to ensure a good fit and directed the local women, who probably needed very little instruction in such matters. The women went even further and supplied shoes, socks, and underclothing for the men.[28]

The sewing marathon lasted late into Saturday night. The last of the work was completed Sunday morning, 2 June, in time for a community farewell that would extend through three days of flag waving, speech making, and tearful good-byes.

About noon on Monday, 3 June, a caravan of nearly 40 teams and wagons carrying 350 people arrived from Waverly. The Waverly people were escorting 20 of their young men, who had joined the Greys. A parade was formed led by the Cedar Falls Brass Band in their new wagon drawn by four horses. The band was followed by about 20 veterans of the War of 1812. The Pioneer Greys met the procession in company formation and formally accepted the Waverly volunteers into their ranks with enthusiastic cheers.[29]

At 3:00 P.M., Captain Matthew M. Trumbull of Butler County arrived with his company, the Union Guards. The Guards were also under the governor's order to rendezvous at Keokuk and were on their way to Waterloo, where 20 more volunteers waited.

The Pioneer Greys and the Union Guards greeted each other in military formations and exchanged salutes and cheers. After close to an hour, Trumbull and his Union Guards marched out of town toward Waterloo, where more than 1,000 people had gathered in a celebration and farewell to their soldiers. After Trumbull's company had left town, the Greys held a meeting and by acclamation formally elected their officers: John B. Smith, captain; Fitzroy Sessions, first lieutenant; and Charles Mullarky, second lieutenant.

That evening more than 800 people again filled Overman Hall for more speeches, songs, and prayers. Zimri Streeter was one of the speakers, and he begged the men not to lay down their arms until every rebel flag had been trodden underfoot. Another speaker announced that funds had been raised to purchase a sword and epaulets for Captain Smith. Smith thanked the people and said that he considered the gift more a compliment to the company than to himself. Lieutenant Sessions was presented with a Colt navy revolver. When he accepted the weapon, Sessions told the crowd that he would never disgrace his town, his company, or their cause.

On Tuesday morning, Main Street from the river to Second Street was alive with people; more than 5,000 had turned out to see the soldiers off. The great railroad celebration six weeks earlier had been almost as large. It was as if the train had arrived just in time to take the men away. The Pioneer Greys, dressed in their new uniforms, mingled with the crowd, saying farewell to friends and family. When Smith gave the order for the soldiers to march to the depot, a parade formed behind them. Led by the Brass Band and the veterans of the War of 1812, the huge crowd of people followed the Greys across the Millrace Bridge to the new train depot, where an engine and cars sat waiting. The train was decorated with flags and cedar boughs; a plume of smoke rose from the engine's smokestack.

The company broke ranks one last time before boarding, the men grabbing one last chance to say good-bye. The reality of what the departure meant struck one woman very hard, for she broke down in open sobs as she held two small children close and begged her husband not to go. He refused. Moved by her appeal, three young men offered to take the man's place in the company, but he refused them as well.

Five passenger cars reserved for the soldiers were quickly filled as the band and about 50 citizens boarded with the troops. The train's first stop was in Waterloo, where Captain Trumbull and his company, conspicuous in their civilian clothes next to the uniformed men from Cedar Falls, also boarded.[30]

The train took the two companies and their guests to Dubuque, where they were met at the station by another volunteer company, the Washington Guards, a militia company organized in 1859.[31] The Washington Guards led the other volunteers through Dubuque to a park for another rally, at which Fitzroy Sessions gave an impassioned speech. He charged that there were secessionists in Dubuque as well as down south, and that it was the opinion of the people of the Cedar Valley that their mouths ought to be shut. He referred to the Democratic newspaper, the *Dubuque Herald*, as a nuisance and closed his speech by asking the people of Dubuque not to let anyone fire upon his men from the rear after they had gone forth to defend the old flag.[32]

The troops were quartered overnight in a large brick building by the river, near the steamboat landing. Wednesday morning the farewells were reversed, with the Greys escorting the Cedar Falls people to the Dubuque train depot. Captain Smith had to travel back with them in order to finish some business matters but planned to rejoin his men in Keokuk. The good-byes were, once again, very emotional. Lieutenant Sessions tearfully called for three cheers for the folks back home in Cedar Falls.

Thursday evening the volunteers boarded the steamboat *Key City*, which would take them down the Mississippi to Keokuk. A large crowd gathered at the wharf to see the men off. There were some Southern sympathizers in the crowd who called out insults as the men boarded the boat. A member of the Greys became enraged, grabbed a wooden bucket from the deck, and hurled it down at them. One of the men on the dock immediately grabbed a missile and threw it back; it struck Sessions in the chest. The angry young lieutenant drew his new revolver and a Bowie knife and in an instant, with the knife clenched between his teeth and the pistol in one hand, he jumped from the moving steamboat back into the crowd. With one well-placed punch, Sessions knocked the rock thrower to the ground. As the *Key City* pulled away from the dock, he was forced to leap several feet across the water to the reaching hands of his men. The Pioneer Greys were on their way to war.[33]

> From Cedar Falls we took our leave
> The fourth of June, We went by steam
> Look away, look away
> Look away, look away
> At Keokuk we first encamped
> Many miles we had to tramp
> Look away, look away
> Look away, look away
> Then we wished we was in Dixie, Oh! Oh! Oh!
> In Dixie land we take our stand
> To win or die in Dixie land;
> Away down South in Dixie.[34]

3

Missouri

E arly in the morning on 8 June 1861, the *Key City* arrived in Keokuk. The steamboat's passengers, the Pioneer Greys, the Union Guards, and the Washington Guards, were the last companies that would make up the 3d Iowa Volunteer Infantry. The military camp was located just north of town, not far from the Mississippi River.[1] The 1st and 2d Iowa regiments, as well as the first seven companies of the 3d Iowa, were already encamped and had given the place the name Camp Ellsworth. There was not enough barrack space yet available in the camp, so the Greys and other new men were quartered temporarily in town.

As the various companies and their officers arrived in camp, they were put in formation, and Lieutenant Alexander Chambers of the regular army read the men the Articles of War. The Articles spelled out the duties of a soldier and the military punishments for failure to carry out those duties. The men then took the required oath and enlisted for three years of service.[2] The Pioneer Greys was the last company sworn in because Captain Smith was still in Cedar Falls and did not rejoin them until 11 June. The volunteer companies were then given their letter designations in the regiment. The standard organization of a Civil War regiment was 10 companies lettered A through K, with the letter J being omitted.[3] The Pioneer Greys were assigned as K Company, Dubuque's Washington Guards as A Company, and Matthew Trumbull's Butler County Union Guards as I Company.[4]

On 10 June, the 10 companies of the 3d Iowa were first formed into a full regimental line, more than 900 strong. They were an odd-looking regiment: they had no arms and no regular uniforms. The companies made the formation a patchwork quilt of colors and styles. The Pioneer Greys wore their grey trousers, navy blue shirts, and caps. Another company wore dark blue coats with green trim and light blue trousers and caps. Still another wore grey jackets with black striped trousers. Others, like the Union Guards, simply wore their civilian clothing.[5] After they were in proper regimental formation, the companies of the 3d Iowa marched through the streets of Keokuk. Both the soldiers and the citizens were impressed at the sight of the long, moving column of men.

On 12 June, both the 1st and 2d Iowa regiments were ordered to active duty in Missouri. This allowed the 3d Iowa to move into the camp barracks. They immediately renamed the camp Camp Kirkwood. In the course of the next few days, the men of the 3d began to learn the life of a soldier. The troops learned to march in close formation, form battle lines, and load and fire their weapons on command. They drilled for a minimum of six hours a day. They learned how to go from a long marching column into a full battle-line and back, how to wheel the line as needed, and how to advance or retreat in good order, all to the rhythms of drums and the shouted commands of their officers.

The tactics of the 1860s had changed little since the days of Napoleon. They still emphasized tight formations, in which each man's shoulders were in constant contact with the shoulders of the men on either side. The tight formations were in deference to the limited range of 18th- and 19th-century smoothbore, black-powder muskets. Such weapons were difficult to load and had a killing range of about 100 yards. An attacking line could expect to advance to within 100 yards of the enemy, exchange volleys, and then attack with bayonets before the defending soldiers could reload and fire again. The rifled muskets which came to be the standard weapon of the Civil War had a killing range of more than 600 yards and, combined with rifled artillery and well-fortified breastworks, made such close-order attacks suicidal.

The regiment received its first pay on 24 June, $7 per man, a down payment from the government toward the $13 per month that each private was supposed to receive. Line officers were to receive $15 a month. The Pioneer Greys were learning that late and insufficient pay were also part of a soldier's life.[6]

That same day the men finally received their arms. They had hoped to be issued the latest military weapon, the British-made Enfield rifle, and were very disappointed to find that they were given Springfield smoothbore muskets dated 1848. While they received their muskets and bayonets, they were not issued other necessary accouterments, such as cartridge and cap boxes, knapsacks or haversacks; nor were they issued ammunition.[7]

Seventeen days after the Pioneer Greys had been sworn into service, the 3d Iowa received its travel orders. The next day, 29 June, they were to board ship and proceed down the Mississippi River to Hannibal, Missouri.

By the terms of the Compromise of 1820, Missouri was a slave state, yet as a border state it had close ties with both the North and the

South. There were many militant secessionists in Missouri, but they were not a majority, nor were the militant Unionists a majority. Missouri's moderate elements sought to defuse the slavery issue and keep peace in the state, something that was becoming increasingly difficult after the election of 1860, when Claiborne F. Jackson, a strong supporter of the South, was elected governor.

After the Republican presidential victory in 1860, a convention was called to consider Missouri's response to the secession crisis. The convention was held in St. Louis on 4 March 1861. The delegates refused to support a resolution calling for secession, but they also refused to back resolutions calling for military action against their Southern neighbors.[8]

Neutrality did not last long. With both sides claiming Missouri, it was merely a matter of what spark would set off the explosion and which side would move first.

Both secessionists and Unionists organized militia companies. The pro-Southern companies were, under the authority of Governor Jackson, incorporated into the Missouri State Militia. The Union companies, under the leadership of Republican legislator Frank Blair, organized themselves as Home Guard units. Blair set up a Union Committee of Public Safety as their parent organization.[9]

On 10 May 1861, General Nathaniel Lyon, the Union commander under the authority of the U.S. War Department, moved his troops against Camp Jackson, a newly established secessionist fort on the outskirts of St. Louis. The militia troops in Camp Jackson surrendered to Lyon, who had them placed under arrest and marched through the streets of St. Louis. A crowd had gathered to watch the affair, and as the militia members were paraded before it, the crowd became unruly. People in the crowd began to curse Lyon and his men and then began to throw rocks at them. Someone in the mob fired a shot, and one of Lyon's soldiers fell dead. An officer gave an order to return the fire, and the soldiers obeyed. When the shooting stopped, 28 people were dead and many more wounded.[10]

Governor Jackson called out 50,000 state militia troops to repel what he described as an invasion of the state. Lyon advanced his forces on Missouri's capital, Jefferson City, forcing Governor Jackson to flee, along with most members of Missouri's elected government. Jackson moved his government to Neosho in the southwest part of the state. The Neosho government then passed a resolution of secession taking Missouri out of the Union. However, a provisional pro-Union government was called together at Jefferson City, and its members deposed Jackson and the rest of his government. President Lincoln immediately recognized the provisional government as the lawful government of the state. As a result, Missouri became both a Union and a Confederate state at the same time, never truly part of either.

At 3:00 A.M., 29 June 1861, reveille sounded, and the men of the 3d Iowa rolled out of their bunks. They were ordered to pack their equipment and stand ready to board ship. The packing was done in a hurry and did not go well. Because the men had no knapsacks, all of their personal baggage had to be packed in large boxes along with the tents and other regimental equipment. At 10:00 A.M., they marched to the wharf, where two steamboats lay lashed together on the water. A large crowd had gathered on shore to see the men off. Bands played martial music, flags flew, and people waved and cheered as the boats, crowded with soldiers, steamed downriver.[11]

The boats arrived at Hannibal, Missouri, later that evening, and within a few hours the men formed ranks for a dress parade.[12]

At 7:00 A.M. on 1 July, after a quick breakfast, the men boarded two 20-car trains of the Hannibal and St. Joseph Railroad. There was a refreshing morning breeze, and the weather was cool as the men rode west through the state. Farmers were cutting their grain, timothy grass was in blossom, and wild roses were in bloom. There were thick forests and small clearings where corn was planted. The trip along the rails seemed more like a summer outing than a war. As pleasant as the day was, the men were aware that they were now in a disputed state, a war zone. They knew that they were vulnerable targets; any band of guerrillas could easily stop or derail the trains. If they got into a fight, the Iowa troops would be in a hard place, as they still had not received ammunition for their smoothbore muskets.[13] The ride, however, was uneventful, and the men were able to see for themselves the divided sentiments in the state. One of the Pioneer Greys frequently wrote letters to the *Cedar Falls Gazette* under the pen name "Udonoho." He described the train journey:

> Had you seen the 3d regiment on their journey you would have thought they were on a Fourth of July excursion, singing on their way and as they passed houses and villages, cheering, waving and swinging their hats and handkerchiefs.
>
> The troops upon their way were greeted by an abundance of Union demonstration.—Now and then they passed places where the occupants would look gloomy and sullen, but a majority of the people seemed heartily to welcome the protectors of the Union. As we passed one slave owner who was riding a horse upon the opposite side of a wheat field he greeted us by patting the seat of his unmentionables: while his slave upon the other side, crouched down behind the grain showing two rows of pearly white teeth and swinging his hat.[14]

After leaving one company at Chillicothe, 130 miles west of

Hannibal, and another to guard a bridge three miles from Chillicothe, the regiment arrived at Utica, Missouri, late in the evening. The men slept in the station house and on the cars that night and in the morning pitched their tents just south of town.[15] Once in camp they were issued four rounds of ammunition per man.

On 5 July, the men finally received their new, state-issued uniforms. The new uniform consisted of a grey dress coat and grey pants with blue piping. They were pleased with the uniform; their old hometown uniforms were worn out, and the new ones seemed to be of good quality. It was a winter uniform, made of wool and heavily padded. The only objection was to the color, grey. While Union and Confederate uniforms had not yet been standardized, the men knew that Confederates frequently wore grey, and they had heard stories of deadly mix-ups in the confusion of battle. The heavy wool clothes could also be a problem in the Missouri heat. The first time the men wore them on dress parade, the coats properly buttoned to the throat, five men keeled over in the July sun.[16]

While the 3d Iowa was encamped at Utica, its commanding colonel, Nelson G. Williams, arrived. Williams had received military training at West Point but had not graduated or held rank in the regular army. The colonel carried with him commissions for other officers. Captain John Scott of E Company, a veteran of the Mexican War, was appointed lieutenant colonel, and Captain William Stone of B Company was promoted to major.[17]

Williams and Captain John B. Smith of K Company found that they got along well together and that the Pioneer Greys accepted their new commander. The same was not true for everyone. Officer commissions in the new, volunteer army were political appointments. Every man who sought such a post knew that he could carry the rank with him through the rest of his career. Political infighting over rank and authority became a problem on all levels of the system. An incapable officer could get his men killed, and service under such an officer could damage the reputations of those around him and hurt their chances for advancement. Before the 3d Iowa was fully organized, political bickering began to undermine Williams's authority.

There were other officers with more experience than Williams, and many of them felt that he was a bad choice. John Scott and regimental surgeon Thomas Edwards were two officers who objected to Williams. Scott, a friend of Governor Kirkwood, was with the regiment at Keokuk when he heard of Williams's appointment. He wrote the governor a letter from Keokuk describing the disorganized condition of the regiment and the need for a strong leader. He wrote that he was not seeking the job himself but that he wanted Kirkwood to know that many thought Williams was unfit for command. He quoted a letter from a friend of his in Dubuque who knew Williams:

> How under heaven that man Nels Williams could secure such a position is a mystery to me. The idea of his claiming to be a West Point Graduate! He was there, when a youth, less than a year, and was then *expelled* for insubordination, as I learn from credible authority. Dubuque has been sufficiently disgraced.[18]

Scott, Edwards, and the rest of the officers and men were forced to accept Williams's rank, but they made no secret of their dislike and disrespect for him. Captain Smith and the Greys, who liked and respected Williams, seemed to be in the minority.

On 8 July 1861, six companies of the 3d Iowa, including K Company, were sent east on the Hannibal and St. Joseph Railroad to a place called Monroe Station, 25 miles west of Hannibal. At Monroe Station the Iowa troops were joined by two companies of Colonel R. F. Smith's 16th Illinois regiment. Colonel Smith then took command of the expedition, the purpose of which was to intercept the Confederate general Thomas Harris, who threatened to capture the Hannibal and St. Joseph Railroad. Colonel Smith's Northern troops were accompanied by a company of the Hannibal Home Guards, who brought along an iron, six-pound swivel cannon. This brought the total number of Union troops to around 550 men.[19]

After they arrived at Monroe Station, the sky opened up in a fierce rainstorm, and the men were forced to take cover for the night. The night was wet and uncomfortable, but many welcomed the storm because it prevented the Confederates from launching a surprise attack of their own. The next morning the soldiers marched in the direction of Florida, Missouri, 16 miles to the south. The detachment from the 16th Illinois led the column and were fully equipped, each man supplied with 20 rounds of ammunition. The Illinois troops were followed by the 3d Iowa companies, whose men still had not received their accouterments. They had received eight more cartridges but were forced to carry their 12 cartridges in their pockets. The Iowa soldiers were followed by the Hannibal Home Guards and their six-pound gun. The march was over rugged terrain in the July heat, and the Iowa troops, without so much as a canteen, had a rough time of it.[20]

About 2:00 P.M., they came in sight of a party of Confederates posted along the edge of a tree line. Thinking that they had surprised the enemy, Fitzroy Sessions, who had been appointed regimental adjutant, cried out excitedly, "We have met the enemy and they are ours, boys!"[21] and he took off after them. The other men quickly followed him, throwing away their blanket rolls as they ran. Though the Union men ran

PIONEER GREYS IN MISSOURI
Map by Andrew J. Karl

a good race, the Confederates escaped. Sessions and his winded men were forced to gather up their belongings and continue the march.

At about 4:00, they entered a place called Hager's Woods, a small crossroads with several abandoned buildings. The old buildings made ideal cover for the Confederate troops waiting there in ambush. In an instant, they opened up on the Union soldiers. This was the first time that the 3d Iowa had come under enemy fire. "Udonoho" described the experience:

> When we were within five rods of the cross lane we were suddenly fired upon by the foe from behind fences, buildings and woods. We halted a little, as you may have seen a balky horse sometimes, formed into line and immediately began to reply to their fire, wherever a man showed his head. The bullets whistled around our heads, but the boys stood the fire well, and all were eager to get a shot at the foe. The firing lasted perhaps ten minutes, when our cannon sent a grist of shot and grape among the fences and bushes, and in a short time none but Union scouts could be found.[22]

The Union troops had three men wounded in the brief exchange but no one was killed at Hager's Woods, and the men rested at the crossroads before withdrawing. Escaped Union prisoners had confirmed reports that the enemy numbered well over 1,000 men and had at least two artillery pieces. Colonel Smith decided to retreat from the larger force. That evening, the men made camp in a wheat field two miles from the woods and in the morning marched back to Monroe Station. Confederate cavalry kept up a harassing action during the retreat, and twice the cannon had to be used to scatter them. When the Union column got back to the station, the men found that their train was in flames, the rails ripped up, and the telegraph lines cut.

Fearing attack and not sure when, or if, reinforcements would arrive, they dug in. They piled fence rails into breastworks, dug trenches, and, most important, secured a supply of fresh water. They took control of the highest point in the area, a three-story brick building that had once been a seminary. That night they lay on their arms, waiting for the expected attack which did not come.[23] "Udonoho" described the next morning:

> As we arose from our trenches in the morning we cast our eyes to the top of the seminary building and found the stars and stripes proudly waving over all. The heart of each soldier leaped at the sight, and I could see the muscles of the soldiers harden as a new determination sprang to his bosom to defend the good old flag to the last.[24]

Though the attack had not yet come, the situation at Monroe Station was bleak. Provisions were nearly gone, and few men had many cartridges left. One attack or a few hours of serious sniping from the enemy would force the men to expend their last rounds.

At 2:00 P.M., the Confederates opened up with their six- and nine-pound guns. Shots fell inside the compound, whizzed over the men's heads, and destroyed the cannon carriage, but no one was injured by enemy fire. The men were even able to enjoy a few good laughs as they watched their comrades dive into their holes and get covered by dust and debris when a shot came too close. One man, Private Cyrus West of H Company, was killed when his musket accidentally discharged.[25]

As the battle raged, a train was seen approaching from the west. Colonel Smith, watching with his field glasses from the top of the semi-nary, was overjoyed to see Union flags on the cars. Reinforcements at last! The arrival of the troop train and the cannon's accurate fire soon had the enemy on the run. As the train's engine approached the station, it struck a spot where the Confederates had ripped up a section of track. The engineer could not see the break in the rails, and the first two cars in line were derailed and sent tumbling down the embankment, spilling men and equipment in all directions. Fortunately, no one was injured.[26]

The soldiers returned to Chillicothe and remained there until early August. After the fighting at Hager's Woods and Monroe Station, the men considered themselves veterans. They had been under fire, had seen men shot down, and had faced privations on the march. The long march-es, especially without such necessary items as canteens and haversacks, had taken their toll. The rest soon had them back in shape, as "X" wrote from camp:

> Truly the "boys" have passed through a severe ordeal. Their powers of endurance, bravery, and good nature, have all been put to the test, and they have without exception acquitted themselves nobly; done them-selves much credit, a credit to the Cedar Valley—to the state of Iowa—to the whole country. To see them on this bright moonlight night—here a cotillian party tripping the "sore bombastic toe" to the music of a cracked fiddle and a pair of bones, there a squad of "warblers" declar-ing in *flute like tones*, their undying affection for "Dinah Rose" or somebody else "way down in Tennessee"—one would not suppose it the same party who had just passed through a series of sleepless nights and hungry days. But such is their temperment. Within twenty-four hours of returning to camp from the Monroe expedition, with their hunger appeased, one good night's rest, they are as ready to "fall in" as ever.[27]

On 4 August, the 3d Iowa finally received its military accouter-ments, and the men were supplied with proper cartridge and cap boxes, canteens, waist belts, and haversacks. They were not issued regulation knapsacks, and rather than go back to packing their personal belongings in boxes, the men continued to roll them up in their blankets. The blanket rolls, thrown over the left shoulder to keep the right free for firing their muskets, were easily carried on the march.[28] The blanket rolls served so well that most soldiers continued to use them even after knapsacks became available.

On 7 August, the seven companies of the 3d Iowa encamped at Chillicothe were placed under the command of Lieutenant Colonel John Scott. Scott's force, consisting of most of the 3d Iowa and a few companies of Missouri Home Guards, was sent to Kirksville with orders to hold the place against Confederate General Martin Green. The Confederate force did not attack, and a few days later Brigadier General Stephen Hurlbut and the 16th Illinois arrived. General Hurlbut tried to show the Missouri Confederates both the velvet glove and the iron fist by issuing a proclamation giving them five days to lay down their arms or be treated as outlaws. The attempt at diplomacy failed, and Green used the five days to move his troops out of danger. Scott's troops were sent in pursuit, the only positive result of which was that the men were treated to a good meal by the German residents of Bethel, Missouri. Hurlbut was severely criticized for his proclamation and failure to move more rapidly.[29]

While Lieutenant Colonel Scott had been campaigning near Kirksville and Bethel, Colonel Williams had received orders to move against Paris, Missouri, with the remainder of the 3d, six companies of the 2d Kansas, and a company of Missouri Home Guard cavalry, a total of nearly 700 men.[30] Williams went by rail to Shelbina and then marched on Paris, where he remained for one day. He then retreated back to Shelbina, having heard that Green's force was nearly twice the size of his own. Green attacked Shelbina on 4 September, and Williams put his men on a train and continued to retreat. The men lost much of their personal baggage in the retreat, and the Confederates were able to capture and loot two Union warehouses.[31]

The failure to capture Green at Kirksville, the retreat from Shelbina, the ambush at Hager's Woods, and the short siege of Monroe Station had all but wrecked the morale of the regiment. The constant marching and countermarching with no positive results were wearing on the men.

Many blamed Colonel Williams and General Hurlbut for the military failures. Rumors of their being drunk on duty spread through camp. The regimental surgeon, Thomas Edwards of Dubuque, was also viewed as a problem, both as a doctor and as an officer. He was placed under arrest for neglect of duty in early September.

Things seemed to change for the better with the arrival of General John Pope, the Union commander in northern Missouri. Pope was a graduate of West Point, a veteran of the Mexican War, and, most important, he was a man who spoke of victory and not defeat.[32] One of the first things General Pope did upon his arrival was examine the leadership of the 3d Iowa. The result was that both General Hurlbut and Colonel Williams were placed under arrest, accused of being drunk while on duty.

The Pioneer Greys were not acquainted with Hurlbut but were willing to give him the benefit of the doubt. They did know Williams and came to his defense. While they had not been a part of his Shelbina expedition, they believed that the retreat was a military necessity caused by his being abandoned by the 2d Kansas: the Kansas troops had insisted on going home, thus leaving Williams and his Iowa troops hopelessly outnumbered. They also felt that Williams's junior officers, under the leadership of Dr. Edwards, had conspired and lied about him. As "Udonoho" explained,

> In the month of August a list of charges and speculations were drawn up against Colonel Williams signed by a majority of the officers of the regiment, charging him with disorderly conduct, etc., etc., in the handwriting and sided and abetted by one T. O. Edwards of Dubuque, Iowa.—To start with, I will simply say that anyone who says that Col. Williams has been incapacitated from duty, through the effects of liquor *lies*. As to the other charges they amount to nothing, being wholly untrue. One signature to the paper was affixed without the knowledge and in the absence of the owner. On his return he wrote to the Colonel denying all complicity in the affair. Three others have already expressed a change in sentiments having acted heretofore entirely on misrepresentations made by Dr. Edwards and a few office seeking, unprincipled politicians, with which we are like other regiments, cursed. . . . Concerning Dr. Edwards it is sufficient to say that he was under arrest for three weeks for gross neglect of duty, and the opinion of the regiment is that an excessive use of opium and other stimulents has driven him into an early doltage.[33]

Both Hurlbut and Williams were ordered to St. Louis to answer the charges against them. Edwards was sent home on an extended furlough, and the assistant regimental surgeon, Daniel M. Cool of Waverly, was placed in charge of the regiment's medical department. The men of the 3d held Dr. Cool in high esteem. During the shelling at Monroe Station, Cool had gone into the thick of the bombardment to attend the wounded. At the Kirksville camp hospital, Cool had "labored day and night with the sick and done all for the boys that one could do under the circumstances."[34]

While the Pioneer Greys and the rest of the 3d Iowa were campaigning in northern Missouri, the situation in the southwest part of the state had turned worse. General Nathaniel Lyon had advanced to

Springfield on 13 July. There he faced a large Confederate force under General Sterling Price. Lyon had repeatedly asked General John C. Fremont, in command of the Department of the West, for reinforcements. Lyon received no reinforcements and little encouragement from Fremont, so he acted on his own initiative. Lyon believed that his force of slightly fewer than 6,000 men was the only means of saving southwest Missouri, and he decided to attack Price and his army of 11,000.[35] Lyon moved on Price at a place called Wilson's Creek, south of Springfield, on 10 August. The battle lasted from 4:00 A.M. until early afternoon and resulted in a Confederate victory. General Lyon was wounded twice, in the leg and the head, before finally being killed while leading a charge at about 10:30 A.M. The Union force, now under Major Samuel D. Sturgis, retreated in the early afternoon, and Price took possession of Springfield. The Union force lost 1,235 men, including those killed, wounded, and missing; the Confederates had 1,184 men killed, wounded, or missing.[36]

Following the Confederate victory at Wilson's Creek, General Price advanced north toward the Federal fortress at Lexington, Missouri, located on the Missouri River about 50 miles east of Kansas City.

Generals Harris and Green, who were still operating in northern Missouri, had to get their troops across the Missouri River near the town of Liberty in order to join forces with Price. General Pope sent a force to prevent the link-up. Lieutenant Colonel John Scott, who had replaced Colonel Williams, was put in charge of the expedition. He commanded most of the 3d Iowa, the 16th Illinois, several companies of the 39th Ohio, and the Missouri Home Guards. The different sections of Scott's force were scattered across the state and were supposed to meet at Liberty on 16 September.

Bad weather and muddy roads prevented many of Scott's troops from reaching Liberty in time. The 3d Iowa, accompanied by some mounted Missouri soldiers and a German-Missouri artillery battery with a six-pound field piece, were the only ones there on time. Confederates were already crossing the Missouri at a place called Blue Mills Ferry five miles south of Liberty. Scott feared that this march would be, like so many others, a failure unless he acted. He bivouacked his men on a hill just north of Liberty, sent couriers to find the rest of his command, and prepared to attack with his immediate force if necessary. He waited throughout the night, and the next day he sent more couriers to search for the approaching reinforcements. The couriers carried the message that Scott intended to attack at Blue Mills and would hold until help arrived.[37]

The Missouri mounted Home Guard forces struck the Confederate rear guard about noon and in a fierce fight had four men killed and several wounded. Scott began his main attack in the early afternoon. When the advance part of his command reached the spot where the Missouri horsemen had fought, they found the four dead men stretched out on their backs alongside the road, their faces twisted in death. Major William Stone became excited and tried to prevent his men from seeing the bodies. Colonel Scott remained calm and quietly rode past the dead soldiers. The men pushed past the grisly sight and on through the heavy timber and dense undergrowth of the river bottom. Scott had a platoon deployed on either side and in advance of the main column to act as skirmishers. He halted the column once, brought them to a front, and had each man inspect his rounds and load his weapon. He cautioned them all to be steady and to fire low and then continued the advance, leading the way on his small roan horse.[38]

The tangle of underbrush and trees was so thick that the men lost their order, and the main column, complete with their one field piece, was lured into a full-scale ambush. The Confederates were drawn up in a long, crescent-shaped line that spanned the narrow road and extended deep into the timber, so they were able to fire into Scott's front and flanks at the same time. The artillery piece was rushed far to the front and hurried into action. The gun was so close that the Confederates were able to fire buckshot at the crew, killing and wounding several of the horses and more than half the men in just a few moments. The German-Missouri gunners were able to get off a single round before the survivors were forced to abandon the piece. Captain Matthew Trumbull was in the front of the line leading I Company, his old Union Guards, when he saw the cannon on the field. He and two lieutenants hurried forward, seized the gun, and dragged it to safety by hand. The horses pulling the gun's caisson took off in panic, wedging the wagon between two trees. The horses were then killed. Trumbull and his men could not free the caisson by hand, and it had to be left behind.[39]

Captain John B. Smith was ill and could not command the company, so Adjutant Sessions took charge of the Pioneer Greys. As the line advanced, Sessions got off his horse, preferring to go into the brush fight on foot. He carried a rifle and cartridge box taken earlier from a sick soldier. When the enemy struck, he formed his men alongside the narrow road and directed their fire into the woods, where the enemy lay hidden.[40] Many of the Confederates wore bright red shirts, and the Union troops could see and fire at them through the brush and smoke.[41]

The firing lasted for more than an hour. When the Confederates finally succeeded in flanking the Federal force, Scott ordered the men to pull back. As the men retreated, Scott remained on his horse, in the center of the road directing and encouraging his men. His horse was hit 11 times during the fight and his uniform was pierced more than once, but he remained unhurt. As they retreated, the Confederates tried to pursue, but Scott set up a defensive line and fired a volley into their ranks which ended the chase.[42]

That night and all the next day, the Confederates finished crossing the river. The Union troops fell back to Liberty, carrying their wounded with them. At Liberty, they converted the William Jewell College into a hospital, where Dr. Cool and the assistant surgeon of the 16th Illinois, which had arrived too late for the fight, worked desperately to bring what relief they could to the wounded soldiers.[43]

That evening, the men returned to the battlefield to gather their dead. Buzzards could be seen hovering in the sky and perched on tree branches, waiting for their share. The butcher's bill at Blue Mills was higher than any the men had yet seen. Fourteen Union soldiers had died on the field, seven from the 3d Iowa. Eighty-four were wounded, and 70 of those belonged to the 3d. The Pioneer Greys had their first man killed, Private James Brownell of Grundy County. Corporal Walter W. Wood, a private listed simply as Caller, and Privates Byron E. Taylor, Calvin Jones, and Ross W. Davenport were wounded. Several wounded Union men were captured by the Confederates and treated during the night. The next day they were returned under a flag of truce. The dead were buried with soldiers' honors in a small graveyard just south of the William Jewell College.[44] A member of the Greys, writing under the pen name "Occasional," eulogized the company's first dead man with these words:

> Poor Brownell, has gone to his long home. He fell while reloading his musket, but did not die until the next day. Friends watched over him in his last moments, and friends followed to the grave. Struck down while manfully performing his duty, the first to fall of the ninety-four who so gaily set forth on the 2nd of June, it is the sincere and oft-expressed hope that he has found in heaven a resting place, that when his pulse ceased to beat another angel took his flight.[45]

Lieutenant Colonel Scott was criticized for not waiting for the rest of his command at Blue Mills but praised for his coolness under fire.

> It is due the soldiers of the regiment to record that they fought like brave men and that they deserved a better place in which to fight. It is due too, to Lieutenant Col. Scott that whatever little judgment he might have used in leading us into the ambush he did, and however little skill he used in trying to get us out, that throughout the whole affair he manifested a coolness that amounted almost to stoicism.[46]

After the Battle of Blue Mills, Scott and 400 men of the 3d Iowa, including the Pioneer Greys, were sent to Quincy, Illinois, where they were stationed for the rest of the year. Their service in Missouri was over.

4

Home in Cedar Falls

By the fall of 1861, the war had grown into the largest conflict the nation had yet experienced, and it would not be decided quickly or by the few volunteers called in April and May. President Lincoln had had to call for more troops that summer. Iowa's share was six more regiments of infantry. There was another call in October, and by the end of the year the state had 13 regiments of infantry mustered into service, with five more in the process of formation. State volunteers also raised five regiments of cavalry and three batteries of artillery.[1]

The departure of the Pioneer Greys in June 1861 had been the beginning of a summer of military activity in Cedar Falls. Representatives of existing regiments as well as the new regiments just being organized were sent to the town. Soldiers became familiar sights on the streets as new companies were formed and other companies from farther up-country marched into town to meet the Dubuque-bound train. Public celebrations for the departing volunteers continued throughout the summer. When the Lincoln Guards, a company from Chickasaw County, marched into town in the middle of July, they were met by the remaining members of the Pioneer Greys, which continued, under the leadership of Peter Melendy, as the town military organization. Two other partial companies being formed in town also joined the Greys in welcoming the Chickasaw County soldiers.[2]

A few days later, on 20 July, James Q. Rownd's son, George, and 19 others from the Cedar Falls area left town. The group intended to go down the Mississippi River to Burlington and join a partial company of infantry from Keokuk. Once there, they found that they did not care for the Burlington camp or the volunteers from Keokuk. Rather than enlist in a company they did not like, the Cedar Falls recruits chose to enlist instead in the 1st Iowa Battery under Captain C. H. Fletcher.[3]

Congressman William Vandever of Dubuque resigned his congressional seat and received permission to recruit a regiment of infantry and a battery of artillery. He set up a recruiting office in Cedar Falls, and

William H. McClure, an attorney, acted as his recruiting agent. By the middle of August, they had more than 50 names on the roll. Vandever's regiment was mustered into service on 24 September as the 9th Iowa Volunteer Infantry. Six soldiers from Cedar Falls served in this regiment in C, G, H, and I Companies. Waterloo furnished most of the men in G Company.[4]

William McClure was appointed first lieutenant of the artillery battery. Thirteen men from Cedar Falls were in the battery, which was mustered in as the 3d Iowa Battery under the command of Captain M. M. Hayden.[5]

The suddenness and awful magnitude of the war caught the nation by surprise. There were many volunteers but few facilities for training them, few modern weapons with which to arm them, and a terribly inefficient system of supply. Friends, relatives, and citizens from their hometowns rallied to the support of the soldiers, who without their assistance often sickened and died in camp.

The women of Iowa took the lead in providing care for their soldiers. Ladies' Aid Societies and Soldiers' Aid Societies were formed in most towns across the country. There were 7,000 local aid societies formed in Iowa during the war, all organized and run by women. The most famous of the women volunteers from Iowa was Annie Wittenmyer of Keokuk, a widow who organized that town's first aid society and helped it expand into the major coordinating force for Iowa's relief agencies. Most local aid societies were eventually incorporated into the activities of either the U.S. Sanitary Commission, or, especially in Iowa, the Western Sanitary Commission. The Army Sanitary Commission for the State of Iowa, or the Iowa Sanitary Commission, was created in October 1861 and grew to be one of the state's principal means of supplying much-needed assistance to the soldiers.[6]

The women of Cedar Falls, who had sewn the first uniforms for their Pioneer Greys, organized both a Ladies' Aid Society and Soldiers' Aid Society. Under the leadership of women such as Barbara Boehmler, whose son, Charles, was a member of the Pioneer Greys, and Elmira Sessions, Fitzroy Session's mother, Mrs. J. B. Powers, and many others, the women of Cedar Falls did all they could to aid the soldiers. The women put out requests for massive amounts of food, clothing, and medical supplies and made sure that the goods were delivered to the men. Once each week the members of the aid societies met at a member's home and planned fund-raising activities such as ice cream parties, amateur theatrical shows, and dramatic readings. The meetings and activities of the aid societies became a central part of the social life in the town, particularly for the women. The meetings would often last for hours as the women sorted donations and packed boxes for shipment south. The only problem with the social aspect of the societies was that they were under the control of the older, married women of the town. Young ladies, often with beaus off in the army, did not feel at ease talking about their lives and romances with their mothers looking on. The young women still wished to help the cause, and in the spring of 1862 they left the old clubs and formed one of their own, the Young Women's Soldiers' Aid Society.[7]

The efforts put forth by the women of the aid societies were much appreciated by the men. Few things were as important as a letter or a gift from home. After the fight at Monroe Station, Captain Smith had returned to Cedar Falls on furlough. When he left town to rejoin his company in Missouri, Smith took along the most important gifts possible: three large boxes and two trunks filled with food, clothing, medical supplies, newspapers, and other items the soldiers needed. A private, in a letter to the *Gazette*, described the reaction when the men received the packages:

> It was one of the brief hours in which the brightest sunshine of a soldier's life floods his soul with joy and love; "Oh 'tis sweet to be remembered" . . .
> This morning the Captain procured the boxes (you know what boxes) from the Depot and distributed the almost everlasting quantity of necessities comforts and luxuries to one of the jolliest crowds that ever swore fealty to the Constitution of the United Sates.[8]

The women's task grew as the war grew and they were forced to do jobs that were previously considered unladylike. Iowa had no provisions in its military organization for female nurses, but the tremendous number of sick and wounded needed attention, and women demanded the right to be nurses. Recognizing the need to allow women to care for the sick, a group of women from Cedar Falls sent a petition to Governor Kirkwood. He replied,

> Mrs. R. Herman, Cedar Falls, Iowa—
>
> My Dear Madam: I received today by mail a petition to the General Assembly from yourself and other ladies of Cedar Falls, asking that an appropriation be made for the employment of female nurses in the hospitals of the Iowa troops. It will afford me great pleasure to lay your petition before the General Assembly, and you may rest assured that any influence I may have will be freely exerted for the furtherance of your noble and womanly object.[9]

Many such petitions had been forwarded to the governor, and they helped convince him that women nurses would be a valuable asset in the war effort. His Governor's Message to the General Assembly, delivered in January 1862, contained just such a recommendation: "I am decidedly of the opinion that female nurses in our hospitals would render invaluable service; and I earnestly recommend that provision be made for securing such service to the benefit of our sick and wounded soldiers."[10]

The assembly did not grant Kirkwood's request, but in November 1863, at the convention of the Iowa Sanitary Commission, the subject was again debated. By that time, it had been rendered moot, as volunteer female nurses were already serving in every theater of the war. Further, the U.S. Army Nursing Corps had been in existence under the control of the famous reformer Dorothea Dix since 1861. The U.S. Sanitary Commission, which was an extension of the women's aid societies, employed female nurses in hospitals and on hospital ships and had so impressed the surgeon general that in July 1862 an order was issued requiring that at least one-third of the army nurses in the general hospitals were to be women.[11] The need for quality nurses during the war did much to elevate nursing to a true profession.

The war meant hardship for most women, as their husbands and sons went off to war leaving them to care for both home and livelihood. The farm women of Iowa had to care for their children, plant and harvest the crops, and take care of livestock. Women in town had to care for family businesses as well as their homes. The families of soldiers were often more dependent upon mail from the soldiers than the other way around because the soldiers often sent money. Families had to be fed, animals cared for, buildings and equipment kept in repair, and clothing made or purchased. The men were away at war, but the daily expenses continued at home. There had been money pledged and much good intention shown, but soldiers' pay was still the only support for their families. The pay was often months late and often given in partial payments. The gap between bills and pay sent home put many families in a severe economic pinch. The war rallies in the spring had been filled with rhetoric promising support for the families of the volunteers, but none of the money that had been pledged in the passion of the moment had been collected or distributed. Three months after the first volunteers had left town, Henry and George Perkins appealed for help:

> Our citizens will remember that a considerable sum of money was subscribed for the support of families of volunteers who went with the Pioneer Greys from this place. So far as we can learn none of that amount has been collected or paid out. There are families of members of that company that went from here, that are suffering for the necessities of life,—understand us, *suffering*. Now fellow citizens this must not be allowed. We solemnly promised those brave men who went forth to fight our battles, as well as their own, that we would provide for their families in their absence and we must do it.[12]

Black Hawk County allocated more than $500 to the aid of the soldiers' families in October and organized a system of distribution. Each soldier with a dependent family was expected to send $5 to $8 of his monthly pay home, and the men of the Greys had sent more than $2,000 home by November. If the family had needs they could not afford to meet, the county was authorized to help.[13] The system was new and inefficient, but the combination of pay sent home and county assistance prevented many families from becoming destitute.

The fall of 1861 was election time in Iowa. Governor Kirkwood was running for reelection, and in many respects, the Iowa Republican Party was up for ratification. The local campaigns of 1861 were not as dramatic as the national election of 1860, but they contained a new element —two divided parties.

The Democratic Party contained a strong faction of Northerners, called "Peace Democrats," who opposed the war. Some were against the war for ideological reasons, and others had become disillusioned with the ghastly death rate, corruption, and mounting costs of the war. The Peace Democrats were opposed by the "War Democrats," who supported the war but not the Republican Party, which they viewed as under the control of radicals.

The Republican Party had carried Iowa in 1860, when war had been merely a political threat. The Union and Confederate dead buried from Bull Run to Wilson's Creek and Blue Mills had made the threat real. Once under way, the war had the potential to completely change the nation. The question of what the war should accomplish, not the war itself, divided the Republican Party. The moderate Republicans such as President Abraham Lincoln took the position that the war had but one purpose, to preserve the Union. Radical Republicans took a different position. They believed that the war could only be won by striking at the root of the problem, human slavery. Slavery was to be abolished both as a war measure and as a reformist measure.

Many Republicans took the position that any opposition to the party was unpatriotic and that the War Democrats were disloyal. The splits in both parties were opportunities for rising politicians to make their marks and gain positions. Many pro-Union Democrats and antiabolition Republicans tried to form Union parties as alternatives. The Union Party movement had little impact on the governor's race, as Kirkwood carried the state by a majority of more than 17,000 votes.[14]

The Union Party movement was more pronounced on the local level. The Black Hawk County Republican convention, held in Waterloo on 5 September, was divided between the moderates and the radicals. The delegates from Cedar Falls, Henry Perkins, Colonel Sessions, and George H. Boehmler, became convinced that the radicals could not be

43

appeased and chose to leave the convention.

> Seeing how things were going, and it being apparent that the Convention was controlled by the ultra, radical portion of the party, we might almost say the abolition wing,—men who would not concede an iota in these perilous times when the good and true men of the country are uniting as far as can be to save the Union from the black vortex of secession . . . there remained but one thing for the conservative, fair-minded portion of the Convention to do, and that was to withdraw and leave the radicals to work out their own ends in their own bigoted way. . . . Party lines cannot be drawn this fall as tight as a year ago, and it will not do to crack the whip of radicalism over the heads of the people.[15]

Those who left the convention worked to build a local Union Party but were still Republicans as far as the state and national elections were concerned. Both Republican newspapers, the *Cedar Falls Gazette* and the *Waterloo Courier,* backed the Union movement but still endorsed Governor Kirkwood for reelection.

The Union Party was successful in Cedar Falls township, carrying all but two of the board of supervisors, township trustees, town clerk, assessor, constables, and road supervisor positions.[16]

The war was the most important issue that summer and fall. Soldiers passed through town, young men enlisted in new companies, and sick and wounded soldiers began to return, discharged or on furlough. The war was constantly in evidence, but life in Cedar Falls was far from grim and war-weary that summer and fall. The arrival of the railroad had encouraged expansion. The new depot across the river, with its warehouses, engine house, depot building, and restaurant, was one of the most obvious examples. There were many others as well. That summer 30 new homes, ranging from two-story houses to small cottages, were constructed. Fourteen new stores and warehouses, a new grain elevator, and Edwin Brown's new, six-story, mill were also completed. There were two new churches, Methodist and German Methodist. Near the edge of town, Andrew Mullarky, Samuel Rownd, and others built a series of stables. Plans were being made to construct a telegraph line between Dubuque and Cedar Falls, and in the fall, Peter Melendy and his business partner, A. D. Barnum, began work on an agriculture warehouse that would serve the needs of the farmers in the Cedar Valley.[17] Melendy could not have chosen a better spot for his large warehouse. The building was constructed on an island formed by the Cedar between the Millrace Bridge, the town's first bridge, and its second, the new River Bridge. Traffic from the north, east, south, and west passed over one bridge or the other. With the growing demand by the military for wool, wheat, and other farm produce, a large share of the exports from the Cedar Valley were guaranteed to pass through Melendy's farm depot.[18]

The fall harvest went well. The mills were extremely busy as farmers from up to 100 miles away came to Cedar Falls. One day in early December there were more than 400 wheat-filled wagons in town.[19]

The railroad also allowed for a new social activity, the railroad excursion. About 700 people rode to Cedar Falls from eastern Iowa on 31 July and were met by a brass band. Several hundred citizens escorted the visitors to the town square, where seats had been arranged under the trees and a supply of ice water provided. The temperature rose to more than 100 degrees, and the out-of-towners spent the afternoon lounging in the shade before they boarded the train again.[20]

The summer and fall of 1861 were active seasons in Cedar Falls. There was the excitement of military activities, the day-to-day work of building what was still a very young community, and a range of social functions that kept everyone entertained. One ominous question darkened the picture: How many of Cedar Falls's young men who marched so proudly to war would return?

5

Shiloh

In both eastern and western theaters of the war, the fall of 1861 was a much-needed period of recovery and reorganization. The Army of the Potomac, which had all but turned into a frightened mob at its first battle, Bull Run, was placed under a new commander, George B. McClellan. General McClellan had graduated from West Point, served in the Mexican War, and had a successful civilian career. He soon turned that mob into a real fighting force.

While McClellan readied his eastern army, a general in the West, Ulysses S. Grant of Illinois, was making a name for himself. Grant had also graduated from West Point and was a veteran of the Mexican War, but unlike McClellan, he had never been a great success, either in the military or as a civilian. It took the personal influence of his congressman to finally get him a command. Once in command of troops, Grant had quickly earned a reputation as a tough, efficient officer who was eager to take the war to the enemy. By August of 1861, he was a brigadier general and soon would rise even further.

The Confederate defensive line stretched, roughly, along the Ohio River from Virginia to the Mississippi River. At some point, Union armies had to smash through that line and invade the South. The first attempt to do so, Bull Run, had failed, and Lincoln looked to the West. The president sent a personal envoy to travel the length of the Confederate line, inspect its fortifications, and look for its weakest point. The envoy, a woman named Anna Carrol, reported that the key to winning the West was not an invasion straight down the Mississippi River but through the Tennessee and Cumberland Rivers. The keys to the rivers were two forts, Fort Henry on the Tennessee and Fort Donelson on the Cumberland. If those forts could be captured, the Confederates would have to retreat deep into Tennessee. The way would then be open for a full-scale invasion by both land and water.[1]

Grant was given the task of taking the forts. Central to his plans was something new in American warfare, river gunboats—well-armored, shallow-draft boats armed with up to 13 guns and designed to operate in shallow river water. He planned coordinated attacks by both land and water. The first fort, Fort Henry, was captured on 6 February 1862 by the gunboats alone; the infantry had not even been needed. Fort Donelson fell after two days of hard fighting that cost 500 Union soldiers killed and another 2,108 wounded. Forty of the dead and 251 of the wounded were from Iowa regiments.[2]

While Grant was preparing his winning campaign, another Union victory was in the making. A former Republican congressman, Samuel Curtis, now General Curtis, had taken command of the dead Nathaniel Lyon's Missouri army. Curtis intended to drive Sterling Price's Confederates out of Missouri. The two armies met at a place called Pea Ridge, or Elkhorn Tavern, on the Missouri-Arkansas border on 7 and 8 March 1862. The battle was a sprawling, bloody affair, the worst yet seen in the West, with more than 1,300 Union and 800 Confederate dead and wounded.[3] It was also a Union victory, and that, combined with Grant's success, was the first step toward a final triumph.

The Pioneer Greys were not with Grant or Curtis. After Blue Mills, the 3d Iowa had been so worn out, sick, and in need of rest that the men petitioned their commanding officer to transfer them to a place where they could recover their health and morale. "Occasional" described the regiment's condition:

> Our regiment entered Missouri 965 strong, composed of as healthy, robust and patriotic a body of men as ever entered the field. Sickness and death, the result of severe exposure and neglect, have so thinned our ranks that we cannot now turn out over 300 men for field service. Under all these trying vicisitudes, our men have acted bravely and nobly; they have passed through them almost without a murmur.[4]

A camp at Quincy, Illinois, served the purpose. The scattered companies of the 3d, those who had been too ill to march to Blue Mills and those on detached duty, were reunited. Mail and gifts from home were delivered, and passes into town and furloughs home were allowed. The men were allowed to rest and were issued new regulation-Union-blue uniforms. The people of Quincy seemed to be all Unionists, and an active social life was possible. A private in the Pioneer Greys marveled at the change:

> We have been in camp in this place about two weeks, and during that time we have been pleasantly situated, enjoying ourselves capitally. We have drilled four hours each day, had dress parades, received visits from Quincey's fair ones, had dances on the green, walkings with the ladies, some visits in the city.—This is a great change for the Third Iowa.[5]

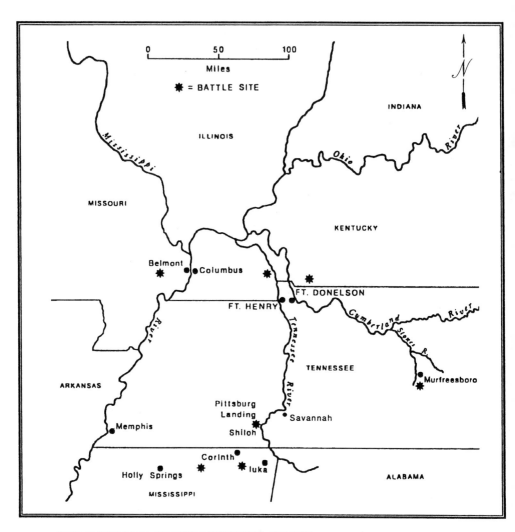

UNION INVASION OF THE MISSISSIPPI VALLEY
Map by Andrew J. Karl

The only complaints were, again, their weapons and their new uniforms. Rifled muskets were becoming increasingly available, and the 3d had served with Illinois troops who had been armed with them. They had not yet been issued to the 3d Iowa, however, and the men still carried their smoothbore Springfields. The new uniforms, federally issued, were the proper color but of extremely poor quality. Their old state-issued grey uniforms may have been heavy and of the wrong color, but they were high quality. "Udonoho" described the new clothes: "We have our new uniforms, a portion of which are a perfect swindle. The pants for instance, some of which have been worn about two weeks, are sadly worn out already. I have seen poor cloth before, but I never saw any so poor as that of which our pants were made."[6]

The regiment remained at Quincy until early November, when it received orders to proceed by river to Benton Barracks at St. Louis, Missouri. Few cheered when surgeon Edwards returned to duty. The Pioneer Greys, in particular, would have preferred that Dr. Cool remain in charge. The worst thing that happened at Benton Barracks was the accidental death of Private Luther Griggs of Cedar Falls. The men were forming for a dress parade when a scuffle began. A musket held by Private John Merrill discharged and blew off the top of Griggs's head.[7]

The day after Christmas, the regiment, under the command of Major William M. Stone, was sent to guard the North Missouri Railroad. The new headquarters was at Mexico, Missouri, a town that had all but been abandoned. There were so many empty houses available that small groups of soldiers were able to move into them instead of setting up their tents. The local farms had an abundance of pigs and poultry that managed to find their way into the men's stew pots. Their military duties consisted chiefly of guarding work details on the railroad, so the winter passed comfortably.[8]

Colonel Nelson G. Williams, declared innocent of all charges against him, returned to duty at the end of February 1862. There were many in the regiment that still disliked the colonel, and he was forced to endure the catcalls of "Shelbina" as he rode into camp. Captain J. B. Smith, Adjutant Sessions, and most of the Greys believed that Williams had been falsely accused. They thought him a good officer, needed by the regiment. They believed that if Colonel Williams had been in charge at Blue Mills they would not have been sent into such an ambush.[9]

On the night of 3 March 1862, the 3d Iowa left Mexico, Missouri, for St. Louis. There they took transport south to a new camp on the Tennessee River called Pittsburg Landing and came under the command of General Grant.

The Union position at Pittsburg Landing was extremely strong because of the layout of the land. The lines faced south and southwest with the Tennessee River on the left, Snake Creek at the rear, and Owl Creek on the right. The federal army could only be attacked along the four-mile line to its front.

The army was divided into five divisions under Generals John McClernand, William Sherman, William H. Wallace, Stephen Hurlbut, and Benjamin Prentiss. A sixth division under General Lew Wallace was encamped at a place called Crump's Landing a few miles below the main camp. Grant kept his headquarters at the town of Savannah because he expected to meet General Don Carlos Buell, who was marching from Nashville with the Army of the Ohio. It would be at Savannah, eight miles north of the main camp, that Buell would first come to the Tennessee River. Once the two armies joined, Grant would have more than 60,000 troops under his command.[10] Included among these were 11 Iowa regiments.

Spring rains had swollen the river, and the Pioneer Greys' journey up the Tennessee aboard a crowded transport boat was unpleasant. They arrived at the landing on 17 March and were put into camp. Muddy roads and swamps criss-crossed the campgrounds; here and there were small clearings and a few farmhouses. A small building made of logs, the Methodist meetinghouse called Shiloh Church, was to the west of the front lines. The camp was a miserable place. Rain had turned the ground to mud, and a constant parade of teams, wagons and new arrivals turned the mud into liquid filth. A spring drizzle kept everyone cold and damp. From up and down the rows of tents came the sound of men coughing. The hospitals back at Savannah were already being filled with men too ill to remain in camp.

The cold rain let up after a week, and the next few days were warm and pleasant. The dry weather and sunshine did much to improve the men's health and good spirits. A private in the Greys described the camp:

> We are still in *status quo*, encamped upon the banks of the now swollen Tennessee.—The condition of the troops is not as we could wish. The long voyage here and the river water which at this season of the year is bad, has produced a distemper in the camps.—From this distemper, which exhibits itself in diarrhea, probably not more than one in five escapes. . . .
>
> I presume that the people of Iowa are congratulating themselves that in a few days the war will be at an end and your volunteers will soon be at home, but you must be patient; the war is not yet over and a single failure may prolong the war for months. In the mean time let us hope that no such failure will happen and that victory will continue to crown our arms.[11]

Confederate generals Albert Sidney Johnston and P. G. T.

Beauregard wanted to inflict just such a failure. In the early morning of Thursday, 3 April 1862, they put their 71 regiments, a total of more than 40,000 men, on the roads toward Pittsburg Landing and Shiloh Church.[12]

Grant's army was more experienced than the Confederate forces. Almost two-thirds of his men had been in action at Wilson's Creek, Blue Mills, Fort Donelson, or Pea Ridge. Few of the Southerners had ever heard a shot fired in battle. In fact, the Confederate army was little more than an armed mob. The men needed training and discipline, but General Johnston could not take the time because he knew that Grant was waiting for Buell. He had to wreck Grant's army quickly. If caught by surprise, Grant could be overwhelmed and driven into the Tennessee River.

The march north was a nightmare of confusion. The Southern recruits, unused to campaigning, fell in and out of line at will, tested their new muskets by firing them, and made the woods ring as they practiced their Confederate battle cries. An April rainstorm broke over the long, winding column on Friday and turned the roads to thick mud, which bogged down the men, artillery, and supply wagons. General Beauregard was discouraged. He believed that the Union troops were surely aware of the Confederate army and would be prepared to meet them from behind well-constructed earthworks.

The Union army began to receive reports of enemy troop movements on 3 and 4 April, but the reports were ignored by the commanding generals. When the colonel of the 53d Ohio reported to General Sherman that his advance pickets had come in contact with a large enemy force, Sherman, thinking it was a false alarm, sternly rebuked him, saying, "Take your damned regiment back to Ohio. Beauregard is not such a fool as to leave his base of operations and attack us in ours. There is no enemy nearer than Corinth."[13] Grant agreed and did nothing extraordinary to prepare for a possible attack.

Generals Grant and Sherman may have believed that there was no enemy force nearby, but the soldiers were not as sure. During a thunderstorm on the night of 4 April, Union and Confederate cavalry clashed in front of Sherman's line. The sound of the fighting caused an alarm, and General Hurlbut rode into the 3d Iowa camp and ordered its drummers to beat the long roll. Hurlbut quickly formed the men and hurried them forward to help Sherman. The cold rain soaked them as they took to the muddy road. The wheels of the artillery pieces and wagons sank to their hubs. Hurlbut had marched them about three-fourths of a mile when he received word that the crisis had passed. The men were glad to march back to camp, as they had no desire to spend the night in the mud awaiting battle without so much as a blanket.[14] As the Pioneer Greys marched through the rain in the dark,

51

they joked about Hurlbut. Many were not pleased with being under his command again, for they believed that he had been drunk during the Shelbina affair and had failed to support Colonel Williams, causing him to retreat.

The next day, while the Union army rested, Johnston and Beauregard deployed their men for a surprise attack in the morning. Beauregard was not convinced that a surprise was still possible and argued until the last minute that the attack should be canceled. Johnston disagreed. There would be no better time for attack, and another retreat, especially without a battle, would demoralize his troops. As dawn broke, both generals could hear the sound of gunfire. Confederate skirmishers had come in contact with a Union reconnaissance party—the battle had started. Johnston mounted his big bay thoroughbred and, as he rode forward, said, "Tonight we will water our horses in the Tennessee River."[15]

General Grant was not at the landing on the morning of 6 March; he was at his headquarters at Savannah. He had no plans to visit the camps that day. During the rainstorm the night of 4 April, his horse had slipped and smashed Grant's leg as it fell. The soft mud prevented the leg from being broken, but it was swollen and extremely painful, and it forced the general to limp about on crutches. His plans were quickly changed when he heard the sounds of battle coming from Pittsburg Landing. Grant boarded his headquarters ship, the *Tigress*, and hurried south toward the sound of the guns. When he arrived by midmorning, the battle was in full progress.

General Sherman's troops, on the right of the Union line, had been the first to receive the Confederate attack. The sun was just rising and there was not a cloud in the sky as Sherman and an orderly rode toward the sounds of musketry. Sherman looked across a large field to his front and saw a solid line of infantry, their bayonets shining in the sunlight. Hundreds of skirmishers advanced in front of the line. Some held their weapons at an angle, as if they were hunting quail. Others dropped to one knee and fired at the Federal line. Volley fire from the infantry line soon replaced the scattered shots of the skirmishers. The Federals' scattered fire could not stand up to the volleys coming against them, and, as more and more men fell, the others turned and ran for the rear.

Sherman rushed to his brigade commanders and warned them of the attack. Leaving their still-cooking breakfasts behind, the men were hurried forward. They saw retreating soldiers along the way but quickly formed a second line along a ridge in front of their camp. They did not have long to stare across the brush-covered valley before a wave of grey infantry surged out of the woods and advanced toward them. These Union troops had never been in battle, but they managed to hold their ridge against four successive attacks. They lost the ridge on the fifth charge but were able to retreat in good order and take up a third position farther to the rear.

The 6th Division under General Benjamin Prentiss caught the Confederate onslaught on the left. General John McClernand had led his men forward to aid Prentiss and managed to fill in a gap between Prentiss and Sherman so that all three divisions made up at least a ragged line. Men from all three divisions dropped out of the line and headed for the rear. The ones who remained were determined not to give ground, but the Confederate advance was too much for them and they were slowly forced back.

When Grant's boat docked, the General had his crutches strapped to his horse's saddle and rode toward the front. Skulkers, panic-stricken soldiers, and wounded men were stumbling to the rear and the shelter of the river bluffs as he rode forward. Grant first established a straggler line to intercept the fleeing troops and then hurried to where Wallace and Hurlbut had formed ranks and were sending their men into the fight as reinforcements for Sherman and Prentiss. He also sent word to General Lew Wallace to send his troops to the landing.

The Pioneer Greys had been eating their Sunday breakfasts when they first heard the sound of muskets. The firing increased in both volume and rapidity, and suddenly they heard cannon fire. Some men buckled on their accouterments and grabbed their guns. Others chose to try to ignore the noise until the long roll was beaten, and then everyone rushed to get their gear. Colonel Williams was in command of the 1st Brigade, and Major Stone was in command of the 3d Iowa. Fitzroy Sessions was acting assistant adjutant general and took the field with division commander Hurlbut and Colonel Williams. Captain Smith led his Pioneer Greys.[16]

Stone moved the regiment forward. As the men passed an Illinois regiment in line, they cheered when they heard an officer tell his men that all those caught straggling would be shot as cowards. Meanwhile, stragglers from the front, many without their weapons, and wagons filled with horribly mangled men poured down the road. The retreating soldiers called out that there were 100,000 rebel soldiers out there, that they had been cut to pieces, and that the enemy had captured their camps. The Pioneer Greys tried to ignore the fleeing men, who shouted that they would soon see for themselves.

The men had been ordered to load their Springfields with buck and ball before marching out of camp. After reaching the battle line, they were told to fix bayonets and be ready. Fleeing soldiers still filled the roads and woods as Captain Smith and the Greys tried to advance. They could hear the sound of Confederate guns behind the retreating troops but were heartened by the sight of battalion after battalion of their division moving in good order to plug the gaps left by the dead, wounded, and retreating men.

The Greys formed their first line at about 8:30 A.M. on the reverse slope of a small ridge covered with trees and brush. Confederate cannon began to shell the ridge, and the men lay on the ground as the shells burst in the treetops. The 3d was ordered forward to support a Union battery at the edge of a cotton field. Beyond the field, visible for the first time that morning, were the Confederates, proudly marching through Prentiss's abandoned camp. The Southern infantry turned, formed a line, and stood ready. The men of the 3d knelt and leveled their smoothbores at them, but they did not fire because their muskets could not carry that far. Then a regiment to the left of the 3d opened fire. The effect was contagious, and soon the whole brigade was shooting. The officers had a difficult time making the men stop wasting their ammunition in such useless firing.

One of the enemy's batteries opened up on the Union battery in the cotton field and succeeded in driving the crews away from their guns. Having silenced the battery, the Confederate gunners began to shell the infantry. The first shots went harmlessly overhead and rattled through the trees, but soon they found the range. Major Stone protested that his men were uselessly exposed. They were moved to the rear and placed in the third reserve line. The position in the reserve line was even more exposed, and shells burst over the men's heads and to their rear. Colonel Williams was severely hurt when a solid shot hit his horse, passing clear through the animal, which fell on top of him. Fitzroy Sessions hurried to Williams's aid and carried the colonel to safety.

Colonel Isaac C. Pugh of the 41st Illinois took command of the brigade, and Adjutant Sessions acted as his courier. The Pioneer Greys lay on their arms for over an hour as shells exploded all around them. The men could hear the sounds of battle to their right as Prentiss tried to hold his position. It was only 10 A.M., and the battle had raged for more than three hours. The Confederates were pushing hard at both Sherman and Prentiss. Sherman was forced back as both his flanks became endangered. As he retreated, the 6th Iowa came under fire, and 52 of its members were killed. The 11th Iowa and the 13th Iowa, as part of McClernand's brigade, came on the run to fill in the gap between Sherman and Prentiss. This was the first time that the two Iowa regiments had been under fire, and they broke, running in confusion. Prentiss fell back slowly, and Hurlbut, on his left, kept his divisions in line with Prentiss's men.[17]

Prentiss had been hit hard that morning, and his division had all but been destroyed, but as he retreated he found an old wagon road along the

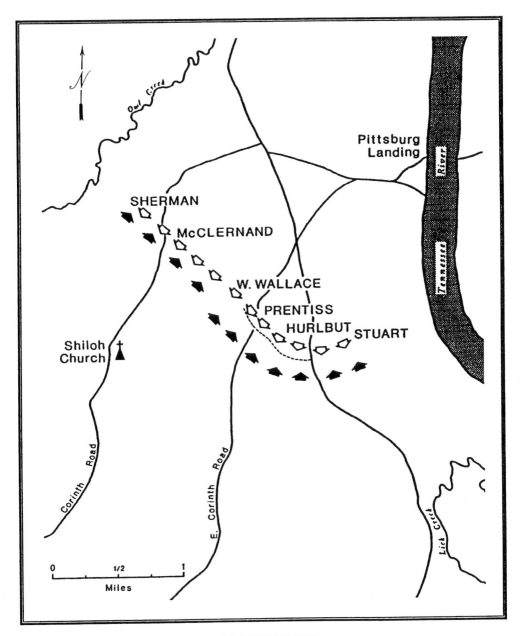

BATTLE OF SHILOH, FIRST DAY, MIDMORNING

Map by Andrew J. Karl

edge of a heavy woods. Rallying as many of his fleeing troops as he was able, Prentiss faced about in the shallow trench formed by the wagon ruts and stood ready. His men lay down in the soft mud of the road, some piling brush and logs in front, and waited for the enemy. There was not long to wait; the Confederates, running as if they still were chasing the Yankees, come straight at them. Prentiss waited until the enemy was well within range and opened fire. A sheet of flame burst along the length of the Union line. The Confederates fell back, crying to each other about finding a hornet's nest of Yankees. The Southerners reformed and charged Prentiss again, and they were once more forced back, leaving more dead men lying in the field. Grant arrived at Prentiss's position in time to see the Confederates fall back.

Along the front to the left of the "Hornet's Nest" was a series of small clearings, some containing peach trees and others having houses or cotton fields. Hurlbut pushed his brigades as far into the clearings as possible. This was the first time that the men from Cedar Falls had an opportunity to see Hurlbut in battle, and they were impressed. If he had been drunk at Shelbina, he was certainly not drunk at Shiloh. He sat on his horse as calmly as if he were on a parade ground and peered through his glasses past the peach trees to the Confederates, who were massing to attack. The artillery shells were still exploding around the men when the attack began. Sergeant J. T. Boggs of the Greys described the next few moments:

> Here they came in battle line through the field. We waited until they got within twenty rods of us when we gave them a full dose of Northern Pills, which took good effect on the gray devils. After the first fire we gave them it put me in mind of a windrow of stumps and chunks piled up. We left a row of their dead and wounded the length of the field.[18]

The Confederates charged across the field four times and were thrown back each time. The cheers of victory were short-lived, however, for the Union men could see regiment after regiment of Confederate soldiers filing along the opposite side of the cotton field to their front. They could hear the firing on the right grow less as the enemy massed in their front, preparing to sweep them aside and flank Prentiss's Hornet's Nest rather than trying to hit it head-on again.

Sidney Johnston's attack, which had begun so well with the surprise in the morning, was by afternoon stalled in front of the Hornet's Nest. Riding forward to break the stalemate, Johnston found that the Confederate troops were not willing to hurl themselves at the Yankee guns again. He rode along the far flank of the Hornet's Nest, opposite Hurlbut's peach orchard and cotton field, and encouraged his men to make one last attempt. Moving to the front and center, Johnston stood in his saddle stirrups and shouted that he would lead them, and as he galloped forward his soldiers followed.

Major Stone rode to the front as the Confederates swept forward. His horse was killed beneath him, and he was badly hurt in the fall. He was cut off from his men and captured. Captain Matthew M. Trumbull then took command of the regiment. The soldiers of the 3d became separated from the rest of the brigade but managed to fight their way back to their original camps. The Confederates pursued, and the 3d then fought through the camp to the landing itself, where Fitzroy Sessions tried to form them into a last line of defense. Captain Trumbull was wounded along with many of his men as they battled their way to the rear. Sergeant Boggs described the retreat:

> After standing under a heavy fire for over seven hours the right and left gave way and we were forced to retreat. The rebels had driven our lines back some four miles, and things began to look rather gloomy. We were within a half a mile of our camp, the rebels received reenforcements, and no one to support us, the most of our Division had left us, when Capt. Smith took command and ordered our retreat. It was just in time to save our bacon.—It was every man for himself. When I got to the camp the rebels were on two sides of it. This took me by surprise, and I thought I was a gone goose. But I had good faith in my running qualities, and said to myself, here it goes. With musket in hand, and my neck stretched out like a sandhill, I started through a heavy cross fire from the rebel musketry. At every jump I thought it would be my last. I could see men fall all around me, and before I reached the brush some cuss shot at my long legged boots, the ball striking the heel and glancing off without doing any damage. This was the only scratch I received. It was nearly sundown when we formed in battle line again, and waited for them to advance. But the sunlight and our fighting was done for the day.[19]

The landing at the river was filled with retreating men. Units were scattered and virtually all organization was gone. Many terrified men were in the river, desperately trying to swim out to the transports or hospital ships. Others cowered on the bank beneath the high bluffs, refusing to move, believing that all had been lost. Mule drivers were frantically whipping their beasts as they tried to save the wagons, while the medical personnel tried to keep the hospital supplies from being trampled as the soldiers ran through the dock area. The men who kept their heads rallied at the river, faced about, and dug in.

The night was dark and filled with clouds. The cries of thousands of wounded could be heard across the fields as hospital orderlies and men taken from the ranks looked for them by lantern light. The gunboats on the river kept up a constant shelling of the Confederate lines. The dark clouds opened up in rain again; lightning flashed across the treetops and thunder accompanied the sound of the booming gunboats. Other sounds could be heard above the cannon fire and thunder: bugles, the steady cadence of drums, and marching feet. Buell's Army of the Ohio had arrived at last and was moving into position along the hills above the river. Grant was being reinforced.

The Confederates had no such reserves. Johnston had expected General Van Dorne and 20,000 men from Arkansas, but Van Dorne had been unable to get across the Mississippi. The fighting would have to be done by the original troops.

Throughout the night, Buell's soldiers continued to be ferried ashore, where they marched up the steep bluffs to the tableland above the river. The troops were ashore by dawn, and at 7:00 A.M. Grant ordered the gunboats to cease fire. The infantry was going to advance.

The second day of the Battle of Shiloh was almost as bloody as the first had been, but this day there was little question as to the outcome. The fresh troops attacked with a fury and pushed the exhausted Confederates out of the old Federal camps toward Corinth. The Pioneer Greys were assigned to the reserves and were able to watch part of the battle from the bluffs.

The battle ended in the early afternoon. Beauregard took his men back to Corinth, and since Grant was satisfied with recapturing his original position, he did not pursue. These were the bloodiest two days of the year-long war. Thousands of dead and dying men lay in the wet grass and mud. Thousands more were at the rear in the field hospitals, or already aboard one of the hospital ships, or in the hospitals at Savannah. The survivors spent the next few days burying the dead of both sides. Grant had approximately 62,682 soldiers under his command at Shiloh; 1,754 had been killed, 8,408 had been wounded, and 2,885 had been reported as missing. The Confederates had 1,723 men killed, 8,012 wounded, and 959 missing.[20]

Nearly 7,000 soldiers from Iowa had been in the battle; 235 of them had been killed, 999 had been wounded, and 1,147 were missing, with most presumed to be captured. The number of Iowa troops listed as missing or captured was large because three Iowa regiments, the 8th, the 12th, and the 14th, had stayed with Prentiss and held the Hornet's Nest. The Iowa troops surrendered with Prentiss after Johnston's last attack finally outflanked their position.[21]

Colonel Williams, Major Stone, and Captain Trumbull of the 3d Iowa had been wounded, and Stone had been captured. The regiment recorded 23 men killed, 134 wounded, and 30 missing.[22] The Pioneer Greys suffered 17 loses at Shiloh. Private George W. Moury was killed while fighting. Privates Atherton Brown and Joseph Ross died of their wounds within a few days. First Lieutenant William Hammill and Second Lieutenant John Wayne were wounded. First Sergeant Gilbert Pulver and Second Sergeant Samuel Taggart also were wounded, as were Corporal Van Ransalaer Rider and Privates Martin Adams, Wallace Briggs, Calvin Jones, Eugene Jefferson, Charles Moulten, Michael Rambach, Norman Woolcott, and George Watson. Second Lieutenant Wayne, Private Calvin Jones, and Private Francis Tyrell were captured.[23] In the 12th Iowa's *E* Company, recruited from the Cedar Falls area, two men were killed, seven wounded, and 33 captured while serving with Prentiss in the Hornet's Nest.[24]

The two days of carnage at Shiloh had resulted in a Union victory. The invasion of the Confederacy, begun at Forts Henry and Donelson, could continue.

6

The Cedar Falls Reserves

The significance of the battle of Shiloh was not immediately clear, and the appalling cost in human lives shocked the nation. The victory carried with it no finality, only the promise of a longer, deadlier struggle. The Confederate army had not been destroyed. In fact, it had been reinforced at Corinth by Van Dorn's Arkansas troops and was as dangerous as the pre-Shiloh army had been. Grant, the hero of Fort Donelson, was branded the bungler of Shiloh. Rumors of the general's having been drunk for several days prior to the battle spread through the ranks and to the press. The victory, such as it was, was credited to the timely arrival of Buell and his men rather than to anything Grant had done. The Pioneer Greys shared the anger toward Grant. One member wrote, "There is a strong feeling here among the soldiers against Gen. Grant for allowing the surprise which happened on the 6th. . . . If Buell was behind time, it was no excuse for Grant not using due precaution in guarding against surprise. On the contrary, he should have used extraordinary precaution."[1]

Grant was not dismissed, but the public feeling against him caused General Halleck to leave Washington, come west, and personally take command of the troops at Pittsburg Landing. Halleck's command consisted of several smaller armies: Grant's Army of the Tennessee, Buell's Army of the Ohio, and John Pope's Army of the Mississippi. Pope and his men had not been at Shiloh but had just returned from capturing a Confederate stronghold on the Mississippi River, which opened Union navigation of the Mississippi to within 50 miles of Memphis, Tennessee. Memphis was protected by another Confederate obstacle, Fort Pillow.

Once in command, Halleck proceeded to advance on the Confederate army, entrenched at Corinth. Grant had been caught unaware at Shiloh, and Halleck had no intention of making the same mistake. He fought his campaign by the book. He advanced his force slowly, methodically, making a few miles' progress and then entrenching for the night.

General P. G. T. Beauregard, commander of the Southern army, wanted to defend Corinth. He saw the position as the key to the entire Mississippi Valley. By mid-May, he had more than 70,000 men under his command, but the force consisted of many who had been wounded at Shiloh and more who were falling ill in camp. Corinth did not have a fresh water supply ample enough for the needs of so many men, and their filth and refuse polluted what water there was. The longer Beauregard tried to hold Corinth, the more men he lost to disease. So, on 25 May, while Halleck was bringing up his siege guns, Beauregard decided to evacuate and leave the filthy town to the Union troops. One of the Greys described what they found:

> Many of the buildings were on fire; warehouses, containing army stores, in some cases, guns, brass instruments, and every class of hardware imaginable. The fat from burning meat ran out into the streets. In the road lay a huge pile of beans burning, and here and there bales of cotton. . . . Here and there a wagon which had given out was left burning, and beyond the railroad was a bridge which the fleeing rebels had attempted to burn.[2]

After capturing Corinth, Halleck did not pursue the Confederates and instead dispersed his large army. Grant's Army of the Tennessee was assigned to guard and repair key railroads, while Buell and the Army of the Ohio were sent east against the Confederate city of Chattanooga. Lincoln called John Pope east in early June to take command of the newly created Army of Virginia. It seemed that most Union offensive action had ended in the West.

Halleck was recalled in July and promoted to general-in-chief. The promotion allowed his second-in-command, Grant, to assume active leadership again.

The key target of 1862 was the Mississippi River. Whichever side owned the river owned the advantage. Troops could be landed up and down its length, and supplies could be easily transported into the deepest recesses of the Confederacy. The river meant access to the world through the Gulf of Mexico, and Union control of the river would divide the Confederacy. The capture of New Orleans by Admiral David Farragut left only one Confederate fortress on the river, Vicksburg, Mississippi, and General Grant had ideas on that subject.

Confederate leaders had not thrown up their arms in surrender after Shiloh or New Orleans but instead made plans to strike. General Beauregard had been replaced. His successor was General Braxton Bragg, a West Point graduate and Mexican War veteran, who desired nothing more than a chance to recoup Southern losses. Bragg left 32,000 men in Mississippi under Generals Earl Van Dorne and Sterling Price to defend the city of Vicksburg and central Mississippi. He then took the rest of his army, some 32,000 men, and transported them by a round-about journey through Mobile and Atlanta, then north to Chattanooga. By mid-August, he was in place for a counterinvasion.

Bragg's hopes were smashed at the battles of Iuka, Mississippi, on 19 September; Corinth, Mississippi, on 3 and 4 October; and Perryville, Kentucky, on 8 October. The three battles were Union victories, and, once again, the Confederate armies were forced to retreat further south.

Iowa troops were conspicuous at the battles of Iuka and Corinth. The 5th, 10th, 16th, and 17th Iowa regiments fought at Iuka and lost a total of 354 men.[3] The Union Brigade, which fought at Corinth, contained the remnants of the 8th, 12th, and 14th Iowa regiments, men who had escaped being captured with Prentiss at Shiloh. Five hundred thirty-one Iowans were listed as killed, wounded, or missing at Corinth.[4] The 3d Iowa was not engaged in either battle.

On 5 October, as Price's Confederates were retreating from Corinth, they were met by Hurlbut's 4th Division. The battle, known as the Battle of the Hatchie, or Matamora Heights, was another Union victory. The 3d Iowa distinguished itself by making a heroic charge across a bridge and up a steep hill into the enemy works. The regiment's casualties were 62 men killed and wounded, most of whom were hit while crossing the bridge.[5] The Pioneer Greys had no one killed, but several were wounded. "St. Charles" described the fight:

> Captain Trumbull led the 3d into the fight and a better specimen of bravery was never seen. After we crossed the bridge and received the iron hail of war, he said to the boys that he was not going to retreat that day but would sooner die there. The 3d Iowa beat her own good name for pluck. One of Gen. Ord's staff who witnessed the whole fight, told me that the 3d in charging across the bridge as they did, and holding their ground, saved a stampede and gained the day.
>
> Most of our wounded are severely so, because nearly all were hit with canister shot, perhaps in our regiment, all but six or eight.
>
> There were of course a few instances of cowardice shown. Two poor frightened fellows attempted to cross the bridge and were driven back by the guards, when they went back a little way, placed their left hands over the muzzles of their guns and shot their fingers off. One artillery man undertook to run when he was caught by three of his fellow artillery men thrown upon the ground and pounded well nigh to death, the boys all the while singing out "kill him, kill him."[6]

The slow but definite Union advances in the West during the summer and fall of 1862 were not matched in the East. General McClellan had proven to be marvelously organized but too slow, according to President Lincoln.

McClellan launched a massive campaign against the city of

Richmond in late June, the Peninsular Campaign. After seven days of fierce fighting and the deaths of thousands of soldiers, McClellan was turned away and forced to seek the shelter of his gunboats on the James River. Disappointed with McClellan, Lincoln looked to the West to find a general capable of winning. He thought the man might be John Pope.

The Peninsular Campaign was significant in that it introduced a new general to the field, Robert E. Lee of Virginia. Lee's Army of Northern Virginia would have to be defeated if Richmond was ever to be captured. The task was assigned to Pope.

Pope did no better against Lee than had McClellan. Lee sent Pope and his army retreating across the Potomac after a second battle at Bull Run, in August. Lincoln then shelved Pope and put McClellan back in command.

McClellan next met Lee's army at a small Maryland town called Sharpsburg on Antietam Creek. The battle was the single bloodiest day of the war, with more than 24,000 men being shot. The battle was far from a Union victory, but Lee had been forced to abandon the field to the enemy and retreat to Virginia. Lincoln was eager to cheer the first battle in the East that looked like a victory, but he knew that McClellan's army had outnumbered Lee's and that McClellan should have destroyed the Southern army.

Lincoln again dismissed McClellan and gave command of the Army of the Potomac to General Ambrose Burnside. Burnside insisted that he was not capable of leading such a large force. The result was a wholesale slaughter of Union soldiers at Fredericksburg in December 1862. Burnside, too, would have to go.

The war in the East, near the capitals of the two sides and under the eyes of the entire world, seemed, at the end of 1862, to be a failure. Fresh troops were needed in all theaters. Troops were now enlisted for three years rather than the three months asked of the first volunteers. The recruiting service, which had been closed in early April, was reopened on 2 June 1862, and on 1 July Lincoln issued a call for 300,000 soldiers.

Iowa's quota was 10,570 men to serve for three years in either old or new regiments and 10,570 militia to be drafted for nine months to fill the old regiments. The War Department of Iowa, however, accepted 24,438 volunteers for three years service and ordered 8,005 more men to fill the old regiments, refusing to allow any nine-month enlistments.[7] The state quotas were to be filled by 15 August, and any state not able to meet the required numbers would have its deficiency made up by a draft. Volunteering progressed slowly through July, but with the threat of a fall draft, which would be the height of disgrace, recruiting went faster later in the summer. Twenty-two new Iowa regiments were being formed by the end of the summer. The 19th to 40th regiments were mustered into service between August and December.[8] There was even serious discussion of enlisting black men, but nothing was done at this time.

A major problem with the system of raising recruits was that it was difficult to fill the old, experienced regiments at the same time as new ones were being formed. Politics—the desire for rank and authority— was a primary reason for the difficulty. Each new regiment would need a complete complement of officers, and men with ambition could rise faster in a new regiment than in an old one. The result was that veteran regiments, their original membership dwindled to a skeleton force, had to beg for recruits while new regiments were filled to capacity. Those recruiting from Cedar Falls were no different. The *Gazette* ran a suitable comment: "We hear of at least half a dozen men in this town who have applied for commissions to raise companies for the war, and about as many more as that who intend doing so. We apprehend that there would be no difficulty whatever in recruiting a company of captains."[9]

Volunteering in 1862 was also stimulated by money. The first volunteers had been promised their army pay, clothing, rations, and an opportunity to serve their country. Such inducements were not enough a year later, so a system of bounty payments was established. Each three-year recruit was to receive a $100 bonus paid over a period of time. At the time of enlistment, a private received a month's pay in advance ($13), one-fourth of the $100 bounty, and a $2 enlistment payment, for a total of $40.[10] States were also permitted to offer their own bounty plan in addition to federal money. Iowa did not offer a state bounty, but many counties, including Black Hawk, offered their own. Iowa's 5th and 6th congressional districts raised a $1,200 bounty fund, with the local communities free to decide how it was to be spent.[11]

One of the reasons that new recruits were needed was that the first volunteers and the old regiments were both becoming worn out. Many of the first enlistees had been shot or had fallen ill because of the exertions of military life. Military politics also took a toll on the regiments as officers vied for recognition and favor.

No member of the Pioneer Greys was as violently patriotic as Adjutant Fitzroy Sessions, but, by the end of his first year of service, he too was wearing down.

Sessions's service record was excellent. He was regimental adjutant and had led the Pioneer Greys at Blue Mills. He had served heroically at Shiloh. Both General Hurlbut and Colonel Pugh of the 41st Illinois praised Sessions in their official reports, saying that he acted "with gallantry, bravery, and self possession."[12] After Shiloh, Sessions began to consider resigning. He asked Dr. Cool to help him get a long furlough so that he could recover his health without having to resign his commission. Dr. Cool explained:

> Lieut. Sessions has been unwell for over two months doing not only his duty as Adjutant of the regiment, but for a long time acted as A.A.A. General. But his failing health compelled him to quit work and finally, after much advice from his friends, he concluded to ask for a leave of absence for a few days. I went with him to the Division Surgeon in order to assist him to get the necessary leave. The surgeon's reply was that he must resign if not able to do duty. This he refused to do until he became firmly convinced that he could not recover if compelled to remain in camp. . . . Under these circumstances he handed in his resignation, being thouroughly convinced that this was his only hope. I took the document myself to Gen. Laumen, now commanding this Brigade. The General said that this would never do; that he was one of our best officers, and that we could not afford to lose him. I laid the case fairly before the General, who recommended that instead of accepting his resignation a leave of absence be granted him. I then went to Gen. Hurlbut who made the same remarks. . . . I then went to Dr. Derby, the Division Surgeon, who heartily approved the matter, and the result was that, instead of being compelled to give up his commission and go out of the service, he has just what he wanted, and so much needs, a long furlough.[13]

Sessions returned to Cedar Falls and stayed until August. That same month, Colonel Williams wrote Governor Kirkwood and tried to get Sessions a well-deserved promotion:

> Your Excellency,
>   Amongst the deserving officers in the 3d Iowa none stand higher as an efficient officer than Adjutant Fitzroy Sessions.
>   Without fear of contradiction I can say there has no officer in this regiment exhibited more zeal in the performance of his duties than the Adjutant. He has been faithful and untiring in the discharge of the duties of his office at all times.
>   At the battle of Pittsburg Landing he acted as Asst. Ajt. Genl. and behaved with such gallantry as to receive special mention by the Commanding General in his Official Report. The position of Adj. in a regiment is isolated and removes the incumbant from the line of promotion, for these reasons I feel it my bounden duty and pleasure to recommend the Adjutant to your Excellency for promotion and therefore most earnestly and respectfully ask that your Excellency make him a Major or Lt. Col. in one of the new regiments.[14]

Colonel Williams's recommendation probably carried little political weight; he was an officer who had been up on charges of cowardice and public drunkeness, and whether cleared or not, he would always be suspect. General Hurlbut, who had endorsed the letter, was probably no more help in that respect, as rumors of drunken behavior and corruption had also been spread about him. Sessions's health did not improve after his return to duty, and in early October he resubmitted his resignation. This time it was accepted.

Every old regiment had lost some of its best men to wounds, diseases, and resignations. The recruiting drive of 1862, with its bounties and commissions in new regiments, was designed to remedy that situation.

The mounting cost of the seemingly never-ending struggle caused many to harden their opinions on the war. Those who supported the war began to take a more critical attitude; those who opposed the war became more bitter in its denunciation. There was little middle ground left. Local politics reflected the polarization of the two sides.

The most important issue of the war was slavery. Conservatives had traditionally rejected the idea of outright abolition as too radical, but by the summer of 1862, it had become obvious that slavery was a war issue. Suggestions of a year earlier, such as freedom for the slaves of the Confederacy or allowing black men to serve their country as soldiers, were no longer considered radical. Henry Perkins, of the *Cedar Falls Gazette*, had been a leader of the Union movement and had condemned the county's radical Republicans as abolitionists. Perkins had changed his mind as the war continued; by the summer of 1862, he called for the support of Lincoln's plan of gradual emancipation, and he urged that black men be allowed to serve as soldiers. In an article in the *Gazette,* he explained his views.

> Let all loyal men, whether white or black, be accepted into the Union cause. If a negro offers his services to the Government why should he be refused? The rebels use them in every department of military service, and if they can make them available why not the North? . . . We never could see why a black skin should prevent a man from fighting for the Union. We were never in favor of making this war simply a crusade against slavery, but if this gigantic rebellion can be crushed more easily and promptly by annihilating the accursed institution in the name of humanity let it be done, and the people as with one voice will say amen.[15]

The Peace Democrats were also becoming more radical. The outspoken opinions of Dennis Mahoney of the *Dubuque Herald* were strong enough that he was arrested and hauled off to jail in Washington, D.C. Perkins cheered the arrest: "So another one of treason's props has been cut down and the only fault we have to find is that it was not done sooner. But better late than never."[16]

The Democratic Party had never had a strong following in Cedar Falls, but as the war continued, the Peace Democrats became more visible. A Democratic paper, the *Northwest Democrat*, was established, and, under a series of at least four editors, it served as an opposition voice to Perkins, Melendy, and the other Republicans. The paper was not in business for long. Unfortunately, no copies have survived, but articles in reference to the *Democrat* appearing in the *Gazette* brand it as a treasonous publication.

The condemnation of the *Democrat* was explained in an article titled "Treason in Cedar Falls—The Evidence!"

> The character of this print has been well known here from its birth. Some, however, may have been deceived by its protestations of Unionism and of its affinity with Democracy, but there is no longer palliation under such a plea, for the most simple-minded of all its supporters. Read its platform:
>
> "The South is engaged in an earnest struggle for independence. The avowed object of the leaders, and the end for which the people labor is to throw off the old Government with its burdens, and to establish a new one, better calculated in every respect to advance the interests of the South. They are fighting for their homes, institutions, and their liberty, and it is useless, nay folly, to longer disguise the fact that they are terribly in earnest, death will be welcomed by them rather than submit to subjugation. We must honor them for their zeal and courage."
>
> Such are the sentiments of the *Northwest Democrat!* We are shocked and chagrined at the audacity of its utterences—utterences which for spleen and vileness, and perversion of truth, could not be outdone by any red-mouthed rebel in Rebeldom. Mahoney in all his career, never gave vent to such rank, disgusting treason. Democrats of the Cedar Valley: do you endorse the *Democrat?* If so, you are aiding and abetting rebellion. Every man who contributes to the support of this pestiferous sheet, contributes to the breaking up of the Union and the destruction of his country.[17]

The issue of slavery as a war aim was settled on 22 September 1862, when Abraham Lincoln issued the famous preliminary Emancipation Proclamation.

Peace Democrats condemned the proclamation as proof that the abolitionists controlled the Republican Party. Perkins, Melendy, and the other Cedar Falls Republicans supported it. The soldiers were mixed in their reactions, but the majority seemed to believe that it was time such an act was taken. A letter from a Cedar Falls resident serving in the 1st Iowa Battery explained the reaction of men in that unit:

> The President's Emancipation Proclamation has been differently received by the members of this Battery; but the majority think it is the quickest, and surest way of putting down this rebellion. We have been in the South long enough to see that slavery is the mainstay of the rebel army. They can press their whole white population into the field and

have an army of between three and four millions of slaves at home to raise the produce necessary to support them.[18]

Support for the proclamation and the Republicans' enlarged war policies came in November with the congressional elections. The Republican Party swept the Iowa elections, winning all six contested seats. An important factor in the election was that soldiers were allowed to vote where they were stationed rather than having to come home. The Republican Party, more radical than it had been at the start of the war, was the principal party in Iowa, the 6th congressional district, and Cedar Falls.

Military activities continued in Cedar Falls throughout the summer. Recruiters from the new regiments found Cedar Falls a good town in which to find willing volunteers. Some of the recruiters were well known in town. Captain Smith returned to find volunteers for his Pioneer Greys but had little success. William McClure, recovered from Pea Ridge injuries, came to recruit soldiers for the 6th Iowa Cavalry. Men from the Cedar Falls area also enlisted in the 21st, 32d, and 37th regiments. The 37th Iowa was a unique regiment, composed of men more than 45 years old who were to be used for garrison duties so that younger men could be freed to go to war. The men of the 37th proudly took the name "Greybeards." Five men from Cedar Falls joined the Greybeards in October 1862.[19]

Lincoln's July call for troops included at least a full regiment from the 5th and 6th districts. The people of Cedar Falls were determined that no draft would be required of their district. Meetings and rallies were held and financial inducements discussed. It was decided that, in addition to the government bounty of $100, each man who agreed to enlist in the regiment from the district would receive $15 from the local fund.[20]

A large Union rally was held in Overman Hall on the night of 30 July. Colonel Sessions chaired the meeting, Henry Perkins was secretary, and Zimri Streeter was one of the guest speakers. The rally had an ambitious purpose—to raise another full company of volunteers from Cedar Falls. Local businessman Thomas Walkup offered a bounty of $5 to any man who would join then and there. At least six men took him up on the offer. Andrew Mullarky offered deeds for tracts of land for those who joined. By the end of the month, the roll was complete.[21]

The Cedar Falls Pioneer Greys had been made up of many of the town's young men, eager for adventure and able to leave their homes to become soldiers. This second company, the Cedar Falls Reserves, was much different. The average age of the original Pioneer Greys was 23, but the average age of the Reserves was 27. Many of the Reserves were businessmen: successful men who could, if they chose, hire substitute soldiers if they were in danger of being drafted or simply pay the

68

government $300 to buy their way out. They did neither.

The captain of the Reserves was Robert P. Speer, a 34-year-old lawyer and one of the earliest residents of Cedar Falls. Speer had been the first justice of the peace as well as a land surveyor, tracing section lines for settlers seeking government land.[22] Theodore Stimming, 32 years old, was first lieutenant. Stimming had been a member of H Company of the 1st Iowa and was a veteran of the battle of Wilson's Creek.[23] Edward Townsend, age 30, was second lieutenant. Townsend was a partner in the banking firm of Townsend and Knapp.[24] Thomas Salisbury, age 31, was orderly sergeant. Salisbury had been one of the original organizers of the Pioneer Greys and had accompanied Charles Mullarky on his recruiting trip to Charles City.[25] Edwin Brown, now age 43, took a partner in the mill so that he could join. John Rath, the young German immigrant employed by Brown, enlisted as well.[26] George Perkins, 23 years old, coeditor and publisher of the *Gazette*, left the newspaper in his brother's care and joined the company.[27]

Samuel Rownd and his brother James watched their two sons, Samuel, Jr., and John, join the Reserves. James's other son, George, was a member of the 1st Iowa Battery and had fought at the battle of Pea Ridge.[28] Colonel William Sessions's youngest son, Daniel, also joined the Reserves.[29]

There were many other businessmen, relatives, and friends in the new company. The unmarried men chose to give their county bounty money to the married men, who had greater needs, and in early September, the company was ready to leave town.[30]

Thursday morning, 4 September 1862, the Cedar Falls Reserves and 95 members of a company from Floyd County boarded the train for Dubuque. This time there was no parade for the volunteers, no brass band playing martial music, and no passenger cars reserved for the troops. The two companies rode to Dubuque on the flatcars of a gravel train, and the crowd of relatives and friends was not cheering: "Streaming eyes bore testimony how great was the sacrifice being offered upon the altar of our country."[31]

The 100-mile trip might have been uncomfortable, considering the rough accommodations, were it not for a kindly railroad employee. Conductor James Northrup supplied the volunteers with two kegs of ale for the journey. The men were most appreciative.[32]

When the men arrived in Dubuque, they were quartered for a week at the Minnesota House hotel and the Armory Hall. They were not assigned or mustered into service but were drilled as if they were enlisted.

The Reserves expected to be assigned to the 32d Infantry commanded by John Scott, who had recently resigned as lieutenant colonel of the 3d Iowa. Scott had been unpopular with the Pioneer Greys; they blamed him both for the charges brought against Colonel Williams and for leading the regiment into ambush at Blue Mills. Rather than risk any conflicts in his new regiment, Colonel Scott refused to take any companies from Black Hawk County.[33] The Reserves were left at Camp Franklin through the month of September, waiting to be assigned.

The Cedar Falls volunteers were stationed at Camp Franklin, just north of Dubuque. While there, they had many opportunities to visit with friends from home. One chance came when more than 1,300 people from the Cedar Falls area boarded cars on the Dubuque and Sioux City Railroad for an excursion to Dubuque and Camp Franklin. The excursion was the largest such outing in the railroad's year-and-a-half history. The crowd filled 22 cars, and the train was pulled by two locomotives.[34] The last opportunity for visiting came when Captain Speer brought the company home to participate in the town's annual Agricultural Fair.

The high point of the last day of the fair was a formal ceremony honoring the Cedar Falls Reserves. The Ladies of Cedar Falls presented Lieutenant Stimming with a sword and Captain Speer with a silk flag. The flag was four and one-half feet by six and one-half feet, and across the stripes in gold letters were written the words, "Presented by the Ladies of Cedar Falls." Joseph B. Powers had the privilege of presenting the gifts on behalf of the women. With the Reserves lined up in formation before the speaker's stand, Powers said, "Soldiers this is your country's flag, which in lisping boyhood you were taught to revere and respect and which it is your duty with the energy and strength of manhood to cherish and protect."[35]

Captain Speer and Lieutenant Stimming accepted the gifts on behalf of the entire company. The men of the Reserves responded with three loud cheers for the ladies and three more for the flag itself. Speer then led his men onto the field, where he put them through a series of military maneuvers. The display ended with the men engaging in a mock skirmish in front of the crowd of fair-goers.

The company had gained a man while they were in Dubuque. John Rath's older brother, George Rath, had been visiting their relatives in Dubuque when John enlisted and the company was transported to Dubuque. When George heard that Cedar Falls soldiers had arrived, he went to visit them at Camp Franklin and was surprised to find his brother in the company. George then followed his younger brother's example and enlisted as well.[36]

On 2 October the Reserves boarded the steamship *Bill Henderson* for transport downriver to Camp Herron, about a mile and a half from Davenport, where they were to be mustered into service and assigned to a regiment.

They received their uniforms on 10 October, and, on 13 October, the

Cedar Falls Reserves were sworn into the army as B Company, 31st Iowa Volunteer Infantry. There were two other companies from Black Hawk County in the regiment: I Company, from Waterloo, and D Company, from La Porte City. Other individuals from the Cedar Falls area served in C, E, F, and G companies of the 31st.[37]

The colonel of the regiment was William Smyth, a well-known lawyer and judge from Linn County. Smyth had been on the commission that revised Iowa's territorial statutes in preparation for statehood. He was a self-educated, capable man but had not had any military experience or training and had achieved his rank through political influence alone.[38] Smyth's lieutenant colonel was Jeremiah Jenkins, from Maquoketa.

The Reserves were extremely fortunate when the regiment was issued its muskets. A and B companies, the regiment's flanking companies, were issued new British-made Enfield rifles, the best military weapon available. The other companies were angry, for they had been issued old Prussian-made smoothbore muskets. A member of K Company described the Prussian guns:

> Our arms are old muskets and in the worst kind of order. A great many of them are not fit for service at all. The boys blame our Col. for allowing such arms to be sent to his men. Some of the Coms. would not take them at first—but—finally knucked under.[39]

On 1 November, the steamship *Sucker State* pulled up to the levee, and the officers were told to get their men ready. The *Sucker State* was a large boat, but with more than 900 men aboard, it was extremely crowded. Many men were forced to try to sleep on the open "hurricane deck." The weather turned bad in the early morning, with cold rain and wet, blowing snow. The men caught on deck retreated below and were crowded into the ship's hold.[40]

The next day, Sunday, was a pleasant fall day, and the men enjoyed themselves on deck. The members of A and B companies, much to the annoyance of the others, practiced with their Enfields by shooting at the many flocks of geese along the river. Some made close shots at a distance of almost half a mile; many birds were killed at several hundred yards. The shooting demonstrated the need for the entire regiment to be armed with such weapons.[41]

The *Sucker State* arrived at St. Louis on 5 November. The men were curious as to their destination but were told to stay on the boat. They stayed aboard all that night and all the next day until evening, when they were ordered to get their weapons, blankets, and accouterments together for a march to Benton Barracks, about four miles from the levee. They were pleased with the spacious accommodations at the famous camp but were not going to be allowed to enjoy them; they were to leave the next day. The men of the other companies were happy to hear that their Prussian smoothbores were to be exchanged for Enfield rifles.[42]

The 31st Iowa marched away from Benton Barracks on the evening of 9 November and boarded the steamboat *Continental*. There were many rumors as to where they were going; none was confirmed, but most mentioned Helena, Arkansas. It was said that a huge army was being assembled at Helena for an expedition down the Mississippi River to the city of Vicksburg.

CEDAR FALLS MILLRACE
Courtesy of the
Cedar Falls Historical Society

WILLIAM STURGIS
Courtesy of the
Cedar Falls Historical Society

JOHN M. OVERMAN
Courtesy of the
Cedar Falls Historical Society

DEMPSEY OVERMAN
Courtesy of the
Cedar Falls Historical Society

PETER MELENDY
Courtesy of the
Cedar Falls Historical Society

GEORGE PERKINS
Courtesy of the
Cedar Falls Historical Society

HENRY PERKINS
Courtesy of the
Cedar Falls Historical Society

BARBARA S. BOEHMLER
Courtesy of the
Cedar Falls Historical Society

NELSON G. WILLIAMS
Courtesy of the State Historical Society
of Iowa, Special Collections

ROBERT P. SPEER
Courtesy of the
Cedar Falls Historical Society

THEODORE STIMMING
Courtesy of the
Cedar Falls Historical Society

WILLIAM SMYTH
Courtesy of the
State Historical Society of Iowa

JEREMIAH JENKINS
Courtesy of the
Cedar Falls Historical Society

JAMES M. TUTTLE
Courtesy of the
State Historical Society of Iowa

WILLIAM M. STONE
Courtesy of the
State Historical Society of Iowa

JOHN RATH
Courtesy of the
Cedar Falls Historical Society

**CIVIL WAR SOLDIERS'
ORPHANS' HOME**
*Courtesy of the
Cedar Falls Historical Society*

IN MEMORY
OF OUR
SOLDIERS DEAD

**CIVIL WAR MONUMENT,
GREENWOOD CEMETERY**
Photograph by Mark Shore

7

Vicksburg

After the capture of New Orleans in the spring, Vicksburg, Mississippi, remained the last Southern bastion on the Mississippi River. Confederate guns on the bluffs on the east side commanded the river, and the high, steep banks were ideal for infantry defense. It was not a city that could be captured easily.

There were, however, several ways to get at the city. The most obvious way was to simply transport an army downriver by steamer, unload the soldiers, and have them storm the works. Another way was to march troops south from Memphis to the state capital of Jackson, take the capital, and then turn west toward Vicksburg. The least desirable way was to march soldiers down the west side of the river and then transport them across at a good spot. The problem was that the Union boats were north of the city, and if they were to steam south, they could be shot out of the water as they passed the batteries on the bluffs. A well-fortified and well-defended position south of the city, Port Hudson prevented Union boats from steaming upriver. Vicksburg had to be taken from the north, by one means or another.

The first person to approach President Lincoln with a plan of action was General John McClernand. McClernand had commanded a division at Shiloh but was more well known as a prominent War Democrat from Illinois. His independent call on Lincoln violated military protocol, for Vicksburg was in Grant's area of command. McClernand wanted to try the direct river approach and even volunteered to use his political influence to personally raise the troops needed. Lincoln listened and, it seemed to McClernand, agreed to let him try. The meeting was secret, and while Grant was shaping his own plans for the city, he was left in the dark about this new operation.

Grant had an ally in the White House, General-in-Chief Halleck, who resented McClernand. While the Illinois general was back home raising new troops, Halleck was seeing to it that, once mustered, those troops were sent to Memphis and Helena, both directly under Grant's command. Halleck also informed Grant, as much as possible, about McClernand's plans.

Both McClernand and Grant complained to Lincoln about what each believed to be interference. Lincoln, a wise and experienced politician, was quite willing to make good use of McClernand. He was not, however, willing to give an operation of such importance to the powerful Democrat. Lincoln upheld Grant's authority and reduced McClernand from an independent commander to a corps commander under Grant. McClernand had been hoping to gain good political mileage out of the preparations for the campaign. He had even planned to begin his honeymoon by taking his new bride and the full reception party down to Memphis, where he would personally take command of his troops.

Grant was making his own plans, and they did not include McClernand. He didn't need the general, but he did need his soldiers, so with Halleck's approval, he put them under the command of his trusted friend, General William T. Sherman. While McClernand was busy with his wedding plans, Grant and Sherman were hurrying their Vicksburg plans so as to be on their way by the time he returned from Illinois.[1]

Between the generals and their ambitious plans were thousands of soldiers, most of them volunteers from Lincoln's call in July. They were, for the most part, inexperienced recruits, and they were expected to carry out one of the most important and difficult assignments of the war. The Cedar Falls Reserves, B Company, 31st Iowa, were among their number.

The regiment's river journey from Benton Barracks near St. Louis to Helena, Arkansas, was difficult. The *Continental* was a large steamer, but it was severely overloaded with men and cargo. The trip gave the men their first taste of a soldier's diet; all they received during the 20-day journey was pilot bread, often called hardtack, a heavy flour cracker that was the infantry's mainstay. The camp at Helena was huge: the ground along the river was white with military tents for over two miles. The Reserves were pleased to find many old friends among the thousands of soldiers assembled there. The 9th Iowa Infantry and the 1st and 3d Iowa batteries, all with members from Cedar Falls, were at the Helena encampment. John Rownd was able to visit his brother, George, from the 1st Iowa Battery, and write their parents that "george is fat and looks just like he did when he left he has not changed in the least i guess he will be glad to be home once more."[2] George's weight may have been due to the fact that some of his friends had hired him at $8 a month to cook for them.[3]

The regiment was assigned to General Sherman's command as part of the 1st Division, under General Frederick Steele, and the 2d Brigade, under General Alvin Hovey. They were only in camp a few days when they were ordered to march to a place called Cold Water, Mississippi. The Cold Water expedition was a part of Grant's maneuvers designed to drive the Confederate army away from Holly Springs and allow him to establish a supply base there. The 31st did not have to go into battle during the march, but the hurried pace and infantryman's load gave the men an idea of what war was really about.

The men were not yet used to hard campaigning, and the expedition was extremely difficult. They had not learned to roll their shelter-tent halves and blankets into bedrolls, which could be carried comfortably over their shoulders. Instead, they carried the regulation army knapsack, which pulled at a man's shoulders and upper arms as he marched. John Rownd had an advantage. The 1st Iowa Battery was also on the expedition, traveling near the 31st Infantry, and George was able to carry his brother's pack on one of the artillery wagons. Even with his brother's assistance, John was exhausted.

> It was a very hard trip on me being the first one and having to carry such a big load on our backs we had to carry our blankets canteens of watter and three days rations the second days march i was done out entirely I could not get my coat off and it was most impossible for me to feed myself that night on account of my shoulders being so tired and sore the next morning i was some better but my back and shoulders was quite stiff yet. . . .
> George was along and he took my knapsack i was very thankful for it lighted my load a great deal.[4]

The expedition returned to Helena on 7 December. There had been seven cotton gins, two houses, and thousands of dollars worth of cotton burned during the march. The 31st Iowa was accused of doing the burning. Colonel Smyth insisted that the burning had been done by other regiments. Lieutenant Stimming was enraged that the subject had even come up and insisted that he had not come south to protect the property of traitors, and, if that was the army's policy, then they could have his sword.[5]

The regiment remained at Helena for most of December. Winter in Arkansas did not come with Iowa-like blizzards, but there was much rain, and soon the camps were sitting in seas of mud. The men were able to store their shelter tents temporarily and construct small, comfortable log cabins.

The Reserves were not allowed to enjoy their little cabins for long. They received their marching orders on 22 December. The date was no accident; McClernand's wedding was to be on 23 December. When the wedding party steamed into Memphis on 28 December, all they found were empty docks. There were no transports or troops; they all had gone off with Sherman.

What McClernand and his party did not know was that the next day the soldiers they expected to meet in Memphis would be slaughtered just north of Vicksburg. Grant's plans were to fail.

The plans were simple enough. The campaign was to have been a cooperative effort between Sherman, on the river, and Grant, on land. The Southern army would meet Grant's army somewhere near Grenada, and while he fought them, Sherman could attack and destroy the city's defensive garrison. Whereas the plans were simple, their execution was difficult. The two forces were widely separated, and their lines of communication weak. Grant was dependent upon the long railroad back to Holly Springs and Columbus, and Sherman's force would not be strong enough to do the job alone if Grant were to run into trouble.

And run into trouble he did. Confederate cavalry, under Generals Bedford Forrest and Earl Van Dorne, raided deep into Mississippi and wrecked Grant's railroad and supply base at Holly Springs, cutting him off. He was deep in enemy territory without supplies, out of touch with Sherman and everyone else. He would be fortunate to get his army back to Memphis unharmed under such conditions; any ideas of continuing the advance were out of the question. Sherman was on his own.

Sherman had taken his troops up the Yazoo River north of Vicksburg, intending to strike at the city's northern defenses at a place called Chickasaw Bluffs. The Confederate army, free from any danger from Grant, was hurried back to the northern defenses and lay in the trenches waiting.

Sherman, still ignorant of Grant's whereabouts, launched his attack on 29 December. The result was a disaster. Nearly 1,800 men were shot down in front of the Confederate trenches. Union soldiers, looking up at the enemy forts, were so exposed that many were forced to dig into the embankments with their hands and scoop out little sheltering caves as the Southerners fired down at them. Many of the men huddled there until after dark, when they were withdrawn one at a time. Sherman was forced to pull back to the river a dozen miles north of the city.[6]

The assault on Chickasaw Bluffs was the first test of battle for the Cedar Falls Reserves. Captain Speer described the company's participation:

> About half an hour after sunrise our army attacked the enemy, and before evening the rebels were driven to their entrenchments, and on the following morning the attack was renewed. About noon our entire regiment was ordered to the field, but did not have an opportunity to participate in the action. . . . Before the battle closed a rain storm set in and continued through the night; and many were the thoughts of home

as our soldiers lay in the mud, wet to the skin. On Tuesday the battle was not renewed, and on Wednesday we sent out a flag of truce and brought in our dead. One hundred and twenty-six bodies were brought to one point for buriel. Every one was stripped by the rebels of cap, coat, pants and shoes. And what was more remarkable four-fifths of the number were shot square in the forehead; besides being wounded in the legs, arms and other parts. From the appearance on the wounds, I am so well satisfied of the fact, that I would be willing to go it blindly, and swear that they were murdered as they lay wounded upon the battle- field. . . . On Wednesday evening, seventeen regiments, including ours, were ordered to draw the loads from their pieces and under cover of the night we marched to the river and embarked on six of the largest steamers without making a sound above a whisper.[7]

After the disaster, Sherman loaded his troops on transport boats and took them back to their starting point of Milliken's Bend. Before he arrived, Sherman received word that General McClernand was waiting there aboard his steamship, intending to take command of the army. William Sherman shared Grant's and Halleck's low opinion of McClernand, but he was a soldier, and McClernand outranked him; much as he hated to, he turned his command over to McClernand.

McClernand had the personal pleasure of informing Sherman of Grant's failure. He then went back to the idea of an independent com- mand. He renamed Sherman's force the Army of the Mississippi and reorganized it into two corps, one under Sherman and the other under General George Morgan, with himself in charge of both. He then looked for a way to cancel the recent defeat.

Twenty miles up the Arkansas River was the Confederate fort of Arkansas Post, or Fort Hindman, garrisoned by some 5,000 Confederate troops.[8] The fort was a potential threat, as men and supplies were often sent from there to Vicksburg, but its major attraction was its availability. McClernand and Sherman resolved to capture the place. This time it was McClernand's turn to move without Grant's knowledge.

The expedition was under way by 5 January 1863. The Army of the Mississippi consisted of about 30,000 troops, 50 transport boats, and 13 gunboats. The transports and gunboats made their way upriver to a point three miles below the enemy fort, where they were then tied up. The next day, the Confederates were driven from their outer works into the fort itself. McClernand prepared to storm the fort and ordered the gun- boats to begin a preattack bombardment. The Federal gunboats moved to within range and engaged the fort's batteries. The land attack, however, was delayed, and the gunboats were forced to back off. The next day, a coordinated land and water assault was made. The Union gunboats knocked the Confederate batteries out of action, and, while the infantry was engaged on the fort's outer works, the Confederates manning the inside works began to wave white flags. Shortly afterward, the Confederates fighting in the outer trenches also quit. Union losses were 1,016, and Confederate losses were fewer than 100 killed or wounded. McClernand had lost more men, but he had captured almost 5,000 Confederates, along with tons of military supplies.[9]

Arkansas Post was the second battle for the 31st Iowa. A charge was ordered from the right, and the brigade was formed into line and moved forward, with the 31st in support of the 3d Missouri. The line became tangled during the movement, which created a good deal of confusion and caused General Hovey to criticize the 31st for its lack of discipline.[10] The brigade advanced across an open field under infantry and artillery fire and was forced to withdraw after getting to within 100 yards of the enemy position. The brigade's companies and regiments were reorganized and a new attack had just begun when the men spotted the white flags on the Confederate works. No one from the regiment had been killed, but 11 men had been wounded, including James Richardson of the Reserves.[11]

The next day, the brigade boarded one of the steamboats and proceeded down the Arkansas River. The boat was so crowded with men and supplies that most members of the 31st were forced to sleep on the open hurricane deck. The rain continued and soon turned to snow, which piled up more than six inches as the men lay on deck wrapped in their wool blankets.

McClernand's report on the battle gave little credit to Sherman, who had personally commanded the infantry, or to Admiral David Porter, who had commanded the gunboats. Sherman and Porter were furious and wired Grant in Memphis asking that he come to take command himself. General-in-Chief Halleck wired Grant that he had permission to replace McClernand if he saw reason. Grant saw many reasons, and on 30 January he rejoined the army, now encamped on the west bank of the Mississippi at Young's Point, a few miles north and opposite of Vicksburg.

The issue had, at long last, been resolved. There was to be one commanding general in the department, and that general was to be Grant. McClernand's short-lived Army of the Mississippi was disbanded and its organizations incorporated into Grant's Army of the Tennessee, in which McClernand and Sherman were corps commanders. Sherman's corps, the 15th, included the 31st Iowa.

Grant was in a difficult position. The repulse of Sherman's troops at Chickasaw Bluffs and his own failure to secure his base and supply line east of the river had shown that an advance on Vicksburg from the east or north was all but impossible. His army now lay west of the river and north of the town, spread out over a wide area. The main camp was at Milliken's Bend, a crescent-shaped edge of the river bank about 20 miles upstream from Vicksburg. At the lower end of the crescent was Young's Point, where Grant kept his headquarters. Below the point was low ground directly opposite the city, where a railroad from Monroe, Louisiana terminated. Union soldiers, nearly 40,000 of them, were camped at all of these places and at isolated spots farther upriver, with another 15,000 still at Memphis.[12]

Grant's problem had not changed since the first expedition. The only way that an army large enough to take Vicksburg could succeed was from the eastern side, through Jackson and Raymond. He could either pull his entire force back to Memphis, calling the whole campaign a failure, and come up with a new campaign down the eastern side, or he could find a way to get his army down the west side of the river and across to the east side. Abandoning the campaign and returning to Memphis would be almost giving back what had been won at Fort Donelson, Shiloh, and Corinth. Continuing the campaign from the western shore meant possible disaster, but he chose to go on.

The winter campaign against Vicksburg was one of the most severe tests of endurance and patriotism yet experienced by the Union soldiers. The camps at Milliken's Bend and Young's Point were death traps of filth and disease. The men of the 31st had begun to fall sick while in Helena and on the Cold Water expedition, and the situation became worse after they went into camp. The hospitals were filled to overflowing, and the night air was filled with the sound of pneumonia-stricken men coughing and wheezing for air. The latrines were bloody with the discharge of thousands of men sick with dysentery. Whole companies seemed to be ill. Often, less than half the regiment was able to report for morning roll call. Morale was as low as it could possibly be without the men throwing down their weapons and going home. Private John Rath described the situation:

> Everything looked gloomy at this place everybody sick. Only five to eleven men for duty out of eighty-five, and four or five dying out of the regiment everyday. Everyone wished to be somewhere else but in Uncle Sam's army. We buried our comrade Ed Culver in this camp.[13]

An officer of the regiment wrote that

> Our army is in the worst possible shape. I am well satisfied that there are ten thousand sick in this army at the present time, and no chance to get more than one in ten into a hospital. Day before yesterday, only seventeen were carried from one hospital boat, who had died during the preceding night. We have received no pay yet, but we are getting used to sickness, death and no pay.[14]

By mid-March, 96 members of the 31st Iowa had died, only one of battle wounds; the rest had been killed by disease as they worked in the rain and mud or lay under their shelter halves in the damp winter air. Three of the Reserves—Orlando Bradley, Erastus Wells, and Edward Culver—had sickened and died by March. Almost a dozen others, including Edwin Brown and George Perkins, had been discharged from the army because of illness.[15]

The soldiers suffered with illness and death, but the constant lack of regular pay was another matter, for their families depended on what was sent home. The people of Cedar Falls and Black Hawk County were very concerned about the soldiers' families and tried, with the county relief fund, to provide for them. A major problem, however, was how this was to be done. Were these families paupers, wards of the county, and should they be forced to prove dire need before being given assistance? The soldiers did not think so. They had volunteered to fight for the cause which was everyone's cause, and they expected to have their families cared for while they were away.

The county board of supervisors first tried to determine a family's need by the amount of property owned. A family with $300 worth of property or more was not entitled to any assistance. A family without such property was entitled to the sum of 50 cents per week per child under 12 years of age. The wife of the volunteer and mother to the children was entitled to an additional $1 per week, provided that she receive from a doctor a certificate saying she was unable to work. The terms set by the board of supervisors angered the soldiers. Most financial problems could be eliminated if their pay arrived on time, but it seldom did, which left the families in need. They were neither paupers nor charity cases, and the soldiers did not want them treated as such. The companies of the 31st Iowa from Black Hawk County held a meeting and forwarded an angry letter to the board, which stated

> We have left our homes and sacrificed ourselves to danger and suffering to sustain that government which you undoubtedly value very highly. . . . In every respect the cause in which we have enlisted is as much yours as ours. . . . Pay-day has long since passed and we have not received our wages. Some of our families have been suffering for the necessaries of life, and some of our children have cried for bread. How have you paid us for running your share of the risks, and paying your share of the debt which every man owes to his country in times like these? . . . It is evident from the manner in which you would treat suffering women and children that you have forgotten the golden rule.[16]

Peter Melendy and others tried to remedy the confusing situation by organizing a Relief Society for the families of soldiers. The purpose of the society was to find soldiers' families in need and to offer aid.

The county board of supervisors also tried to help by scrapping the $300 qualification and adopting the suggestion of the Relief Society that need be the only factor in considering a family for assistance. The former mayor, Bryon Culver, and Reverend Waterbury were appointed from Cedar Falls to aid the board of supervisors in finding needy families and deciding how much aid was needed. As an article in the *Gazette* explained,

> As it now stands the Supervisors, in concert with a committee of two, determine upon the wants of families of volunteers in their respective townships, and are authorized to draw a monthly sum, not to exceed ten dollars per month, for their support. . . . As it now stands those really needy will receive aid according to their wants. If a family needs no help it will get none; if another family needs five dollars a month to make it comfortable it will get it; and if another family requires ten dollars a month it will receive it.[17]

The work of the Ladies' Aid Society, the Young Ladies' Soldiers' Aid Society, and the Soldiers' Aid Society became more important than ever. There were now two companies of soldiers from home in the field, and they had to be cared for. The packages from home were often life-savers for the men lying in the wet camps above Vicksburg. The Reserves were supplied with food, vegetables, clothing, medicines, and blankets by the women of Cedar Falls. On New Year's Day 1863, they were treated to a New Year's dinner. The total weight of the five large boxes containing the food was 1,517 pounds.[18] The women's societies forwarded similar packages to their sons and husbands in other units every month.

One of the war's hardest impacts was economic. The increased demand for war materials was a boon to production and shipping, but there was also inflation, the growing cost of day-to-day living. Cedar Falls was economically better off than many Iowa communities. As it was the railhead for the entire Cedar Valley, most of the produce and the troops from the valley came through Cedar Falls. The mills on the river were busy. In the fall, there were days when the streets were clogged with hundreds of grain-filled wagons from the up-country. An article in a January 1863 issue of the *Gazette* painted an enthusiastic picture:

> The amount of produce which daily finds a market in our streets is truely astonishing. It was estimated by those competent to judge, that more than ten thousand dollars in currency, was paid last Friday for produce, and during the week not less than forty thousand. The farmers are getting large prices for all they have to sell, and are prosperous, as their numerous improvements abundantly testify. The merchants are also thriving and the abundant stocks purchased in the Autumn are found to be none too liberal for the demand.[19]

The records of the town's hotels showed that more than 25,000 travelers visited the town in 1862. More than 4,000 railroad tickets were sold during the year, not including the tickets used by soldiers. The railroad used 3,304 cars to carry produce out of town in 1862 but only 980 cars to bring in outside imports.[20]

Wartime inflation negated much of the prosperity. As coffee rose to more than $1 per pound, people served substitutes made of wheat, bran, and rye mixed with molasses and sweet potatoes browned in sugar. Muslin rose to more than $1 a yard, and the costs of other fabrics rose even higher.[21] Families were forced to make do with their old clothes.

Annie Wittenmyer, in her capacity as agent of the State Sanitary Commission, visited the camps near Vicksburg and was appalled at the lack of proper food for the soldiers. Cases of scurvy and other diseases of malnutrition had broken out. The men needed fruits and vegetables. She issued an urgent appeal to the people of Iowa, asking them to donate all they could, including the contents of their root cellars.

The Cedar Falls relief societies responded by shipping hundreds of pounds of needed goods to Wittenmyer's organization. Dempsey Overman offered to lend the Soldiers' Aid Society one acre of land, tilled and ready to plant, if they wanted to raise fresh potatoes for the soldiers. The proposal was accepted, and Overman's acre became the society's "Tater Patch." Local merchants supplied the cuttings and on 3 June the ladies held a "Potato Planting Bee." There were a dozen men and close to 30 women at the planting bee. The men dug the rows, and the women followed behind, dropping potato cuttings in the furrows. The affair took on a holiday atmosphere, and, when the day's work was done, the women served a large picnic dinner. A similar festival was held in early July when the patch needed weeding. The men went to work with their hoes, and the women fixed ham sandwiches, pound cake, and, as a coffee substitute, oven-browned barley. The harvest of the "taters" came in mid-October, a time when farmers had their heaviest work schedule; only four men showed up to dig. The women took their spades and went to work, and by nightfall they had the potatoes dug up and piled nearby. The society was able to send 60 bushels of potatoes to the Iowa Sanitary Commission and still keep 40 more bushels for the needs of soldiers' families during the winter.[22]

In April, Grant chose to take the all-or-nothing chance and send his transport boats downriver to Vicksburg, risking the Southern guns on the bluffs.

Admiral Porter's ships were ready to run the line of guns by the 15th. He had eight gunboats, one ram, and three river steamers loaded with supplies. Each had water-soaked bales of cotton and hay lashed around the boilers and banked against the sterns. A large column of cavalry raiding down the east side of the river toward Newton's Station acted as a diversion. The Union infantry was marched down the west side to a point opposite New Carthage to await the boats.

Porter's boats proceeded down the river on the night of 16 April. Grant watched from the upper deck of his headquarters steamer. The night was clear, but the boats carried no lights and appeared like shadows on the water. As the boats rounded the point and drifted past the heights, the Confederate gunners opened up. Southern pickets quickly put the torch to some abandoned houses on the shore, and the flames served as flickering searchlights for the gunners.

The firing lasted until past midnight, then stopped. The Union fleet had passed the Vicksburg batteries. One of Porter's transports had been sunk, another had been put out of action, and several coal barges had been lost. Most of the other boats had been at least slightly damaged, a small price for such an accomplishment.

The presence of the boats below the Vicksburg defenses meant that the Union infantry would be able to be ferried across to the east side. The campaign for the city of Vicksburg had begun in earnest.

8

A Third Summer

While the Emancipation Proclamation had made slavery a primary issue of the war, it was the war itself that forced many
Northerners to consider black people as human beings and not
just Southern slaves. Many Iowans had never met or known black people
and had never seen the institution of Southern slavery in practice. When
Iowans, along with most Northern soldiers, marched south, blacks
became an intregal part of their war experience. Most soldiers became
acquainted with black people through the thousands of former slaves
who ran away from their owners and sought refuge within the Union
lines. The escaped slaves were, like most refugees, very poor and desperate, willing to do the dirtiest of camp chores for little pay, and willing to
put up with much abuse rather than be returned to their masters. The
Union soldiers treated them with a combination of contempt, curiosity,
and sympathy. Racist humor, often at the expense of a black person, was
common. Cedar Falls soldier George Rownd wrote home and described a
bit of "fun" in camp:

> Well I suppose I must tell of a little scene that i saw in front of the
> sutler the other day the sutler is young and fond of fun there was two
> darkies about as large as Charles [George's 11 year old brother] came
> along the sutler took up a couple of figs and showed them to the boys
> and told them whichever one could out-bunt should have the figs down
> they went on there hands and feet like two rams and went at it an kept it
> up five minutes to the great amusements of the bystanders finally one
> found a softspot on the others head and he caved in the other eat his
> figs and declard he was not hurt.[1]

At other times, the Cedar Falls troops were appalled at the brutal
treatment of slaves by their masters. In the course of their service, the
troops found blacks lynched near the Union picket lines, or saw the scars
of the lash on both male and female slaves who fled to them for
protection. Shortly after his Cedar Falls Reserves went into active

service, Captain Robert Speer wrote home and described the treatment of blacks by both Union and Confederate troops:

> Hundreds of slaves are now within our lines at Helena. When our army moves hundreds of them are driven off like sheep in droves to the hills. In some instances, masters attempted to conceal their slaves until our army should pass by, tying their hands and feet, stretching them at full length on the ground and driving a stake between their wrists, and another between their feet and gagging them and covering them with brush. In this condition some have lain for days without food. They are now considered by their masters "property of unsteady habits," and consequently valued very low. If I should ever return to Cedar Falls I think I shall take a pair of Negroes and a pair of mules with me.[2]

Frederick Jacob, an English-born Cedar Falls farmer, wrote home describing black children to his own sons and mentioning the arming of former slaves.

> You boys would like to see the Little niggers you would laugh to see their wooly heads; I see one quite a white nigger it has red eyes it was about eight months old. . . . Our soldiers are taken all the nigger men they can we are going to furnish them with arms and let them do some of the fighting that seems to annoy the rebels.[3]

Jacob was correct, for the arming of blacks struck at the very heart of the matter. The use of former slaves as soldiers was, for Southerners, the ultimate act of Northern savagery. No federal violation of states' rights was as serious as the arming of blacks. Every Southern state had strict laws forbidding blacks to own weapons or act violently toward whites. Black soldiers dressed in the uniform of the federal government negated each of those laws.

Those in the North who favored the enlistment of black men often did so for pragmatic reasons. The Emancipation Proclamation had spread like wildfire through the communication network of the black communities and it encouraged many slaves to flee to the Union, thus denying the South much valuable labor, both at home and in the armies. Each black person who had once dug ditches for the South could now toil for the Union, freeing white soldiers for combat. After 1 January 1863, President Lincoln called for at least four regiments of black troops.

The first black regiments were not organized in Iowa until the fall of 1863, but the idea had many supporters, ranging from Henry Perkins, editor of the *Cedar Falls Gazette*, to the governor of Iowa, Samuel J. Kirkwood. Kirkwood had recently made a visit to Vicksburg, and he toured a spot near Milliken's Bend which had been defended by black soldiers from Louisiana in early June. Kirkwood expressed his views on the subject in a speech at West Union, Iowa, on 8 September 1863:

> I thought that by the help of these blacks the enemy had been prevented from boasting a victory for rebel arms, and I thanked God that they had the manliness and the bravery to come forward and help us. I thought it made little difference whether men were white or black or what color they were. Let men be pea green, or sky blue, or any other color under the heavens, if they have the manliness and the courage to come up and fight for the old flag, I am ready to say Godspeed them.[4]

Helping blacks earn citizenship had never been a primary motive for enlisting them, but once the door was open, military service could be used as a stepping-stone to full equality. Captain Speer, who early in his service had written home saying that he wanted to bring "a pair of Negroes and a pair of mules" back with him, had witnessed the June battle at Milliken's Bend, and his tone concerning black people was decidedly more respectful.

> When the rebels came within sight the negroes manifested great anxiety to attack them. And when the attack was made they exhibited more of the tiger than the man. After the battle, negroes pointed with pride to their fallen comrades, and the wounded appeared to act as though "it is sweet to die for one's country."
>
> I am of the opinion that a few regiments of them would be sufficient to give relief to any community suffering with copperhead fever.[5]

The word "copperhead" was a catchall term pertaining to those who did not support the war. As the war continued, the peace faction of the Democratic Party and other antiwar elements became more active. There were peace meetings across the state of Iowa, many in southeast Iowa.

Rumors began to circulate concerning Iowans who belonged to such organizations as the Knights of the Golden Circle and the Sons of '76, which were secret societies designed to disrupt the war effort by discouraging enlistments, sheltering deserters, and resisting the draft. Such groups were said to be very well organized and well armed, capable of becoming a military threat behind the Union lines. Little was ever proven as to the extent of such organizations, but the threat of an active fifth column seemed real enough.

A major source of friction was the wearing of so-called copperhead or butternut pins. The copperhead pins were usually made from pennies and the butternut pins from home-dyed wool. Unionists thought that they were the secret recognition signals of a vast, traitorous conspiracy, but while the pins may have had such uses, they were actually a form of defiance. The pins separated the Peace Democrats from the War Democrats and stuck an arrogant thumb out at the Republicans and the abolitionists.

Unionists responded to the perceived internal threat by organizing Union Leagues, locally based groups which sought to silence all traitors. Henry Perkins called for such a league in Cedar Falls:

> We are no alarmist but if we read the signs of the times aright there is danger ahead of us,—not far off, but in our own midst,—and it is time for loyal men to arouse from the apathy which seems to envelope them. The traitors are active and vigilant, organized and armed. . . . We believe it is time for all unconditional Union men to be active and vigilant. . . . If they see that we are prepared for any emergency they will probably keep their fangs concealed; but if on the contrary they find us unprepared for successful opposition we may expect to suffer heinous wrong at their hands. We must pluck this budding treason before its bloom.[6]

The Union League of Cedar Falls was formed in late March and early April, another was formed in Waterloo, and more than a hundred more were organized across the state. The Cedar Falls league hosted war rallies and invited well-known speakers, such as Matthew M. Trumbull of the old 3d Iowa, to address the gatherings.[7] Cedar Falls became known as one of the most intolerant towns in the state when it came to disloyal activities. The *Northwest Democrat* had ceased publication because of lack of support, as well as unofficial harassment. Peter Melendy, Henry Perkins, and other leaders of the community tracked down rumors concerning anti-Union activities and did their best to drive the disloyal from town.

The leading advocate of the Southern cause in the state of Iowa was still the *Dubuque Herald*, and, in Cedar Falls, anyone connected with the *Herald* was considered a traitor. One *Herald* editorial said that the people of Cedar Falls were so intolerant that the town was "a Sodom in comparison with other towns in Iowa."[8] After the *Herald*'s editor, Dennis Mahoney, was arrested and taken to Washington, the editor's position passed to Stilson Hutchins, of Des Moines. Hutchins was even more outspoken than Mahoney had been, and was, of course, hated in Cedar Falls. Hutchins visited Cedar Falls in March 1863 and met with several local Democrats. Few others knew of his visit until a Sunday evening, when he chose to have his evening meal at the Carter House Hotel. One of the guests at the hotel was the veteran soldier, lately resigned, Fitzroy Sessions.

Sessions had not met the Dubuque editor, but Hutchins, while editor of another paper, had accused Sessions of threatening the *Dubuque Herald* during Sessions's speech in Dubuque almost two years earlier, and the two had exchanged insults through newspaper letters about the incident. Sessions was informed as to who the man was and followed him into the hall and confronted him. He asked Hutchins if he was the man who had accused him of trying to urge a mob to burn down the *Herald* office. Hutchins replied that he was, and Sessions demanded an apology. Hutchins refused, and Sessions called him a liar and a coward, and invited him to step out into the street. Hutchins did not accept the challenge, so Sessions slapped him across the face. Before Hutchins could react, Sessions piled into him, fists swinging, and beat him bloody. Hutchins cried for mercy, and the former soldier let him up. While the editor was wiping the blood from his face, Sessions tore into him again, knocking him down and viciously kicking him again and again.[9]

Hutchins returned to Dubuque and wrote: "The town of Cedar Falls is thoroughly abolitionist and this man Sessions is reported to be its bully."[10]

Another such confrontation concerned Peter Melendy and a member of the *Dubuque Herald* staff, John Hodnett. Hodnett visited Cedar Falls in late May 1863 and was overheard expressing ideas that many in Cedar Falls considered treasonous. Melendy, Perkins, and others had long taken the position that "we, as a community, allow no outspoken treason in our midst."[11] They decided to do something about Hodnett.

A citizens' committee was formed to drive the *Herald* man from town. Hodnett was told of the committee's plans and quickly changed hotels, but he was soon discovered. The committee members surrounded the hotel while Melendy and several others searched the premises. Hodnett was found in a darkened room on the top floor. He was searched for weapons and was given 10 minutes to leave town. He asked which direction he was to travel and was told that it did not matter as long as he left immediately. As Hodnett and a friend who had accompanied him to Cedar Falls walked out of town, they were closely followed by the committee members. The men followed faster, and when the two men heard the rapid footsteps behind them, they took off running with the Cedar Falls Unionists in hot pursuit. The Dubuque men escaped the mob and hid for the night. The next day, they headed home on the railroad tracks by way of a handcar.[12]

The *Dubuque Herald* made much of both Sessions's attack on Hutchins and the committee's attack on Hodnett. Fitzroy Sessions, appointed deputy provost marshal in June, responded to the charges of mob activity in a letter published in the *Dubuque Times*:

> Now we do not approve of mobs or rowdyism, and there is no more
> law abiding people than those in this vicinity; and they are patriotic, as
> is shown by the fact that our county has furnished about two hundred
> and fifty men more than our quota for the putting down of the rebellion.
> But we do think that it is our duty, while our sons, brothers and fathers

are absent fighting for us, to keep down home traitors, and in view of the fact that the authorities are so backward in attending to these matters, we are determined to let the consequences be what they may.

I will say, for the benefit of Hutchins, that the citizens of this place *do approve* of his chastisement and of Hodnett's banishment; and that this is to be our settled policy from this time forward, and they can govern themselves accordingly.[13]

The only other violence connected to the incidents came in mid-July when Peter Melendy and fellow Cedar Falls resident George Walkup were visiting Dubuque on business. As the two were walking toward the railroad depot, they were stopped by John Hodnett and a gang of his supporters. Hodnett was on his home ground, and his friends were armed with clubs and stones. He approached Melendy and demanded to know if he had been one of those who had driven him out of Cedar Falls. Melendy reached into his pocket. Hodnett saw the move, and, thinking that Melendy was reaching for a gun, drew his own. Melendy looked at the armed man and his crowd of friends, then defiantly threw down his satchel, squared off against Hodnett, and announced that he was indeed one of the men. And, he added, if Hodnett ever again spouted treason in Cedar Falls, he would be sure that he got the same treatment again. Melendy then looked the man in the eye and told him to shoot and be damned. Hodnett and his friends backed off.[14]

While the Unionists of Cedar Falls struggled to silence those considered to be unpatriotic, their soldiers marched with General Grant against Vicksburg. The fortified town of Port Gibson was the first objective, and it fell to the Union forces on 1 May. From Port Gibson, Grant's army was able to march toward the state capital of Jackson, Mississippi. A large Confederate force was hurried to the town of Raymond, which lay between Grant's troops and Jackson.

The Confederates at Raymond were not part of John C. Pemberton's Vicksburg army but a part of General Joseph E. Johnston's force. Grant was faced with two enemies: Pemberton's army near Vicksburg and this new army under Johnston. Grant defeated the enemy at Raymond and then captured Jackson itself, pushing Johnston out of the way before advancing against Pemberton.

Johnston, while in retreat from Jackson, sent General Pemberton a message instructing him to move his troops in such a way as to trap Grant between them. One of Johnston's couriers was a spy, and he took his copy of the order to the Union camp. Aware of his enemy's plans, Grant ordered the captured stores at Jackson to be destroyed, broke off his pursuit of Johnston, and turned to meet Pemberton. Grant and Pemberton's troops met at a place called Champion Hill on 16 May. The fight for the hill lasted four hours, with the Union losing 2,400 men to death and battle wounds, 590 of them from Iowa.[15] The Confederates lost more than 3,800 killed, wounded, and missing.[16] The hill changed hands several times during the fight, but finally it was taken and held by the Union. Pemberton's troops were forced to retreat toward the Vicksburg entrenchments. They made one more stand at the Big Black River and shot another 279 Union soldiers, 221 from Iowa.[17] After the fight at the Big Black, Pemberton retreated into the Vicksburg lines. Penned up in the city, he was cut off from Johnston in the north, with Grant already advancing on his position.

The Cedar Falls Reserves were in the rear of the march and did not suffer any casualties in the fighting at Raymond, Jackson, Champion Hill, or the Big Black.

The steamboat *Crescent City* arrived at Vicksburg on 19 May with the men of Cedar Falls's Pioneer Greys aboard. The Greys, as part of Grant's 16th Corps under General Stephen Hurlbut, had not been involved in any of the early maneuvers against Vicksburg. Hurlbut's corps had been stationed in Moscow and Memphis, Tennessee, for most of the winter.

Captain John B. Smith had still not received a long-overdue promotion, but his skill and long service were rewarded when he was transferred to General Jacob Lauman's staff. Lauman had succeeded General Hurlbut in command of the 16th Corps's 4th Division when Hurlbut was promoted to major general and placed in command of the entire corps.[18]

The Pioneer Greys and the rest of the 3d Iowa left Memphis in late April and headed for Vicksburg by way of St. Louis. "St. Charles" described the first part of their journey:

> We left St. Louis on the fine steamer Von Phul. We had for company a detachment from the 14th Illinois.—To say that we had a "time" would hardly be expressive enough. My readers can term it what they please after I tell them that we used up the contents of about 20 casks of beer besides a few boxes of wine for trimmings.
>
> At Cape Giraradeau we got up considerable of a fuss with the 1st Nebraska. It was commenced by the Nebraska men being a little rough with some of our boys, who had just stepped a shore to enquire after some friends stationed there. The guards pushed one of our boys over and set out to strike one with his musket. This led to words fierce and loud, pretty soon one of the officers ordered the guard to fire upon us, in an instant the shuck of balls going down guns co'd be heard all over the boat. The affair quieted down however, until just as the boat was pushing off when the boys let drive with a perfect shower of eggs, and well covered the guards, who beat a hasty retreat amid shouts of those on board the boat and from the crowd that had collected on shore. . . .

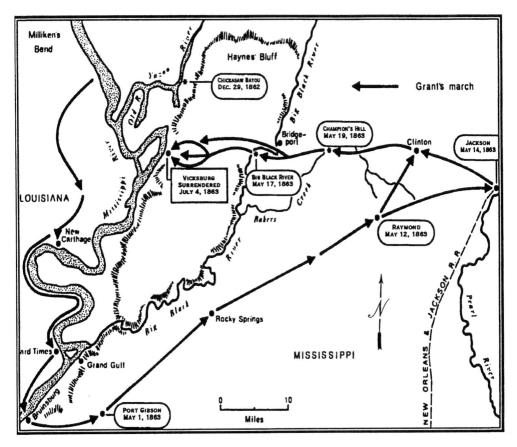

Miliken's
Bend

Haynes' Bluff

CHICKASAW BAYOU
DEC. 29, 1862

Grant's march

Bridge-
port

CHAMPION's HILL
MAY 19, 1863

Clinton

JACKSON
MAY 14, 1863

VICKSBURG
SURRENDERED
JULY 4, 1863

BIG BLACK RIVER
MAY 17, 1863

LOUISIANA

New
Carthage

Bakers

RAYMOND
MAY 12, 1863

N

Rocky Springs

MISSISSIPPI

rd Times

Grand Gulf

NEW ORLEANS & JACKSON R.R.

Pearl River

0   10
Miles

PORT GIBSON
MAY 1, 1863

VICKSBURG CAMPAIGN
Map by Andrew J. Karl

> We have just received orders to pack for Milliken's Bend, one tent
> to the company, so good-by to light bread, good grub and quiet camp
> life, and welcome to hard tack, night watching and the iron hail of war.
> The old 3d that has proved herself true upon so many a field is not
> going to miss the campaign against Vicksburg.[19]

The men waited for transport until 17 May, when they received
orders to board the *Crescent City*. The next day, a few miles above
Greenville, Mississippi, the boat was fired on from shore by hundreds of
Southern soldiers supported by three field pieces. The Union troops on
board sprang for their weapons and, with the aid of a piece of artillery on
board, drove the Confederates from the bank. The next day, the men
went ashore at Haines's Bluff, just north of Vicksburg. As the Pioneer
Greys took their places in the trenches, they could hear artillery bursts,
musket volleys, and shouted orders. A battle was in progress.

Since crossing the Mississippi, General Grant had enjoyed a successful campaign. His troops had driven the Confederates from Port Gibson,
Raymond, the state capital of Jackson, the bloody slopes of Champion
Hill, and into Vicksburg itself. As the Union troops surrounded the city,
it seemed that just one more push was all that was needed to finish the
job. At noon on 19 May, as the Pioneer Greys were going ashore, Grant
ordered an assault. Pemberton's Southerners may have been pushed into
the city, but they were not about to quit so easily. Grant's attack was
repulsed along the entire line, with a loss of almost 1,000 men.[20] Many of
the 20 regiments from Iowa were under fire on 19 May, but only the 4th
and 12th had any casualties that day.[21] The Cedar Falls Reserves, as part
of Sherman's corps, were close by and under fire but did not take part in
the assault.

The failure on 19 May did not convince Grant that the city could not
be taken by storm, and he prepared one more full-scale attack. At 2:00
A.M. on 22 May, Grant launched his second attack up the high, steep
slopes of the Vicksburg entrenchments. Few positions were as easy to
defend as the Vicksburg hills. The Confederates were able to wait until
just the right moment, aiming their weapons down at the attacking blue
soldiers who were struggling to keep their footing in the loose
Mississippi dirt, and then killing them with ease. The result was a
slaughter. Union dead, wounded, or missing numbered 3,200, while only
500 Confederates were reported lost.[22]

The Pioneer Greys did not participate in the assault on 22 May. They
lay on their arms as part of the support troops but were not sent in. The
Cedar Falls Reserves went into the battle as support for the 9th, 26th,
and 30th Iowa regiments. The attacking route was up a steep hill, with
the men exposed to heavy fire most of the way. The men of the 9th Iowa
pushed forward and got to within a few feet of the top before they were

thrown back, leaving 79 dead or wounded men behind.[23] Once up the hill, the Union troops could not turn their backs on the enemy and run back down the hill; they were trapped where they were. The men took cover wherever they could find it—behind logs, in ravines, or up so close to the Confederate works that the Southern soldiers were forced to shoot high over their heads. The 31st Iowa did not suffer the casualties that the 9th Iowa had, but several members, including Colonel Jeremiah Jenkins, were wounded. Captain Speer described the part played by the 31st:

> Before the charge could be made it was necessary to run two gauntlets, one of about 25 rods and the other 15 rods in length. In running them our regiment lost ten men in killed and wounded. Co. B went through without a scratch. The balls flew like hail, and as many shells as were desirable. The 9th, and three companies of the 30th Iowa regiments, and the 12th Missouri, attempted the assault but were repulsed with a loss of about 225 in killed and wounded. As they failed we were not ordered up, and under cover of night we removed to our original position immediately above the city and near the river.[24]

The failures of 19 May and 22 May ended Grant's string of victories. The wounded suffered and died, and the bodies began to swell and decay. On 25 May, General Pemberton, unable to stand the sight or the smell of the hundreds of blackened Union corpses, sent a message to Grant asking that he accept a temporary cease-fire in order to tend to his casualties. Grant accepted, and for the next two and a half hours, soldiers carried off the few remaining wounded and gathered the dead for burial. Given that they had been trying to kill each other for months, the soldiers of both sides were quite friendly during the short truce. Corporal Soloman Humbert, of the Cedar Falls Reserves, recounted one incident:

> A small squad of us met, about the same number of Gray coats unarmed according to agreement for a chat about events present and past. When the gay young rebel Gen. Dick Taylor approached on his gray steed and interfered by ordering us into our proper limits, this complied with however not without us safely conducting a couple of "Jonnies" into our lines with us.[25]

Union and Confederate troops lived in close proximity to one another for the next six weeks, at times engaging in short, fierce fights and at other times meeting between the lines and exchanging goods and information. The daily lives of the Pioneer Greys in the 3d Iowa and the Cedar Falls Reserves in the 31st were much alike during this time. A letter from "St. Charles," of the Pioneer Greys, described life on the Vicksburg lines:

Our labor has been almost terrible. We were out five days and nights out of six, either supporting batteries or laying in rifle pits. The latter work taxes all the strength and endurance a man has. He is in a little hole with generally no shade, and there he must stay from daylight until dark. If he gets up he has the assurance that at least half a dozen mini-balls will come singing by his head. . . . All day long under a broiling sun we pickets blazed away at each other until about 4 p.m. by which time our ammunition was getting low, so we concluded to go talking with each other. The upshot of the affair was, that about 80 on a side of us, concluded to hold a party; so we went out and met each other half way between the lines and had a general good time. I never saw strangers come together with more cordiality and general good feeling. The regiment we met was the 59th Tennessee. We carried over coffee to them and they supplied our boys with tobacco. We concluded that the 59th were "bully good boys," and they "do" of the 3d Iowa. We made a truce to fire at each other no more that evening, and in fact at no time when we were on Picket. Finally bidding each other "good-bye boys" we each went to our own lines; but not a picket shot was heard after that though each party kept exposed.[26]

The siege lasted through the month of June, and, though Pemberton had taken care to bring in all available food and supplies, the stores became exhausted. Both soldiers and civilians suffered short rations and were in danger of starvation. Both also suffered the dangers of enemy fire. Grant saw little distinction between them, and he had his guns continually shell the city. Whole families learned to live in caves dug into the hills, and these became as important for civilians as the rifle pits and trenches were for the soldiers.

Somewhere outside the siege lines, behind Grant's army, General Johnston was supposedly raising a huge army that would come crashing in on Grant's rear. When that happened, Pemberton's troops could break out and attack Grant's front, and every Confederate loss from Donelson to Corinth would be avenged. As the days dragged on, however, that hope faded. Finally, in late June, Pemberton was forced to recognize the awful reality of defeat: he could not break out and save his army, and Johnston was not going to break in.

At 10:00 A.M., 4 July 1863, General John C. Pemberton surrendered the city of Vicksburg to General Grant. Regiment after regiment of Southern soldiers marched out of their trenches, and, in full view of the assembled Union army, stacked their arms and surrendered their colors. After almost 10 months of effort and a cost of thousands of dead and wounded men, the last Confederate city on the Mississippi River had fallen to Union forces. General Grant, the bungler of Shiloh, once again had become a national hero.

Vicksburg's southern defense, Port Hudson, was surrendered on

9 July. There were no more Confederate obstructions of the Mississippi. It was a Union waterway.

The same day that Pemberton marched out of Vicksburg, General Robert E. Lee began his long retreat home from the bloody fields and hills of Gettysburg, Pennsylvania. For the first time, the Army of the Potomac, now commanded by General George G. Meade, had been victorious. There would be no more great offenses by Lee's army. The Fourth of July would cease being a holiday in the South; instead, it would be a day of mourning for a lost cause.

The news of the fall of Vicksburg reached Cedar Falls on 9 July. Within minutes of the dispatch being read, Main Street became alive with people. There had been no Fourth of July celebration in town. There had been little reason for celebration, and no one had the enthusiasm to organize one. Instantly, all was changed. Flags went up on poles and were hung in windows and from porches. The available members of the Brass Band ran home for their instruments, and soon the air was filled with martial music. A procession was organized behind the band and a man carried a large flag. The parade marched up and down Main Street with more and more people joining in each time. An outhouse was hauled into the center of the street, and set ablaze. Someone made an effigy of the Confederate president, Jefferson Davis, and turned it over to the crowd; in a few moments it was swinging in the wind, lynched. Later, the effigy was added to the bonfire. People who had not been known to take a drink made repeated visits to the saloons, while the crowd in the street continued to holler and cheer.[27]

The soldiers from Cedar Falls had little opportunity to celebrate. Since Pemberton's army had surrendered and Vicksburg was safely occupied, Grant could now turn his attention to General Johnston's force. Grant ordered Sherman to go after the Southern army located near Jackson once again. Both the Pioneer Greys and the Cedar Falls Reserves were a part of Sherman's 50,000 men. They marched along the dusty summertime roads toward Jackson while the rest of Grant's army celebrated in Vicksburg.

The Pioneer Greys were ordered to cross the railroad south of Jackson on the morning of 12 July, which brought them within a mile of the Confederate works. The Greys were part of a brigade which included three Illinois regiments and a battery from Ohio, all under the command of Isaac Pugh. General Jacob Lauman, commanding the division, ordered Pugh's brigade forward to within 300 yards of the enemy trenches. The brigade was well in front of the Union line, but Lauman ordered the advance to continue. There was no support on either flank, and, as they advanced, the Union troops came under fire from three Confederate brigades supported by 12 pieces of artillery. They advanced alone to within 75 yards of the Southern trenches but could go no farther. The men stood the fire for less than half an hour and then fell back, leaving their wounded and dead behind. The brigade was all but destroyed.

There were 241 men of the 3d Iowa in action that day, and almost half of them were shot, including Colonel Aaron Brown. Privates Martin Adams, Ellsworth Gorhum, Samuel Grove, Austin Leversee, and Francis Thyne, all of the Pioneer Greys, were wounded. Private John F. Troutner was captured, Private Martin Cain was missing, and Private John Blinn was wounded. Blinn was captured and later died in enemy hands.[28]

General Johnston retreated from Jackson, and Sherman pursued him across the state of Mississippi before quitting the chase and returning to Vicksburg. The long campaign had been very costly to Iowa. Thirty Iowa regiments participated at one time or another. Reportedly, 330 Iowa soldiers were killed and another 1,347 wounded.[29] Many thousands more had their health ruined or, worse, died in the camps.

9

Chattanooga

U nion triumphs at Gettysburg and Vicksburg showed the people of the North that victory was possible, providing they were willing to continue paying the bloody cost. The Southern capital of Richmond had not been captured, and there were half a dozen Confederate states that had not yet been invaded. Most important, though, were the several hundred thousand well-led and well-armed Confederate soldiers still prepared to defend their homes.

The state of Iowa was spared the physical ravages of battling armies and the economic disaster of the dying Confederacy. The war, in fact, helped boost Iowa's farm economy. Soldiers had to be fed and clothed. Cedar Falls, the railhead of the Cedar Valley, became a leading town in northeast Iowa. Goods from the length of the valley passed through Cedar Falls on their way east to Cedar Rapids, Dubuque, and the Mississippi River. The demand for farm produce worked in favor of the farmers and the merchants, mill owners, and mechanics who serviced them. There had been about 1,500 people in Cedar Falls when the Pioneer Greys boarded the cars for the war in 1861; by the end of 1863, the population had grown to almost 2,400. There had been 272 new buildings erected since 1861: private dwellings, stores, churches, warehouses, barns, and stables. Cedar Falls's six hotels had registered more than 25,000 guests in 1862; in 1863 the total was more than 32,000. The three large mills were busy, especially during the fall harvest, when hundreds of farmers, teams, and grain-filled wagons crowded the streets.[1] The *Gazette* proudly proclaimed that "the business of Cedar Falls has increased over one hundred per cent in 1863, as compared with that of 1862,—footing up for the year ending Dec. 31st, $2,575,110, and this independent of the transactions of transient dealers, which amount to a large sum."[2]

While the war had not physically damaged the town, a price was being paid. Young men, such as Pennsylvania-born farmer Samuel Grove, who lost a leg in the disastrous charge at Jackson, came home crippled. Others came home too physically broken down ever to work on the farms or in the mills again. George Perkins, for example, spent a year recovering from the fever he caught at Vicksburg. It was worse for families whose sons would never come home. Those men, such as Ed Culver, Lathrop Ladd, Charles Lusch, and many others were buried in Southern graves.

James Q. Rownd and his wife, Caroline, had watched both their sons go to war, George with the 1st Iowa Battery and John with the Cedar Falls Reserves. They had sweated out the news from Pea Ridge, Shiloh, Chickasaw Bluffs, and many other battles. Both sons came home. John was hit in the hand during the fighting at Vicksburg and had lost several fingers. He was discharged in November 1863. After the fall of Vicksburg, George Rownd had taken ill and was transferred to the military hospital at Helena, Arkansas, where he was discharged from the army. His father wanted to bring his son home to recuperate, so in December he traveled to Helena to get him. He brought the boy as far as Dubuque, but George's health was so bad that he died before reaching home.³ The Cedar Falls casualty list continued to grow throughout the fall as the men fought with U. S. Grant.

At the request of Governor Kirkwood, the loyal citizens of Iowa began to organize actual Home Guard militia companies to combat the perceived threat from local traitors. A Cedar Falls militia company, the Governor's Greys, was organized in July and August 1863. Many of the members were older men, such as Colonel William Sessions and John H. Overman, or former soldiers, such as Fitzroy Sessions. The company served as both a show company, designed to intimidate local copperheads, and as a means of keeping the Unionists deeply involved in the war effort. The Governor's Greys were accepted as part of the Iowa State Militia and issued 100 stands of arms and 1,000 rounds of ammunition. Veteran soldier John Wayne, who had been wounded and taken captive at Shiloh, was elected captain. Peter Melendy was elected first lieutenant.⁴

Women could not join the militia companies, but they could form Union Leagues of their own. The Ladies' Union Leagues, however, were aid societies whose activities were primarily directed toward aiding the widows and families of the soldiers. Carrie Lovell, a state organizer of the Ladies' Union League of Iowa, explained the goals of the organization in a November 1863 article published in the *Gazette*:

> First, this is no women's rights institution, or anything of the kind, gotten up by those aspiring to occupy the place of the sterner sex. There is a sphere in which woman can act, and her influence, like the gentle dews of heaven, will be felt and appreciated. The present is no time to

be idle. Disinterestedness is cowardice if not treason. . . . It is our design to throw our whole, *our united influence, in favor of the Union.* To have little as possible to do with those who sympathize with secession. To aid our brave soldiers, and their families. To this last feature I wish particularly to direct the attention of my loyal sisters, as I think it is not fully met in any other organization in the State. Our "Soldiers Aid Societies" and "Loyal Leagues" have their missions, and we wish them God Speed. But I would ask have not the families of the defenders of our country an equal claim upon our sympathies? . . . Even now there are soldiers' families enduring untold privations.—One during last summer lived for weeks on green corn and potatoes. Another, with tears in her eyes told that no one but herself knew what she endured last winter. . . . Each league is requested to appoint a committee to visit soldier's families and ascertain their wants. Now my sisters, we can make this organization spread its wings like an angel of mercy over our beautiful prairies. We can bring sunshine and gladness to many a heart. Will you do it?[5]

The Ladies' Union League of Cedar Falls was organized and added to the list of aid organizations run by women. Through their efforts, both the soldiers in the field and their families at home received much-needed help from their community.

Politics was an important issue that fall, since Iowa voters would elect a new governor. Samuel J. Kirkwood would not be a candidate, and many Republicans feared that, in spite of the recent Union victories, the Democrats could appeal to a war-weary public and win the office.

The Iowa Democrats selected General James M. Tuttle as their candidate. Tuttle's nomination reflected the almost impossible position of any Democratic candidate. He was an outspoken War Democrat who had fought heroically at Fort Donelson and Shiloh; he could not repudiate the war itself. While such a candidate could appeal to Iowa War Democrats and non-Republican Unionists, he could not expect any Republican crossover votes and could lose the Peace Democrats.

The Republicans nominated their own war hero, Colonel William M. Stone of the old 3d Iowa. Stone had fought at Blue Mills, Shiloh, and Vicksburg. He had been wounded twice and captured once.

Governor Kirkwood was not a candidate for any office that fall, but he actively campaigned for the Republican ticket. Late in August, he began a month-long speaking tour of northeast Iowa. His host in Cedar Falls was the leading Republican organizer in that part of the state, Peter Melendy.

Melendy and Kirkwood had known each other for several years. They had first met while helping to organize the Iowa State Fair in 1859. When the war broke out, Kirkwood had appointed Melendy to the post of military recruiter for Black Hawk County.[6]

Martha Melendy prepared an evening meal and had instructed the two children, Charles and Etta, in the proper way to speak to the governor. After her husband, a professional horticulturalist, had taken Kirkwood on a tour of the large Melendy garden and orchard, the meal was served. As family and guest were finishing their dinner, Captain John Wayne marched his Governor's Guards through the garden gate. Wayne formally introduced the company and called for three cheers for the governor. Kirkwood made a few informal remarks and was then given a military escort through the streets of Cedar Falls to the Overman Building, where a large rally was already in progress.[7]

The Cedar Falls Republicans, led by Melendy, Henry Perkins, Thomas Walkup, and others, fielded a full Union ticket for the local elections, which included former mayor Bryon Culver and Thomas Walkup, running for the board of trustees, and Fitzroy Sessions, up for the position of town constable.

Both the governor's race and the local elections were Republican successes. Stone won 60.5 percent of the total vote, defeating Tuttle 85,896 to 56,169. The soldiers voted overwhelmingly in favor of Stone. In spite of Tuttle's impressive military record, he won only 3,279 soldier votes, as opposed to Stone's 18,426.[8] The Union ticket in Black Hawk County and Cedar Falls Township won by large majorities.[9]

The election of 1863 was, in many ways, a trial run for the all-important presidential race coming in 1864. The war and the way it had been conducted were sure to be the key issues. If Lincoln and his party were to retain their positions, there had to be more Union victories. A seemingly endless stalemate might make Northerners so sick of the war that they would vote Lincoln and his party out of office.

The Confederacy found a much needed victory at a place called Chickamauga on the Tennessee-Georgia border on 19 September 1863. A mistake in the Union line during the second day allowed the Confederates to pour thousands of men through a momentary gap. The Union line was split, and General William Rosecrans and most of the troops from his Army of the Cumberland fled toward Chattanooga. General George Thomas, a Southern-born Union man, earned the name "the Rock of Chickamauga" by holding with his division until nearly sundown, but by evening he too was retreating toward Chattanooga. The bloody field belonged to the South, won at a cost of 16,170 Union dead and wounded and 18,450 Confederate casualties.[10]

General Rosecrans could either continue his retreat and save his army, or he could try to hold Chattanooga and risk watching his men starve in a besieged city. The first meant the most severe setback yet in a war that had only recently been favorable to the Union. The second risked the same thing.

Lincoln called upon General Grant. The victory at Vicksburg had not automatically proven that Grant was the general most able to win the war. Each of his successes, from Donelson to Vicksburg, could be explained as the work of more capable subordinates or simply sheer chance. Amid all the rumors and charges lay one thing that could not be ignored—he won. He had forced the surrender of two full Southern armies and driven the Confederacy off the Mississippi River. Chattanooga would prove, one way or another, if he was really as capable as it seemed.

Secretary of War Edwin Stanton created the Military Division of the Mississippi, a new organization under Grant's command that would unite his Army of the Tennessee, Rosecrans's Army of the Cumberland, and the Army of the Ohio. Included in the new organization were two corps, the 12th and 11th, from the Army of the Potomac, under Generals "Fighting Joe" Hooker and Oliver Otis Howard, respectively.

Grant relieved Rosecrans and placed "the Rock of Chickamauga," George Thomas, in command with specific instructions that the city was to be held. Thomas wired back, "We will hold the town until we starve."[11]

The Pioneer Greys' 3rd Iowa and its brigade had been wrecked at the mistaken assault on Jackson on 12 July. The surviving members of the brigade were transferred to Natchez, Mississippi, for rest and reorganization, so they did not travel east with Grant.

The Cedar Falls Reserves marched with General Sherman's 15th Corps, commanded by Major General Frank P. Blair, Jr. Their regiment was a part of the corps's 1st Division, under the command of Brigadier General Peter J. Osterhaus. Their brigade, the 2d, under Colonel James A. Williamson, was known as the Iowa Brigade because it included the 4th, 9th, 25th, 26th, and 30th Iowa regiments, in addition to the Cedar Falls Reserves' 31st Iowa.

Captain Speer reflected upon the condition of the regiment after almost a year's service:

> When we left Davenport, Iowa our regiment numbered 960 men. More than two thirds of the regiment have either died, been discharged, or are now in the hospital. If we live until tomorrow, we will have served one third of our time, as we were mustered into the U.S. service on the 13th of October, A.D. 1862. If we can judge the future by the past when our time of service shall expire but few will be left to tell the tale.[12]

Grant arrived at Chattanooga on 23 October prepared to take personal charge. His journey had shown him just how serious the situation was. The weak, drawn faces of Thomas's men gave evidence of the lack of rations. Feeding the army inside the city was Grant's first priority. Once that was done, the Confederates could be handled, for reinforcements were on the way. The Southerners had to be driven from the heights of Raccoon Mountain and the river crossing of Brown's Ferry in order for Grant to open a new supply line. This was accomplished by the end of the month, and ample supplies were soon flowing into the city.

The keys to Chattanooga were Raccoon Mountain and Lookout Mountain, on the right of the advancing Union forces; Tunnel Hill, across the river to the left; and Missionary Ridge, opposite the city itself in the center. Grant's plan depended on a three-pronged attack from the west. Hooker was to take Raccoon Mountain and Lookout Mountain and advance through Rossville Gap to a position beyond Missionary Ridge. Sherman was to cross the river and attack on the left through Tunnel Hill. Thomas and his army were to hold the center, advance against the base of Missionary Ridge, and hold while Sherman and Hooker came in on both flanks. Grant had about 75,000 troops under his command; the Confederates had about 43,000.[13] The attack began near noon on 24 November.

The Cedar Falls Reserves were to have gone in with Sherman but were unable to cross the river after the Confederates destroyed the Union pontoon bridge. Rather than waste time rebuilding the bridge, Grant assigned Osterhaus's division to Hooker. The men had been issued 100 rounds of ammunition apiece, and they knew they faced a fierce fight. It had rained two days earlier, and the clouds hung thick and low that morning. From where they stood in formation waiting to advance, the Reserves could see the flames of hundreds of Confederate campfires through the haze on Lookout Mountain, the smoke mixing with the morning fog.

General Thomas had not been pleased with his assignment. The decision to have him hold the center while Sherman and Hooker rescued his army offended both him and his soldiers. When it came time to move, the men of the Army of the Cumberland were eager and ready. At 1:30 P.M., they moved forward, drums and bugles sounding the charge. Thomas's men advanced with a fury and captured the first Confederate outposts, chasing the defenders back to their main line on Missionary Ridge. Thomas's men then grabbed picks and shovels and rebuilt the Confederate works so that they faced the opposite direction. Then they dug in for the night, expecting that the next day Sherman and Hooker would be in position to strike at both ends of Missionary Ridge.

Sherman's advance the next day was delayed by both the terrain and stubborn resistance; he made little progress. Hooker and his 12,000

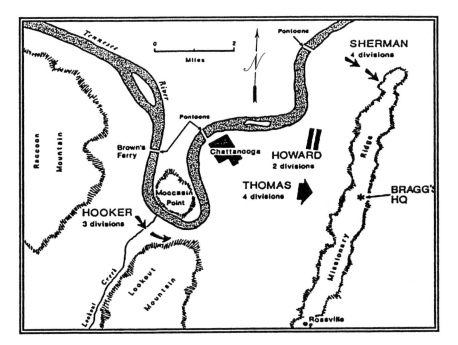

UNION ATTACK ON MISSIONARY RIDGE
Map by Andrew J. Karl

troops were more successful against Lookout Mountain. The men attacked the steep heights, which were not only lightly defended but also too steep for the artillery to be used effectively. The fog still hung thick around the mountain; the white mist was so thick that the battle became known as the Battle above the Clouds.

The Cedar Falls Reserves and the Iowa Brigade fought on Lookout Mountain all day. That night, they held their hard-won positions against repeated Confederate attacks. During the nighttime fighting, Captain Speer tried to raise the fighting, defiant spirit of the Cedar Falls soldiers by ordering Private Horace T. Cooper to sing while the men rested between assaults. While they prepared to storm the Yankee works again, the Southerners were astonished to hear music, as Cooper loudly sang "Root Hog or Die" and "The Low Backed Cat."[14]

The fighting ended just after midnight, and the soldiers collapsed on their arms, exhausted, cold, and very hungry. No campfires were allowed until morning. The day had been a Union success. While Sherman had not smashed through Tunnel Hill, Thomas was in position to assault Missionary Ridge. Hooker's troops were still on Lookout Mountain, but after 2:00 A.M., all of the Confederate troops left on the mountain had been withdrawn to defend Missionary Ridge. Hooker was ready to advance past the mountain and across to Rossville and drive north up the ridge while Sherman drove south. Private John Rath described the sight that greeted the Cedar Falls Reserves the next morning:

> It had again cleared up and we could now for the first time see the Beautiful Valley of the Chattanooga and we now could see the valley swarming with the Army of the Cumberland that we had just saved from starvation by taking Lookout and Sherman could allso be seen and heard on the extreme left on Missionary Ridge as far as the Eye could carry Booming away and oure Flag could be seen for miles on the peak of the Mountain and the signal Corps was allso Buisy communicating with Thomas and Sherman, and all was right after a little rest for one hour we moved down the mountain and we now saw one of the Grandest sights ever wittnest by man. there was a line of Battle as far as the Eye could see down the valley driving the Rebels before them toward Missionary Ridge at times nothing could be seen from the smok of powder.[15]

What Rath witnessed was the almost spontaneous attack by the Army of the Cumberland up the slopes of Missionary Ridge. Anxious to redeem their loss of two months earlier, Thomas's men were screaming "Chickamauga!" as they charged. The officers tried to stop them, but when they saw that their troops wanted nothing more than to get at their foes, they turned around and helped lead the charge. Missionary Ridge was carried.

While the Army of the Cumberland fought their way up the center of the ridge, Osterhaus's division, including the Cedar Falls Reserves, was charging up the reverse slope. During the attack, John Rath suffered one of the worst losses that can hit a man, the death of his brother. Rath described the battle:

> Oure company was again sent out as skirmishers again drove what Rebs there was in front of us through the Gap on the Right of Missionary Ridge on the Rosswell Road taking cannons prisoners Wagons &c and we was now on the south side of the Ridge and in the rear of the Rebs that were yet left on the Ridge. we now charged on Breckenridges Brigade (only oure Brigade) oure co out as skirmishers as usual drove the Rebs up the Hill and into theire works put up by Oure army on theire Retreat from Chikamauga we now charged these works after about 1 houres hard fight in which poor Bro George was instantly killed by a Reb bullet. my feelings at this time only a few rods from the Reb work can easier be imagined than described. our flag was the first one on the works and we captured the whole Reb Brigade. D. Orcutt & Thos G. Salisbury were severely wounded, but the Reb loss was afull the ground was covered with dead and wounded it was now dark and we Bivuaked in the Rebel Camp the night was cold and no rations.[16]

The next day, John Rath, Corporal Amos Eyestone, and Private Horace T. Cooper returned to the south side of the ridge as a burial party. They wrapped George Rath's body in an army blanket, dug a shallow grave in the Tennessee dirt, and buried him alongside the graves of two other Iowa soldiers.[17]

The two days of fighting had been very hard on the Iowa Brigade; 155 men were killed or wounded.[18] The Cedar Falls Reserves had three wounded: Private Darius Orcutt, Corporal Spencer Fellows, and Adjutant Thomas Salisbury. George Rath was the only one of the Reserves killed in the fighting.

After burying their dead, the Union soldiers took up their pursuit. The battles for Chattanooga settled the issue as to which of the many Union generals was most able to win the war. Through a special act of Congress, General Ulysses S. Grant was promoted to general-in-chief of all the Union armies.

Grant's promotion was the beginning of the last, most destructive campaign of the war. Grant would travel east and make his headquarters with the Army of the Potomac, where he would be up against the South's first team, Robert E. Lee and the Army of Northern Virginia. Grant's friend and most able subordinate, William Sherman, would take command in the West. Chattanooga had opened the way for an invasion of Georgia and the key city of the deep South, Atlanta.

The soldiers Grant and Sherman needed would be raised by the usual combination of bounty incentives and the threat of a draft. The previous March, Congress had approved the National Enrollment Act, which enrolled all male citizens between the ages of 20 and 45, holding them liable for military duty if needed.[19] Voting districts and townships in each state were assigned quotas that, if not met by volunteers, would be filled through conscription.

The people of Cedar Falls and Black Hawk County generally took pride in the fact that no draft had yet been needed. When a new call was issued in July, recruiting continued in the town and county. During the summer and early fall, few men enlisted, and some feared that a draft would finally be necessary, but as the New Year deadline grew closer, recruiting efforts increased.

One new infantry regiment was the 1st Iowa Infantry (African Descent). Six of the regiment's 10 companies were raised in Iowa, which had a black population of less than 1,500. The recruits were enlisted for three years at only 10 dollars a month, three dollars of which went for uniforms and rations. Unlike white volunteers, the black enlistees received no bounty. The 1st Iowa (African Descent) did not see combat but performed guard and garrison duty in St. Louis and other places.[20] Two new regiments of Iowa cavalry were also organized that fall.[21]

Soldiers from the old regiments came to Cedar Falls to find recruits. Matthew Trumbull, who had resigned his commission in the 3d Iowa because of his wounds, had been practicing law in Cedar Falls. When the new call came, Trumbull received a commission as colonel in the newly formed 9th Iowa Cavalry. Joining Trumbull in the 9th was Captain John Wayne of the Cedar Falls Governor's Guards.

Veteran soldiers were generally pleased with the threat of a draft, as it forced a commitment upon those who often cheered for the Union but were not around at enlistment time. Captain Speer expressed a soldier's feelings on the subject shortly after the battles at Chattanooga:

> Our Government calls for men and there are few who can offer a good excuse for not enlisting. Men of wealth you owe a sacred debt and are you waiting your poor neighbors to come forward and pay it? But I beg pardon for speaking rashly. You have asked your County Board of Supervisors to offer large bounties to new recruits and they have granted your request. You are certainly magnanimous. A county tax will be necessary to raise the liberal bounties which you have offered. And the hundreds of Black Hawk County soldiers now in the field will cheerfully give the little bounty which they will receive from the government as their share of the tax rather than see the war prolonged and the country ruined.[22]

The county bounty for the 1863 call was generous. A veteran soldier who reenlisted would receive a $200 county bounty, a $400 federal bounty, and a $2 enlistment bonus. New recruits would receive the $200 county bounty, a $300 federal bounty, and the $2 enlistment bonus. Anyone acting as a recruiting agent would receive a $15 bounty for every soldier enlisted.[23]

Black Hawk County had almost met its quota of 157 recruits by mid-December. The Cedar Falls quota was 37 men, which was met with a surplus of one man by early December. When the town of Waterloo found itself short two men, the Cedar Falls recruiter allowed one of their men to be counted from Waterloo.

This still left Waterloo one man short of its quota. They found him in the person of George Butler. Butler was one of the few black people living in Waterloo. He was 46 years old and ran a small barber shop. A whole crowd of potential recruiters, in addition to the regular recruiters, descended upon Butler's shop. The bounty was attractive, and they succeeded in persuading him to enlist. Henry Perkins, in an article in the *Gazette*, explained: "Thus it was that Waterloo was saved from the draft, and her quota is now filled by twenty-five white men and one darkey."[24]

A few weeks later, after Butler reported to Camp McClellan in Davenport, he complained about how he had been recruited. He claimed he had not been told that he was joining a segregated army. Butler said that he had been told by county recruiting officer O. O. St. John that he could join any branch of service he wished. He was under the impression that he had enlisted in the 4th Iowa Cavalry, but, when he got to Davenport, he was told that black men were only to be enlisted in the 1st Iowa Volunteer Infantry (African Descent).[25]

Henry Perkins had little sympathy for Butler, as he wrote: "Each man there chose his regiment, and this Geo. Butler was put down for the colored regiment on the Provost Marshal's books. He entered no complaint at the time, though he may have been deceived; we are candid in the belief that Mr. St. John had no part in drawing the wool over the darkey's eyes."[26] George Butler then joined the "colored regiment," and within a year became another Union soldier listed as having "died of disease."[27]

Most of the new recruits from Cedar Falls chose to join their townsmen in the 31st Iowa. Thirty-one of the 37 new recruits joined the 31st, two joined the 32nd, one the 7th Iowa Cavalry, and one the 3d Iowa Battery. One man joined the 18th Michigan, and another went to the Department of Texas.[28]

The winter of 1863–1864 was a hard one in Iowa: blizzards and cold weather brought most activities to a halt. The railroad was not running because of excessive snow on the tracks, and the recruits could not travel to their rendezvous site by train, as had the Pioneer Greys and Cedar Falls Reserves. Instead of rail transport, the government provided four large sleighs, which took them to Iowa City. From there, they would travel by rail to Davenport.[29] General Grant would have the men he needed for his spring campaigns.

10

Atlanta

The 1863 winter enlistments and draftees had added thousands to the ranks—5,906 had come from Iowa[1]—but there were still not enough soldiers. Recruiting efforts continued through the winter and into 1864. Two new drafts were threatened, and Governor Stone forbade eligible males from leaving the state until its quota was filled.[2] Enough Iowa men enlisted so that no draft was needed that spring; in fact, by April Iowa had 10,318 enlistments above quota. The governors of Iowa, Ohio, Indiana, and Wisconsin even petitioned President Lincoln for permission to raise 85 regiments of men who would be enlisted, without bounty payments, for 100 days. The 100 men would be assigned to guard borders, man fortifications, and do other duties that would free veteran troops for combat. Iowa's share was to be 10 regiments of 100-day soldiers.[3]

Veterans were the most important soldiers; they were hardened to the rigors of campaigning and camp life, but many of their enlistments were running out. The government stepped up its efforts to induce them to reenlist. Bounties for veterans were $100 more than for new recruits. Reenlisted veterans from Cedar Falls would receive $502 in federal and local bounties.[4] Almost as appealing was the promise of a 30-day furlough for each reenlisted veteran. The number of Iowa veterans who chose to reenlist during the winter and spring of 1864 was 6,529.[5]

Late in March, the people of Cedar Falls heard the exciting news that their veterans from the Pioneer Greys were coming home. Many of the members of the old 3d Iowa had reenlisted and would be reorganized as the 3d Iowa Veteran Infantry. There were fewer than 50 members of the original 93 Pioneer Greys left in the field by February 1864; 13 chose to reenlist, 32 did not.

During February and March, both the reenlisted veterans and those who would be mustering out in June marched with General William Sherman on what was called the Meridian Expedition. The campaign was designed to destroy the railroads and resources of central

Mississippi and to support operations farther south by General Nathaniel Banks. The expedition was only partially successful. Sherman reported losses of 21 men killed, 68 wounded, and 81 missing and presumed captured.[6] The 3d Iowa had one man killed and 10 captured.[7] Two of those captured were from the Pioneer Greys: Private Moses Allan, who had just reenlisted, and Private Edward Shields.[8]

After the Meridian Expedition, the reenlisted veterans of the 3d Iowa were granted their furloughs. The rest of the regiment, along with almost 10,000 other soldiers from the Army of the Tennessee, were sent to reinforce Nathaniel Banks on what became known as his Red River Campaign.[9]

The furloughed veterans were to be home in early April, and Peter Melendy, Zimri Streeter, the Ladies' Soldiers' Aid Society, and many others who had helped see the men off almost three years earlier began to make plans for a reception.

The committee volunteers decorated the train depot with cedar boughs and Union flags. A large arch made of cedar branches was placed over the station platform. Beneath the arch was a sign, made of cedar twigs, spelling out the single word "Welcome." Along the side of the depot building was a large banner, which read "Honor To Whom All Honor Is Due; Iowa Boys, Bully For You!" Another cedar arch was erected over the Race Bridge, and across its length were the words "Welcome Veterans of the Iowa Third." Each side of the arch was decorated with the names of the battles in which the men had fought: Blue Mills, Shiloh, Matamora, Vicksburg, and Jackson. Horticultural Hall in the Overman Building was also decorated with cedar branches, and the battle names were placed inside cedar wreaths decorating the walls of the large room.[10]

As had been done three years earlier, a line was stretched from the Carter House hotel across Main Street to the Overman Building, and a large flag was hung from it so that it fluttered in the breeze above Main Street. More flags were flying from businesses, upstairs windows, and houses. The Cedar Falls Brass Band was on hand and hundreds of people milled about in the street, ready to meet the train. Shortly before train time, Peter Melendy gave the signal, Marshal Fitzroy Sessions formed the people into a parade column, and the whole procession marched across the bridge to the depot.

When the train pulled into the station, other veterans of the 3d Iowa and the reenlisted Pioneer Greys marched out of the passenger cars and formed a military line. They were formally greeted by former military chaplain Reverend A. G. Eberhart. Eberhart was chosen for the duty because he was well known for his oratory skills and because his son,

George, was among the veterans, a member of I Company, 3d Iowa, the Union Guards.

The parade was then reformed and the soldiers were escorted across the bridge to the Overman Building. The men were welcomed by the Reverend H. B. Fifield, who had preached their farewell sermon three years earlier.

After the formal speeches, the men were treated to a real home-cooked meal, prepared by the same self-sacrificing women who had, for three years, supplemented the soldiers' military diet with food from home. All veterans in Cedar Falls were invited to the feast; the hall contained men from the 3d Iowa Battery and the 9th Iowa Infantry, as well as the Cedar Falls Reserves. Beyond beautifully decorated cakes and cookies was an abundance of good food: mashed potatoes, roast beef, cold meats, hot coffee, homemade preserves, and much more. After the meal, a veteran expressed the soldiers' feelings as he enjoyed an after-dinner cigar at the Carter House: "That was just a bully supper—the best they had given us anywhere; why they had enough to feed a regiment of men."[11]

The 30-day furlough passed quickly, and on Tuesday, 3 May, the veterans again boarded the Dubuque-bound train. They had not been idle while at home but had recruited nine volunteers for the regiment. Charles Boehmler, a member of the original Pioneer Greys, was accompanied by two of his four brothers, Edward and Jacob.

While the reenlisted veterans enjoyed their furloughs and visits home, the rest of the Pioneer Greys marched into Texas toward the Red River with General Banks. One of the worst fears of the Union leadership was that the major European powers, particularly France and England, would formally recognize the sovereignty of the Confederacy. Worse yet was the possibility that those nations might send military aid to the South, such as an invading army from British-held Canada, or a French-English fleet capable of breaking the Union naval blockade of Southern ports.

French Emperor Napoleon III had never hidden his pro-Southern views. The emperor was also trying to extend French influence into North America by placing a French-controlled government in Mexico. Lincoln recognized the potential threat and insisted that the U.S. flag be placed over some part of Texas as a warning to the French. To that end, General Banks was given authority over 42,000 men and ordered into Texas. The Red River Campaign degenerated into a nightmare of long, grueling marches and brief, vicious battles that had little effect on the war. By the time the campaign ended in May, Banks had been relieved of command and other generals had resigned in disgust. The affair became the subject of a congressional investigation and official censure.

Fortunately, none of the Pioneer Greys was killed or wounded during the Red River fiasco. But not all soldiers from Cedar Falls were as fortunate. There were 16 Cedar Falls men serving in Colonel John Scott's 32nd Iowa, and Scott's regiment was cut to pieces at the Battle of Pleasant Hill, Louisiana. Frederick J. Carter of Cedar Falls was killed in the battle, Elbert D. Blackman died soon after, Clayton Dow was wounded and captured, and Lewis Charles was captured. Charles died in a Texas prison camp. Another member of the 32nd, Elias Allensworth, was killed in battle in Arkansas a month later.[12] The Greys, along with the other 250 men of the 3d Iowa who had not reenlisted, were then sent to Davenport, Iowa, for an honorable discharge.[13]

Grant's and Sherman's spring campaigns were to begin in early May. The major difference in the 1864 campaigns was that, for the first time in the war, there was a unity of strategy in both the East and the West. Although Grant was in the East, keeping his headquarters with the Army of the Potomac, he was in charge of all theaters. Sherman's drive south toward Atlanta was in concert with Grant's drive toward Richmond: both theaters would press forward together and not let one army stand idle leaving the Confederacy free to shift forces to oppose the other.

Grant and Sherman understood that cities were of little importance as long as the Confederate armies remained in the field. Sherman was out to wreck the army that had been driven from Chattanooga, now reinforced and under the command of General Joseph E. Johnston. Grant was in the East to be sure that the Army of the Potomac not only took the Confederate capital, but destroyed Robert E. Lee's army in the process.

The Cedar Falls Reserves remained with the 15th Corps of the Army of the Tennessee, commanded by the fiery War Democrat from Illinois, John "Black Jack" Logan. The veteran Pioneer Greys, their new recruits, and the rest of the reenlisted 3d Iowa were still with the Army of the Tennessee but were now assigned to the newly organized 17th Corps, commanded by Missouri Republican Francis Blair, Jr.

There were only about 325 men with the reenlisted 3d Iowa, too few to make up a full regiment. Before being reassigned, they were called into line and given several options: they could form an independent battalion; they could form a battalion that would be assigned to one wing of another regiment; or they could be split up and used to replace men of other veteran regiments. The men were asked to vote, and they chose to form an independent battalion. The new battalion was reequipped, and, after three years of using a combination of smoothbore muskets and two kinds of rifled muskets, the men were issued new 1864-model Springfield rifles, the best weapons in the Union army.[14]

The Atlanta campaign presented Sherman with a disadvantage. Unlike the previous campaigns, there was no convenient river to float supporting gunboats or resupply the troops as they advanced. The lack of a river meant that Sherman would be dependent upon wagons and one railroad. The great supply depot for Sherman's troops was in Nashville, and supplies were moved south on the Nashville and Chattanooga Railroad. Beyond Chattanooga was the all-important Western and Atlantic Railroad, the railroad to Atlanta. Sherman planned to capture the line as he advanced and use it to supply his men. His estimate was that he would need 65 cars a day, and if, as he feared, he lost two trains a week to the enemy, he would need 120 cars a day. He planned to use the men of the new 100-day regiments to guard the rails as he and his veterans pushed forward.[15]

After the battles for Chattanooga, the Cedar Falls Reserves, along with the rest of the Iowa Brigade, had gone into winter quarters at Woodsville, Alabama. They had been able to build comfortable log cabins for shelter and were well fed, and except for occasional marches to guard railroads, they had little activity. Late in February, the new recruits from Cedar Falls began to arrive and learn military drill and discipline from the veterans. The comfortable life of winter quarters ended in April. The men were forced to leave their warm cabins and prepare to march. Early in May, the men shouldered their knapsacks and Enfield rifles and marched toward a place called Snake Creek Gap, Georgia.

As the Reserves prepared to march, Captain Speer wrote home expressing his opinions on the beginning of the great campaign:

> The Union and Rebel armies were never in better condition than now, and the coming conflict will undoubtedly be terrible. We will endeavor to do our duty, to wit: March, hope, fight, and curse those who would compromise with rebels, and pray for the enlargement or improvement of the hearts and brains of a majority of the present Congress.
>
> We have unbounded confidence in Grant, Sherman and Thomas— indeed in nearly all our leading Generals, and have strong hopes that the rebel armies will be defeated. But if we should fail the blame will not rest upon Generals or armies, but mainly upon those who opposed a draft.[16]

General Joseph Johnston's army was prepared to resist the coming invasion. The Confederate force, numbering more than 60,000, was drawn up in what seemed to be an impregnable position along the length of a ridge known as Rocky Face, which ran from a point just north of Dalton, Georgia, south to the Oostanaula River.

Rocky Face could be crossed only at three places. The most important was Mill Creek Gap: it was wide, and the all-important railroad ran through it. Dug Gap, five miles to the south, was much narrower but still close to the railroad. The third, Snake Creek Gap, was at the southern edge of the ridge, west of the small town of Resaca. Snake Creek Gap was the farthest from the railroad, but it presented a direct route from Taylor's Ridge to the rear of Johnston's line. The high peaks of Rocky Face could also serve to screen the movements of the Union columns. If Sherman could get one of his armies through the gap and capture Resaca, Johnston's army could be flanked and trapped in the valley between Resaca and Dalton.

Mill Creek Gap and Dug Gap were each vulnerable in their own way, and Johnston, believing that Sherman would strike from the north, gave those two approaches most of his attention. Sherman planned to do just the opposite. Using McPherson's Army of the Tennessee as his leading punch, he cut himself off from the railroad, moved south, and struck at the railroad at Resaca through Snake Creek Gap. If successful, he would again have a rail line, and Johnston would be flanked. On 4 May, all three of Sherman's armies advanced, the Army of the Cumberland toward Mill Creek, the Army of the Ohio toward the town of Dalton, a dozen miles north of Resaca, and the Army of the Tennessee toward Resaca. The well-screened movement caught Johnston unawares. The gap was virtually undefended, and the Army of the Tennessee had a foothold to the south before Johnston realized the danger.

The movement toward Resaca exemplified Sherman's strategy throughout the campaign; rather than smash head on into Johnston's entrenched troops, he would maneuver his own forces so as to flank the Confederate positions. Once that had been accomplished, Johnston would have to fight at a severe disadvantage or retreat. The campaign would not be decided by one or two all-or-nothing battles but by a series of movements, with both armies in almost constant contact with one another.

George Thomas's Army of the Cumberland came into contact with the enemy on 7 May, the day after Grant and the Army of the Potomac met Lee's army at a place called the Wilderness in Virginia. From that point on, both theaters would be scenes of continuous warfare throughout the summer.

The Cedar Falls Reserves were among the first of James B. McPherson's troops to enter Snake Creek Gap, advancing as skirmishers for Logan's 15th Corps on 9 May. The men had heard the sound of gunfire to the north as they marched toward the gap, and they were uncertain as to what lay ahead for them. Fortunately, there was little resistance as they entered the gap. Some Confederate cavalry formed a skirmish line and fired a few shots, but soon they retreated. The full Union column was able to get to within a mile of town before the men came under fire

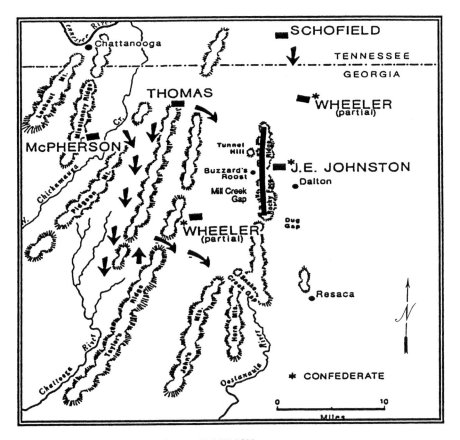

BEGINNING OF THE ATLANTA CAMPAIGN
Map by Andrew J. Karl

from more than 4,000 Southern muskets. The enemy line was strong but not so strong as to stop McPherson's entire army. McPherson, however, much to Sherman's anger and disappointment, chose not to smash through and take Resaca. Instead, the general, fearing a larger, well-entrenched force, chose to withdraw back into the gap and dig in.

For the next few days, the two sides perfected their works and continued to skirmish with each other. The Confederate line stretched for three miles along a series of hills and ridges with the Oostanaula River at the rear. It was a strong position but not impregnable; the hills just to the front of the Southern line were only lightly held, and if they could be captured, Federal guns could rake the length of the line.

McPherson began to form his troops for battle on 12 May. The troops left their works and advanced about a mile without any fighting. The next day, the battle began in earnest as the Union and Confederate cavalries clashed between the lines. The Cedar Falls Reserves were among the troops sent in to relieve the cavalry, which had dismounted and fought behind temporary entrenchments.[17]

The full Iowa Brigade was then formed into battle line in a large field. As the men waited to advance, they came under severe shelling by enemy artillery. One shell exploded near Lieutenant Colonel Jenkins, wounding him severely. The colonel of the regiment, William Smyth, the Linn County politician, had never learned to actually lead the regiment. Smyth had not known anything of drill or tactics when he joined the regiment, and since the beginning of its active service the 31st had actually been led by Jeremiah Jenkins. When Jenkins had been wounded at Vicksburg, the command had passed to the former lieutenant of the Cedar Falls Reserves, Theodore Stimming, since promoted to major. With Jenkins's second wound, the command again passed to Stimming. As John Rath put it, "Colonel Jenkins was severely wounded and the command of the regiment devolved upon Major Stimming as Colonel Smyth did not amount to anything."[18]

The Reserves were again sent out as skirmishers. They crossed the valley toward the Confederate line, waded a small stream, and gained a good position on one of the ridges. The ridge was exposed to the enemy guns and the Reserves quickly dug in. During the fighting, Sergeant Nelson Blakeslee was shot through the right lung, Private James W. Burke was severely wounded in the foot, and Private Horace T. Cooper was hit in the shoulder. The Reserves held the ridge until nightfall, when they were relieved by other troops.[19]

Sherman's full attack took place the next day, 14 May, and for two days the Reserves held their position while the Confederate line collapsed after assaults on both the left and the right. On the night of 15 May, General Johnston pulled his men out of Resaca.

Sherman ordered an immediate pursuit, and while Johnston tried to pull his army out of reach and find a new defensive line, his rear guard battled Union troops every day. The pursuit was exhausting, as the summer sun baked the men in their wool uniforms. There was not enough forage or water for the draft animals and little for them to feed off in the sandy soil of that part of Georgia. Private George Bawn collapsed from sunstroke as the Reserves marched through the desolated countryside; he died less than 24 hours later. Privates Wellington Prouty and Joseph Mills also broke down but were well enough to stay behind and guard the extra baggage. Private John Tirrell was not as fortunate; he had fallen ill at Resaca and had been left at Snake Creek Gap, where he died.[20]

Johnston managed to concentrate his army near the town of Dallas, where a small Methodist church called New Hope was at a key crossroads. The ground was hilly and heavily wooded, cut by deep ravines and creeks, and well fortified. There was skirmishing every day, and on 25 May the Union pressed forward. The fighting was fierce and blind as the men shot at each other through the smoke and trees. New Hope Church became the center of the battle, and the men fighting for the place called it the "Hell Hole."

The Reserves were on the far right of the church and spent the rainy night of 25 May in mud-filled rifle pits on the advance skirmish line. At dawn, they were relieved by fresh pickets and sent forward as skirmishers. As they advanced through the trees, Private Frederick Jacob was hit in the jaw and neck. The skirmish line was halted and forced to turn as a Confederate regiment struck its left flank. The Cedar Falls soldiers fired into the advancing enemy ranks as fast as they could ram balls down the hot barrels of their Enfield rifles. When the Confederates were within 100 yards, they opened fire on the Reserves. Private John Clough was shot through the jaw and died a few days later. Privates Harlow Perry and James Watson were killed as the company tried to pull back to its own line. Private John Rarick was captured, and Private John Parmeter wounded. The wounded men were left lying between the lines for hours.

The battles around Dallas were not Union victories, but Sherman was able to break off, swing east, and once again flank Johnston. The Confederate general was then forced to move his army to Sherman's front. It rained every day as the two armies tried to outdance one another. The constant marching and digging in the red clay took its toll on the men of both sides. Johnston took up a strong position at Acworth, with the heights of Pine Mountain and Lost Mountain as the strongest points. Two miles to the rear of the Acworth line loomed the twin peaks of Big and Little Kennesaw Mountain, another excellent position to which Johnston could retreat. Less than 30 miles beyond Kennesaw was the prize of the campaign—the city of Atlanta.

While the Cedar Falls Reserves battled their way toward Atlanta, everyday life continued at home. Former soldier and, now, town marshal and newly appointed deputy county sheriff Fitzroy Sessions was as busy as any man in town. His duties ranged from tracking down and capturing horse thieves, deserters from the military, and other criminals to more mundane tasks.

One of the primary concerns of the people of Cedar Falls was the fate of their soldiers down south. The casualty lists for the spring and early summer were appalling, and many people had no idea if their wounded relatives were alive or dead. W. B. Boss, whose brother, Sergeant Nelson Blakeslee, had been one of those wounded at Resaca, resolved to bring his brother and a fellow soldier, James Burke, home. The journey was not a fruitful one. As Sherman's troops were still engaged in combat, the military authorities would let Boss travel only as far as Chattanooga. Worse was the news that his brother had died of his wounds, as had James Burke.[21]

Cedar Falls businessmen John Hartman, T. B. Carpenter, and H. H. Carpenter also traveled to Dixie that spring, but they had different motives. Taking a drove of horses and mules along, the men traveled to Mississippi, where, a few miles below Vicksburg, they leased a plantation of more than 300 acres. They had hoped to be able to put more than 200 acres in cotton and then ship the product north, realizing a considerable profit. The venture failed. Several other Northern entrepreneurs had had the same idea and had leased nearby plantations. The people of Mississippi hated the Northern "carpetbaggers" and tried to drive them out. Southern guerrillas made midnight visits to the intruders, and several of the outsiders were murdered. While the Cedar Falls businessmen received no such visits, they did receive warnings. When they received an acceptable offer on the land, they chose to sell out and return home before they too were killed.[22]

The women's aid societies were busy that spring and summer with their local fund-raising projects and aid activities, and also in preparing for the Northeast Iowa Sanitary Fair, held in Dubuque on 21 June. The Sanitary Fair was the area's largest effort of the kind; thousands of dollars were donated, the Reserves donated several evergreen trees, and Fitzroy Sessions used his military connections to gather war relics. The ladies of Cedar Falls contributed many beautifully embroidered articles of clothing.

A year earlier, war weariness had contributed to a lack of interest in celebrating the Fourth of July; this year was to be different. With their soldiers steadily advancing on Atlanta under Sherman and with Grant advancing on Richmond, feelings were far different. Five days before the holiday, Melendy, Henry and George Perkins, Thomas Walkup, Zimri Streeter, the leaders of the aid societies, and others met to organize a real Independence Day celebration.

The weather on the Fourth was beautiful. The streets were filled with people by early morning. There were families with picnic lunches; band music and a general holiday atmosphere prevailed throughout town. At 2:00 P.M., Marshal Sessions formed the holiday parade, which marched through town to Overman Park near the river. There were eight veterans of the War of 1812 in the procession, the Governor's Greys, and many furloughed and discharged soldiers from the current war, as well as more than 150 schoolchildren from Cedar Falls and other nearby communities. Once at the park, the large crowd was entertained by the Brass Band and the local Glee Club. After the concert, there was a large display of fireworks. The holiday ended with a community dance that lasted until dawn.[23]

There were not many people in Cedar Falls or Iowa who had been more active in the cause of the Union than Peter Melendy. His efforts within the Republican Party were rewarded in February when he was elected to be one of the two delegates from the Sixth District to the party's national convention, to be held in Baltimore on 7 June 1864. At the capitol, he took the opportunity to watch Congress in session, and he met with Iowa Senator James W. Grimes and Representatives Asahel W. Hubbard, William B. Allison, and Josiah B. Grinnell. He also had a long visit with the secretary of the treasury, Salmon P. Chase. Chase, also from Cincinnati, had known the Melendy family for years. While in Cincinnati, Chase had earned the nickname the "nigger lawyer" for his many court cases defending the rights of black people. One of his allies had been Melendy's uncle, John Melendy.

Some of Melendy's most moving experiences involved visits to the Washington hospitals set up by the U.S. Sanitary Commission. Grant's eastern campaign had produced almost 2,000 casualties per day, and the hospitals were much needed. Melendy described a visit in a letter to his friend Henry Perkins:

> There are some twenty hospitals in and about the city, containing at this time thirty thousand sick and wounded soldiers from the late battlefields of the Army of the Potomac, and all these sufferers are cared for by the Sanitary Commission. . . . It was wonderful to notice the soothing effect it would have on a man writhing and groaning under a painful wound to have a gentle, sympathizing women step to his side, lay her hand on his fevered brow, and speak to him thoughtful words of consolation while administering a quieting draught. . . .
>
> We cannot do too much for the Sanitary Commission when we remember its noble deeds of charity. Surely no soldiers ever

deserved more attention than ours, and let us show them that we are not ungrateful.[24]

Before leaving Washington for the convention, Senator Grimes arranged a special appointment for the Iowa delegation to meet with President Lincoln. Melendy was much impressed with the man he had supported for so long. Lincoln, the master politician, shook each man's hand, told a few humorous stories, and complimented the Iowa men by saying that they were the "best looking delegation that had called on him, and the first."[25]

On 11 June, General Sherman's soldiers, entrenched in front of Johnston's Confederates, received word of Lincoln's renomination. The result was a wild cheering along the length of the line. Two days earlier Sherman had received another piece of good news: General Frank Blair's newly organized 17th Corps, some 10,000 veteran troops, had rejoined the Army of the Tennessee. There were enough soldiers in the corps to replace all the losses suffered to date in the Atlanta campaign. Among these veterans was the 3d Iowa Veteran Battalion, more than 300 strong and containing the last members of Cedar Falls's Pioneer Greys.

The Cedar Falls Reserves were not on the front lines; instead, from 10 June to 15 June they had been assigned to guard duty, safeguarding the division wagon train. The weather was miserable; a steady rain for over two weeks had turned Georgia's clay into deep, red gumbo. Both Union and Confederate soldiers were exhausted as Johnston retreated from his Acworth line and took up position on Kennesaw Mountain. The Reserves were taken off guard duty on 15 June and put into rifle pits in front of Pine Knob. The next day, 20 members of the company were sent out as skirmishers. The firing was heavy, with both enemy and Union shells bursting above the advancing skirmish line. Private Albert Heldt was killed. A few days later, the last of Johnston's troops made it to Kennesaw. The hot, wet weather and hardships of the campaign took their toll—Captain Robert Speer and others fell ill and were forced to go to the hospital.[26]

Johnston had placed his army in formidable defenses since the beginning of the campaign, but none was as imposing as those on Kennesaw. The mountain was situated on a broad plain and rose to a height of more than 700 feet; its smaller peak, Little Kennesaw, separated from the first by a narrow gorge, rose to more than 400 feet. The two peaks stood right in front of Sherman's advance. His soldiers could hear the sounds of trees falling as the enemy fortified their position, and soon both places were crowned with artillery.

On 22 June, there was a terrible battle between John Schofield's Army of the Ohio and a Confederate corps under John Bell Hood at

Kolb's Farm. Schofield had tried again to flank Johnston's position but failed, proving that there would be no easy way around Kennesaw.

William T. Sherman was not a patient man, and he saw the constant skirmishing and entrenching as detrimental to the aggressive fighting qualities he wanted to maintain in his armies. He also knew the political costs of stagnation: with an election coming up in the fall, he could not afford to besiege Kennesaw all summer. He also remembered the magnificent, successful charge up Missionary Ridge at Chattanooga by the Army of the Cumberland. Another such victory at Kennesaw could very well destroy Johnston's army. He decided that an attack would be made on 27 June.

McPherson's army was to attack Little Kennesaw, and Thomas's men were to have the main job at Big Kennesaw. The ill-fated attack began with an early morning barrage by more than 200 Union guns. It lasted until about 8:00 A.M., and then the infantry moved forward. The attack was a bloody failure: McPherson was halted before noon, as were the rest of the Union troops. Rather than retreat, however, the veteran soldiers dug in on the mountain slopes and continued to fight. Almost 12,000 soldiers had been sent up the slopes; close to 3,000 had been hit. One member of the Cedar Falls Reserves was wounded—Private William H. Palmer. The Pioneer Greys did not suffer any losses. That afternoon, as the wounded men lay in agony on the wooded slopes, it began to rain, and from the heights above, the Confederates added a shower of artillery shells.[27] The men lay in the mud, under fire, for the next two days. Men from both sides met to bury the dead on 30 June.

The assault was the first time in the campaign that Sherman had deviated from his flanking approaches, and the last. The attack was also the only clear Confederate victory, but it did little good. Three days later, on 3 July, Sherman looked through his chief engineer's spyglass and saw Union soldiers on the crest of Kennesaw. Johnston had retreated once more.

While the people of Cedar Falls celebrated the Fourth of July with picnics, a parade, and fireworks, their soldiers celebrated by marching through the Georgia heat to a place called Nickajack Creek, where they dug in and skirmished with Confederate troops. Captain Speer, still in a military hospital at Rome, Georgia, described the Independence Day celebration there:

Between three and four hundred sick and wounded soldiers crawled from their beds and marched around the hospital grounds preceded by a fifer and tenor drummer, playing a tune entitled, "Rally Round the Flag Boys." Their dress was uniform, to wit:—Drawers, shirt and shoes. A large proportion of them were wounded. I noticed that many of them did not keep the step; but I think they were excusable as they had unfortunately lost legs and were obliged to march on crutches. Others again had arms amputated or in slings. Some had strips of cotton cloth wrapped round their heads, but it was not to keep the sun off.[28]

After the retreat from Kennesaw, Johnston's army took up another strong position, this time near Vining's Station. Once again, Sherman maneuvered to flank him, and once again, Johnston pulled back. From the abandoned works at Vining's Station, the Union troops could at long last see the church spires of Atlanta. After more than nine weeks of constant fighting and a loss of more than 17,000 men, the Richmond of the deep South was in sight.[29]

Being in position to view the city, however, was hardly the same as capturing it. Union troops had several times come within gunfire distance of Richmond during the last three years, and it was still in Confederate hands: Atlanta could prove equally strong. There was also a new figure to be reckoned with. Confederate President Jefferson Davis, very much concerned over Johnston's many retreats and afraid that he intended to abandon Atlanta, relieved him of command and replaced him with General John Bell Hood.

The Southern armies had produced few leaders with the fighting qualities of John Hood. He had saved the day for Lee's army at Antietam by his aggressive fighting at the Cornfield. At Gettysburg he had led one of the assaults on the slopes of Little Round Top, which had cost him the use of his left arm. And it had been Hood who led the Confederate attack through the Union gap at Chickamauga, which had won the day for the South. That attack had cost him his right leg. Now, with his mangled arm inside his sleeve and pinned to his side, strapped to his horse because the stump of his leg was too short to allow him to remain seated on his own, he took command of Johnston's army with the expectation that the retreats would end.

Sherman's three armies approached the city from the east and northeast. The Army of the Tennessee, "Black Jack" Logan's 15th Corps, led the way. Early in the afternoon of 20 July, Logan's artillery fired the first shots into the city.

Hood had no intention of waiting behind the city's strong defenses for Sherman's attack. He was determined to seize the initiative and drive the invaders back. His first attempt was an attack on the Army of the Cumberland. His objective was to separate Thomas's army from any possible support, trap it between Peachtree Creek and the Chattahoochie River, and destroy it. The resulting battle of Peachtree Creek was a Confederate failure. Though Thomas suffered heavy losses, he managed to hold his position and drive the enemy back into the city.

The Cedar Falls Reserves were once more acting as guards for the

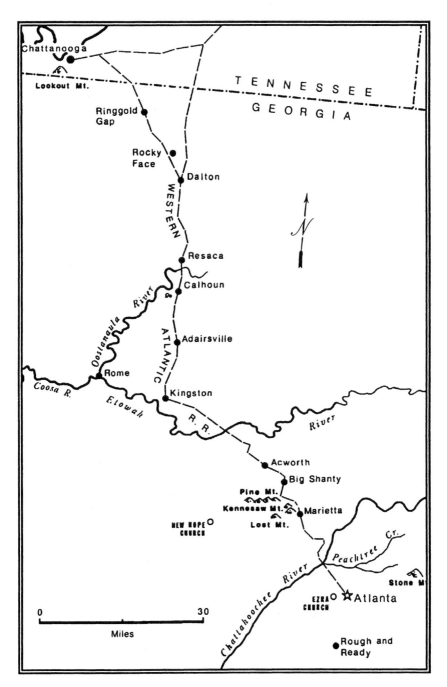

ATLANTA CAMPAIGN
Map by Andrew J. Karl

division wagon train and cattle herd and so were not engaged in the battles for the city. The duty was light, but not without danger. When the regiment moved its camp on 20 July, there were not enough men available to carry all the mess equipment along, and Sergeant Francis F. Fitkin was left to guard the kitchen equipment until others could be sent back to help transport it. Fitkin was then taken captive by Confederate cavalry.[30] Beyond this one prisoner, the Reserves suffered no losses during the battles for Atlanta. The same was not true for the Pioneer Greys.

There was little fighting on 21 July, except along a part of McPherson's line. Between Decatur and Atlanta was an important rise called Bald Hill. The hill, if held by the enemy, endangered the positions of both the 15th and the 17th Corps, so the Union troops were determined to take it. Confederate General Patrick Cleburne was equally determined to hold it. During the previous day, Private Martin Adams, of the Pioneer Greys, had been wounded while on skirmish duty. The next day, 16 members of the Greys were among those ordered to take the hill. They charged forward and gained the crest of the hill but held it for only a moment before they were forced back by heavy fire. As they withdrew, Private John T. Smith was shot through the lung and killed. Smith had not been one of the original members of the company; though he was from Cedar Falls, he had served two years with the 27th New York before joining Company A of the 3d Iowa. He joined the Greys after reenlisting as a veteran.[31] The Union troops charged the hill again, and after more hard fighting, they managed to hold it.

Hood's failures at Peachtree Creek on 20 July and Bald Hill on 21 July did not mean that he intended to retreat and give up the city. He would attack again. Throughout the night of 21 July, General Hood had his men make a forced march that would bring them close to McPherson's left rear, near the town of Decatur. He hoped to surprise McPherson's troops and defeat them while Sherman's other two armies were occupied where they were.

At about 12:30 P.M., 22 July, Sherman and McPherson were at Sherman's headquarters studying plans for a new flanking movement. Neither was expecting an attack. As the two generals conferred, they were startled to hear gunfire from the south. McPherson called his staff together, mounted his horse, and went off to investigate. He rode to a small ridge and saw that a full battle was in progress along his line. General Grenville Dodge's 16th Corps seemed to be holding their own against the heavy Confederate assaults, but Blair's 17th Corps was in serious trouble. McPherson sent his staff officers to Decatur to urge Dodge to hold on. Then, accompanied by one orderly, he rode toward Blair's corps. As the two rode across the rear of Bald Hill, they ran into Southern troops and McPherson was killed.[32]

Hood's surprise attack was achieving at least partial success, especially south of Bald Hill, where a division of the 17th Corps had been nearly surrounded. The 3d Iowa Veteran Battalion was sent in, and the rear of Bald Hill became the center of the battle as the division was struck hard from both the front and the rear. The fighting was so close that the soldiers were thrusting their bayonets through the dirt chinking of the log-reinforced trenches, trying to stab their foes on the other side. Several times, they were forced to leap over the logs and defend the other side of the trench as they were hit from still another direction. General Logan was hurrying reinforcements, but they did not arrive in time. The battle became a desperate fight for survival as the men tried to cut their way out of the trap. About 60 of them managed to escape and were able to run back to the Union line and throw themselves into any entrenchments they could find. The rest of the battalion rallied around the regimental colors and fought on. The color bearer was hit by several bullets and died holding the flag, which was instantly picked up by another soldier. The newly commissioned lieutenant colonel, Jacob Abernathy, was killed, and when it was obvious that the rest had no chance, they finally threw down their new Springfields and surrendered.[33]

There were 15 Pioneer Greys in the fight and only five made it out. They were Sergeant Jesse Cooper and Privates Leonard Castle, James M. Maggart, George Rothemal, and William Payton. Corporal Charles Boehmler, his brother Edward, Corporal Daniel Mabie, and Privates Earl Hoyt, James Baker, Henry King, Henry Rosen, and James Daniels, who was wounded in the shoulder, surrendered with the rest. Private Edward Groom lay dead in one of the lost trenches. Private Charles Blaseberg was captured and died in enemy hands. The third Boehmler brother in the battalion, Jacob, was among the sick and missed the battle.[34]

Several legends grew about the fate of the 3d Iowa colors. The report of Major William A. Taylor, of the 24th Texas Cavalry (dismounted), lists both the state and national colors as having been captured.[35] After the war, a former Confederate general, Patrick Cleburne, returned the national colors, embroidered with the names of the regiment's battles from Blue Mills to Jackson, to Laura J. Massengale of Iowa, who returned the flag to the Iowa adjutant general on 7 August 1883.[36]

A man who claimed to have witnessed the battle and surrender of the battalion wrote that, as the 3d Iowa prisoners were being marched through the streets of Atlanta, they were taunted by Confederate cavalry who waved their captured flag at them. Enraged at the sight, the prisoners were said to have rushed the cavalry, taken back the flag, and ripped it to shreds rather than leave it in enemy hands.[37]

Charles, Edward, and Jacob Boehmler's younger brother, William, who did not serve in the 3d Iowa but in a 100-day regiment and later in the 39th Illinois Infantry, wrote this account of the destruction of the colors:

> Every commissioned and non-commissioned officer had been killed or wounded, except Charles who was a Corporal at the time was in command at the time. When Charles saw that it was either to surrender or be annihilated. He took a vote of the men who voted to surrender.
>
> When Charles walked up to the Color Bearer and tore off our beloved flag which by the way had been badly riddled by rebel bullits. He tore it to pieces and gave each a piece and told the men to wear it next to their hearts.[38]

Whatever the fate of the regiment's colors, the sad fact was that after more than three years of hard service, the 3d Iowa Volunteer Infantry was destroyed at the Battle of Atlanta on 22 July 1864.

The losses on 22 July were terrible for both sides, but the Union troops were able to hold their ground against Hood's attacks. By evening, he again retreated into the city's defenses. Hood lashed out again on 28 July, this time at a place called Ezra Church, three miles west of the city. General Oliver Otis Howard had assumed command of the Army of the Tennessee after McPherson's death, and he too was able to hold off Hood's attacks.

The fighting for Atlanta continued throughout the month of August. At times it was siege warfare similar to that at Vicksburg, and at other times it involved fierce, full-scale battles. The Cedar Falls Reserves were relieved from guard detail and sent back to their brigade on 2 August, and thus they were in the trenches and under fire throughout the month. The Reserves arrived at the town of Jonesboro on the night of 30 August and proceeded to dig in. After a hard night's work, they had prepared formidable defenses. The next day, the 15th Corps was hit by two Confederate corps. Again and again, the Southern troops charged the Union lines only to be thrown back. The Reserves suffered two casualties in the battle. Second Lieutenant Henry E. Williams was shot through the chest and Private Wellington M. Prouty in the hand.[39]

On 1 September, Hood began to evacuate the city. Schofield's troops marched in the next day. The Reserves were far from the city when Hood left, but the men could hear the sounds of explosions as Hood destroyed all the ammunition and supplies he was unable to transport. Sherman launched a pursuit of the escaping Confederate army but failed to corner it. Rather than push his exhausted men any further, he halted the chase and brought his men back to Atlanta for some much needed rest.

While Sherman had not completely destroyed Hood's army, he had caused it considerable damage and driven it out of the most important city in the deep South. His armies had suffered more than 31,000 casualties. A total of 2,515 of those casualties had come from Iowa: 334 killed, 1,085 wounded, and 1,096 captured.[40] While his men rested and he made fresh plans, Sherman was able to send a triumphant telegram to Washington—"Atlanta is ours, and fairly won."[41]

11

Marching through Georgia

W hen General Hood left Atlanta, he took his army north along the same route that had been fought over all summer. Hood hoped that by tearing up Sherman's much-needed and hard-won railroad and endangering the Union garrisons from Chattanooga to Atlanta he could force the Union general to leave Atlanta and pursue him. Initially, Sherman took the bait. He chased Hood past the old battlefields of Kennesaw Mountain, Acworth, and Big Shanty. The garrisons at Big Shanty and Acworth were captured by the Confederates, and Hood seemed on his way to capturing the important Union supply base at Allatoona Pass, halfway between Atlanta and Resaca. Sherman sent Iowa General John M. Corse and the 15th Corps's 4th Division to Allatoona with orders to hold the pass until the rest of the army arrived.

Hood attacked with more than 4,000 troops. The battle lasted all day with terrible casualties on both sides, but the troops managed to hold until relieved. Hood was forced to bypass Allatoona and continue his retreat. He struck at Resaca on 12 October, captured its 1,000-man garrison, and wrecked a good deal of the railroad. He then retreated through Snake Creek Gap and took up a defensive position not far from the Chickamauga battlefield. Sherman arrived on 17 October, but as he was preparing for battle, Hood retreated into Alabama. Sherman then returned to Atlanta.

The month-long chase enraged Sherman. Hood's ability to endanger garrisons and destroy the railroad almost at will showed the fundamental weakness of Sherman's drive into the deep South. He could capture territory and cities, but he could not protect all that had been taken. Large-scale raids by Confederate cavalry under Generals Joseph Wheeler and Bedford Forrest also added to the problem. If Sherman used his men to garrison every captured mile and chase after cavalry raiders, he would watch his tremendous army dissipate before his eyes; all the gains made since May could be destroyed. Sherman had no intention of letting such a thing happen. He expressed his difficulties clearly in a message to Grant on 9 October and he also presented his plan for a new campaign:

> It will be a physical impossibility to protect the roads, now that Hood, Forrest, Wheeler, and the whole batch of devils, are turned loose without home or habitation. . . . I propose that we break up the railroad from Chattanooga forward, and that we strike out with our wagons for Milledgeville, Millen and Savannah. Until we can repopulate Georgia, it is useless for us to occupy it; but the utter destruction of its roads, houses and people, will cripple their military resources. By attempting to hold the roads, we will lose a thousand men each month, and will gain no result. I can make this march, and make Georgia howl![1]

Before retreating north, Hood had exchanged a series of letters with Sherman in which they each declared the other guilty of war crimes and atrocities. One piece of good fortune came out of the exchange: Hood asked for an exchange of prisoners. The prisoner exchange program had all but broken down over the last year. Exchanges still took place, but they were few. Because the Confederate government refused to recognize black Union soldiers as prisoners of war, and because Lincoln and Grant knew that the North could afford to have thousands of its men in prison while the Confederacy could not, few exchanges were made after 1864. The result was a terrible overcrowding of prisons on both sides. The most notorious example was the Southern prison at Andersonville, Georgia, where conditions were described as a living hell. One prisoner left this description:

> I will take a space not larger than a good-sized parlor sitting room. On this there were at least fifty of us. Directly in front of me lay two brothers named Sherwood. . . . They were in the last stages of scurvey and diarrhea. Every particle of muscle and fat about their limbs and bodies had apparently wasted away, leaving the skin clinging close to the bones of the face, arms, hands, ribs and thighs, everywhere except the feet and legs where it was swollen tense and transparent, distended with gallons of purulent matter. Their livid gums from which most of the teeth had already protruded far beyond their lips. To their left lay a sergeant and two others of their company, all three slowly dying of diarrehea. Beyond was a fair-haired German, young and intelligent-looking, whose life was ebbing tediously away. To my right was a handsome young sergeant of an Illinois infantry regiment captured at Kennesaw. His left arm had to be amputated between the shoulder and elbow, and he was turned into the Stockade with the stump all undressed save the litigating of the arteries. Of course, he had not been inside an hour before the maggot flies had laid eggs in the open wound, and before the day was gone the worms were hatched out and rioting amid the inflamed and super-sensitive nerves. . . . I would be happier could I forget his pale drawn face as he wandered uncomplainingly to

and fro, holding his maimed limb with his right hand, occassionally stopping to squeeze it as one does a boil and press from it a stream of maggots and pus. . . .

This was what one could see in every square rod of the prison.[2]

Hundreds of Iowa soldiers spent time in that terrible pen. The records show the names of 202 Iowa men buried in the swampy Georgia field that served as the prison graveyard. Among those were Moses Allen of the Pioneer Greys, who had been captured on the Meridian Expedition in February, and Charles P. Philpot of the Cedar Falls Reserves, who had been captured after the battles for Chattanooga.[3]

Private Edward Shields had also been captured on the Meridian Expedition and had spent more than four months at Andersonville before being transferred to Florence, South Carolina, in September 1864.

The Pioneer Greys who surrendered at the Battle of Atlanta on 22 July also were sent to Andersonville; not many men who went in were as fortunate, for not long after their incarceration General Sherman accepted Hood's offer to exchange prisoners. Sherman had neither the desire, nor the authority, to negotiate a general exchange, but he was willing to swap for men who could be returned to his own army. Corporal Daniel Mabie sent a letter to Henry Perkins describing the return of the Pioneer Greys from Andersonville:

Hank—Here we are after a two months' absence in a Southern prison, and I send you a few lines to say that Charles Boehmler, Ed. Boehmler, Earl Hoyt, Henry Rohssen and myself, of Co. K, A. Edwards, F. Seick, W. Wilder and G. Eberhart of Co. I . . . were exchanged on the 19th. You cannot imagine the feelings of our 750 men when our officers took us in charge and we got upon the train that brought us to this point. Cheer after cheer went up, and many were the thankful expressions made upon our escape from the jaws of hell, as we all call the bull pens at Andersonville.[4]

The exchanged prisoners were disappointed to find that their old regiment no longer existed. There had been 21 Pioneer Greys in the 3d Battalion and now, after the prisoner exchange, there were 17 left. These men were assigned to Company A of the 2d Iowa; the other members of the old 3d were assigned to Company B, 2d Iowa.

General Sherman did not want to waste his manpower by garrisoning the city of Atlanta. He would use the place as a military base but ordered all civilians still inside the city to leave. He did not want impediments to the new campaign.

Sherman had not forgotten about Hood and his army; he had plans for them as well. He detached two corps from George Thomas's Army of the Cumberland and kept them with him; he left the rest of the army to Thomas. Thomas was ordered to keep after Hood and destroy his army while Sherman marched the 300 miles across Georgia to the the city of Savannah and the Atlantic Ocean.

The new organization created two separate armies under Sherman's command, operating as two wings of the same force: the Army of the Tennessee under the command of General O. O. Howard, and the Army of Georgia under the command of General Henry W. Slocum.

The last of the Pioneer Greys, as a part of the 2d Iowa, were assigned to the 4th Division of the 15th Corps under General John M. Corse. The Cedar Falls Reserves's 31st Iowa was assigned to the 1st Division of the same corps, which was part of the Army of the Tennessee. Lieutenant Thomas Salisbury was put in command of the Cedar Falls Reserves.

The new Georgia campaign was part of Lincoln, Grant, and Sherman's efforts to finally bring the weight of the North's industry and manpower pool to bear against the Confederacy. While the South could no longer replace its soldiers, the threat of new drafts in the North kept the troops coming. The threat of a draft as an inducement to voluntary enlistments was an inefficient way to muster men, but it did the job. A call in July required 5,749 recruits from Iowa. Patriotism, combined with the federal and county bounties, caused enough men to enlist so that there was no summer draft.[5] A new draft was threatened in the fall, and recruiting efforts increased. The Cedar Falls quota was, initially, three men. This was met by appointing a special committee to raise enough funds to offer each recruit who helped fill the quota $500. Bryon Culver, who was on the list of potential draftees, hired a substitute in Chicago to enlist in his place, which reduced the town's requirement to two men. Edward Thayer and A. H. Carey agreed to be those two.[6]

The draft in the 6th District took place on 28 September. The people of Cedar Falls thought that they were free from the draft, but a revising of the lists by the adjutant general of Iowa increased the town's quota to eight. More bounties were offered, but there was still a shortage of two men at the end of September.[7] There was much concern over the seemingly endless quotas, and talk of actual resistance. In Cedar Falls those opposed to the draft became more active. The *Gazette* published an ad concerning the issue: "All of our citizens interested in escaping the approaching draft are urged to meet in Horticultural Hall, on Monday evening, January 16th at 7 o'clock, to advise together on ways and means to that end. This meeting is called at the request of Many Citizens."[8]

The meeting did not produce anything beyond more bounties and hired substitutes. The whole issue was resolved at the end of the month when a new count revealed that, because the Iowa troops enlisted for three years and not two, as in some other states, the state was entitled to more credits than was originally supposed. The extra credits meant that Iowa was out of the draft. There would be no more drafts in the state during the war.[9]

The draft was only one means of providing a pool of potential soldiers. The onetime voluntary militia companies, such as Cedar Falls's Governor's Guards, were no longer voluntary. Every man of military age was ordered either to enlist in the army or a recognized militia company. Black Hawk County was divided into three regimental districts. Cedar Falls was in the first district. Peter Melendy was given a lieutenant's commission and put in charge of organization in the district. By January 1865, there were 22 Home Guard companies in the county, five of them in Cedar Falls—one artillery company and four infantry companies.[10]

When Melendy returned from the Republican National Convention in Baltimore, he immediately began to organize to make 1864 a repeat of Lincoln's 1860 election. He was often in Des Moines at the state Republican headquarters, and in Cedar Falls he, Henry Perkins, and Colonel William Sessions formed the Lincoln and Johnson Club, which served as the major Republican organization in town.

The Democratic Party's candidate, General George B. McClellan, suffered from the same political handicap as had Iowa gubernatorial candidate General James Tuttle. As a man who had led soldiers into battle in the cause of the Union, McClellan could not disavow the war itself and get the support of the Peace Democrats. At best, all that he could do was bring into question Lincoln's policies and methods of prosecuting the war. This tactic was undercut by Sherman's victory at Atlanta; it now seemed that those policies were producing results. Still, the long war was taking a toll; there were thousands who were desperate for some sort of settlement.

The election and the war were not just academic issues. The people of Cedar Falls had seen far too many of their friends and loved ones killed or disabled for life to keep their tempers quiet. George Philpot, one of the town's original settlers, exploded in violence one evening. Three of Philpot's sons had joined the army. George, Jr., and John were home safely after serving three years with the Pioneer Greys, but in late September, their father received word that the youngest of his three boys, Charles, had died in the Andersonville prison. Feeling despondent, Philpot spent part of the evening drinking in several of the downtown saloons before returning to the Inman House Hotel, where he was a boarder, for dinner. The conversation around the dinner table turned to politics and the war. The hotel's proprietress, Mary Inman, made the mistake of taking McClellan's side and declared that she did not support Lincoln's war and did not care who knew it. The partially intoxicated Philpot angrily jumped up from the table, grabbed a tea cup, and hurled it at the woman. He then stormed out of the hotel. Once in the street, he turned and smashed the two front windows before friends grabbed the heartbroken father and led him away.[11]

Inman was in the minority, but, while Lincoln and Johnson won the popular vote by 2.2 million to 1.8 million, the large turnout for McClellan showed that many disagreed with Lincoln's policies. McClellan received 76 votes in Cedar Falls, against 357 for Lincoln. Though the results were a clear victory for Lincoln, they revealed a small propeace sentiment in the Republican town. The Democratic Party in Iowa suffered a worse defeat in 1864 than it had two years earlier, and all six Republican representatives were returned to office with larger majorities than before.[12]

Peter Melendy wrote a congratulatory message to all Lincoln supporters. He expressed the same hatred toward those opposed to the war as had been shown by Philpot's violent outburst:

> God have mercy on the degenerate Americans who voted against their country. May they see the enormity of the crime that they have recorded against Liberty. Their names are recorded on high as copartners with the foulest rebellion that ever had a record in the history of man. Down to your dens, and to the gulf prepared for copperheads.[13]

The election gave former state representative Zimri Streeter a unique opportunity to view the war firsthand. Governor Stone appointed the Cedar Falls farmer to be one of the commissioners assigned to travel to Atlanta and bring back the soldiers' ballots from men in the 4th, 6th, 9th, and 30th Iowa regiments.

Streeter arrived in Atlanta as the final preparations for the new campaign were in progress. The railroad back north was destroyed, and with Sherman's main force marching east, it seemed wiser to stay with the army than to travel back home the way he had come. "Old Black Hawk" would accompany the troops on the march across Georgia. His visit was a living reminder of home, as a Cedar Falls soldier wrote: "Old Black Hawk stopped down upon us just before we started. Just the sight made all feel like going home, so natural was he and every inch himself."[14]

General Sherman watched his army leave Atlanta from the top of Bald Hill, not far from where the Pioneer Greys had fought in July. More than a third of the city lay in ruins; many of the fires were still burning, sending a dark cloud into the sky. The smoke and flames added a festive atmosphere to the occasion, and as Sherman watched, he could hear a regimental band playing "John Brown's Body" and "Battle Hymn of the Republic." The soldiers were singing along heartily.

The armies had been stripped to the basic campaign necessities. Every soldier carried 40 rounds in his leather cartridge box, with more in the wagons. They were all well armed with new 1864-model Springfield rifles. There were 8,000 head of beef cattle being driven along, but beyond that, there would be no more, except what could be gleaned from the land they passed through. Sherman had long since learned the value of living off the land that he was conquering. He intended to move fast and destroy all that his armies did not need.

The march was to be made in two separate columns, each with about 30,000 men. This would prevent crowding and delays on the roads and would allow a larger path of destruction, almost 60 miles wide, between the two wings. The right wing was the Army of the Tennessee and the left was the new Army of Georgia. There was little resistance as the invaders smashed and burned their way through the state. The most difficult part was the marching itself, with the men making an average of 15 miles a day. There were few entrenchments to dig. Forage proved abundant as the men searched out food, grain, and valuables hidden by the people of Georgia. The nighttime campfires, made of fence rails and lumber from wrecked buildings, were spectacular. This was a conquering army, eager to avenge three years of warfare and with little pity for those who they felt had started the terrible war.

The only serious fighting took place on 22 November near the town of Griswaldville. The weather had turned colder the night before and there were flurries of snow as the 15th Corps marched into a large pine forest. The men dug in during the dark, the trenches facing the rear. The Pioneer Greys and the Cedar Falls Reserves lay in their works through the night and made sure that there was a strong picket line established. The next day, they could hear the sounds of artillery and rifle fire as their comrades in the 2d Brigade fought off three determined assaults by the Georgia militia. When the battle ended, the 2d Brigade troops cheered their victory and went out to the field, where more than 600 Confederates lay. They found little to cheer about. The Union loss was only 62, but the attacking force consisted mostly of old men and young boys, unfit for regular Confederate service, amateurs at war who had hurled themselves in desperation at the hardened Union veterans.[15]

There were no more battles on the march. The most the men had to fear was capture or death at the hands of roving bands of local Confederates. The men most susceptible to such a fate were the so-called bummers—soldiers who had been released from their commands to swarm over the countryside and seek out hidden supplies, torch buildings, and forage for food. Private Edward Boehmler wrote home and told his family of a narrow escape. He and three friends had been out on forage detail, each mounted on a captured horse, when they found themselves surrounded and forced to surrender. They were taken to a nearby plantation, where they were locked in a room with armed guards placed outside the door. The men wondered if they would be shot in the morning or sent to the prison at Andersonville, a very real terror for Boehmler, who had only recently been released. While the bummers worried over their fate, an elderly house slave came to their aid. The old man went to the cellar and brought back a bottle of peach brandy, which he gave to the guards after teasing the Yankees with the delicacy. The guards enjoyed the treat and were soon fast asleep. While they slept, the old man was able to get into the room, wake the prisoners, and take them to their horses, which he had saddled and waiting. By morning, the bummers were back at their own lines.[16]

The slaves in the deep South were very much aware of the Emancipation Proclamation, and they greeted Sherman's soldiers as liberators. Thousands of former slaves flocked to the Union columns, carrying all their worldly possessions with them. They came on foot, on horseback, and by mule and handcart, chasing the freedom promised in Lincoln's decree. Sherman's rough soldiers had little use for the runaways and often treated them shabbily. Sherman, himself no lover of black freedom, urged the escapees to stay at their homes. He used some former slaves as "pioneers," the men who preceded the column to clear the roads of obstruction, and as teamsters, but beyond that, he wanted no blacks with his army. The soldiers welcomed black women who were willing to be used as prostitutes and mistresses, but few others. Not all Union soldiers were violent racists, but they were a combat army and were not set up to begin Reconstruction then and there. Beyond offering human compassion, of which there was little, there was nothing the soldiers could do for the black residents of a charred land.

The campaign was the easiest the Union troops had yet endured, with easy marching conditions and plenty of food. By 10 December, the outer works of the city of Savannah were visible. The city was located on a peninsula extending east into the Atlantic. The Savannah River was to the north, and the mouth of the Ogeechee River was a dozen miles to the south. On the south bank of the Ogeechee was Fort McAllister; it was well situated to defend the mouth of the river and prevent Union ships from coming upriver, but it was manned by fewer than 250 men. Sherman sent a division under Brigadier General William Hazen to capture the place. The fort fell within minutes of Hazen's ordering his men forward. That night, the steamships began to arrive, bringing rations and, best of all, hundreds of sacks of mail.

The next objective after the capture of Fort McAllister was Hutchinson's Island, north of the city. When the island fell, Savannah would be encircled north and south on the land side. Instead of a desperate battle for the island, the Union troops found themselves hailed as saviors by a colony of slaves who worked in the rice mills.[17]

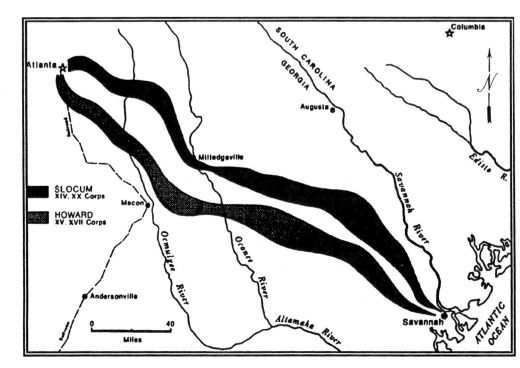

MARCH TO THE SEA
Map by Andrew J. Karl

With both flanks of the city under Union control, Savannah was doomed. Many thought that capture would mean destruction, as at Atlanta. While Sherman's men built earthworks or rebuilt those made by General Francis Marion ("the Swamp Fox") during the Revolutionary War, Confederate General William Hardee gathered as many supplies as he could transport and took the Confederate troops out of the city. The mayor of Savannah, accompanied by a delegation from the board of aldermen, came out of the city on 21 December; they were carrying a white flag and wanted to meet with Sherman. Union troops were triumphantly marching through the streets by afternoon. Sherman himself entered the city the next day and established his headquarters in one of the city's large houses. There was little damage done by the victorious Yankees, and the occupation of the scenic city was an enjoyable duty. Private Earl Hoyt, of the Pioneer Greys, described Savannah as

> by far the prettiest place I have seen in the South. The streets are wide and pleasant, only a little too sandy. The large buildings are mostly constructed of brick, and are very well built. The river has been cleared of obstructions so that other steamers are to be seen running up and down every day. It is a beautiful sight for one who has always lived in the far West to see these large ocean steamers moving majestically through the water with the stars and stripes floating proudly over them, and that too in Southern waters.[18]

Sherman had suffered the loss of fewer than 2,000 men and had marched his armies across the length of Georgia, capturing yet another of the South's important cities. The campaign was a success at all levels. Sherman heard another piece of good news while at Savannah: General Thomas had finally smashed John Bell Hood's army, first at the Battle of Franklin on 30 November, then at the Battle of Nashville on 15 and 16 December. The largest Confederate army in the deep South was in shambles and retreating into Alabama.

Zimri Streeter was able to board ship at Savannah, sail north, and then travel across country by rail, returning to Cedar Falls in late December. The soldiers from Cedar Falls had no delusions that the campaign had been just another march. Earl Hoyt, of the Pioneer Greys, wrote a letter expressing his thoughts on the march:

> We received news yesterday that Gen. Thomas had been cleaning Hood out and taking ten thousand prisoners. This together with our peaceful occupation of Savannah, has brought this army to a lively hope that our warfare will soon be over, and we will be allowed to once more return to our peaceful homes and friends. The general opinion here is that the rebs cannot hold out longer than until the first of July next, and large bets are being offered by the sporting community.[19]

143

The men did not know where Sherman would march next. They enjoyed their stay in Savannah, with its fresh seafood and pleasant climate, and left the planning to "Uncle Billy" Sherman. Each man was issued new clothes, received back pay and mail, and had an opportunity to rest before being ordered to shoulder his Springfield and fall in. As Earl Hoyt wrote, "It is not in the nature of Gen. Sherman to lay still when he can just as well be on the move.—The troops, however, are confident of victory wherever they go, and, therefore, are not very particular which they do."[20]

12

Triumph and Tragedy

The destructive march through Georgia had proven that the deep South was vulnerable. The long campaign against Richmond seemed to be coming to a conclusion as well. General Grant and the Army of the Potomac had cornered Lee's army at the city of Petersburg, Virginia, where it had been starving behind miles of trenches for four months.

The capture of Savannah and the capture, on 27 December, of Fort Fisher, which guarded the port city of Wilmington, North Carolina, put Sherman in position to take his army north, and if need be to deliver the knockout punch at Petersburg. The plan was for Grant to order General John M. Schofield's corps from George Thomas's Army of the Cumberland to Wilmington and reinforce it so that Schofield could then drive west through North Carolina. While Schofield marched through North Carolina, Sherman would be marching north through both South Carolina and North Carolina. The two would meet at Goldsboro, unite their forces, and then continue north to Petersburg.

Sherman's campaign presented many difficulties. The worst of these was the very nature of the land itself. The Carolinas contained innumerable rivers and swampy marshes. The campaign was scheduled to begin in the middle of January, during the worst winter the South had seen in years. There was snow in the air and, worse, rain—day after day of icy, cold rain. All of the rivers were swollen, as were their dozens of tributaries. The land between the rivers and creeks was a flooded swampy marshland, and roads were either under water or had turned to channels of thick, deep mud.

There were Confederate soldiers in the Carolinas as well. General P. G. T. Beauregard had been put in command of the almost 20,000 troops scattered across the two states, including reinforcements from the remnants of Hood's former command who were on their way from Alabama. If the Southern general could concentrate his forces, he could possibly defeat Sherman while the Union armies were bogged down in

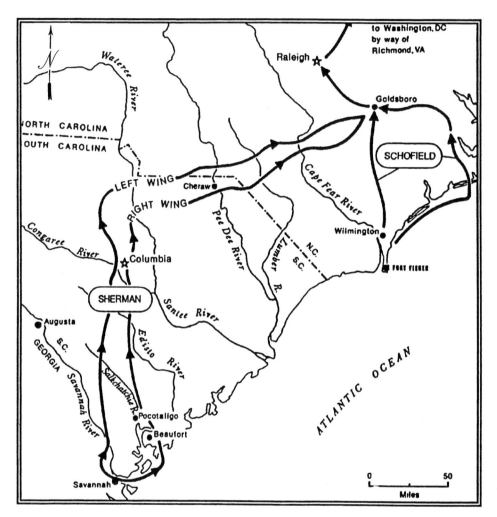

CAROLINAS CAMPAIGN
Map by Andrew J. Karl

the swamps or straddling the rivers.

Sherman and his troops were well aware of the problems involved in the winter campaign, but they were a victorious army and now they were marching into the heart of the rebellion—that would make a difference. The first Southern state convention to pass a resolution of secession had met in the capital of South Carolina, Columbia. The war had been fought up to this time in the border states to the north or in states to the west, but it had not yet touched South Carolina. The new campaign would bring the war full circle, back to where the Union soldiers felt that it had begun. They were ready to avenge themselves.

The organization of the campaign would be little different from the one through Georgia. General Logan was back in command of the 15th Corps but General Howard remained in command of the wing, the 15th and 17th corps. General Slocum commanded the other wing, the 20th and 14th corps. Sherman planned to march with the two wings separated. As in Georgia, the march would both deceive the enemy as to what the final destination would be and prevent Beauregard from concentrating his forces in opposition. It would also allow a huge swath of destruction. The two wings would feint at both the city of Augusta, where Beauregard had his headquarters, and at the key city of Charleston while actually heading for Columbia, which lay between them.

Sherman's plan was for most of his army, including all of Slocum's wing and Judson Kilpatrick's cavalry, to cross the Savannah River and march into South Carolina by land. Most of the 15th Corps, however, were transported downriver to the sea on 13 January, where they were put aboard navy warships and transported to Beaufort on Port Royal Sound. The Cedar Falls Reserves were among those who had the opportunity to experience a short, six-hour "pleasant ride on the Briny deep," aboard the U.S.S. *Pontiac*.[1] Some of the midwesterners did not find the rolling sea pleasant, and they were glad to be on dry land once more, where their stomachs could recover.

After landing on South Carolina soil, they marched to their campsites four miles from town, where they stayed for several miserable days as the cold winter rain soaked the land. The weather cleared up on 27 January, and the Reserves were ordered to break camp and march: the campaign had begun in earnest. Sherman had not told his men what their destination would be, but they knew that they were bringing the war to South Carolina, and that seemed most important. As John Rath wrote, "Allmost everyone Swore Vengeance to South Carolina the Mother of Rebellion and threatening to Burn everything that would Burn and make them feel the War which they had not before in the evening allmost every house was a fire which looked as though the Boys intended to carry out what the said."[2]

The Pioneer Greys did not get a boat ride but left their Savannah camp on 28 January and marched north along the Savannah River. They marched for three days until they reached a place called Sister's Ferry, about 40 miles above Savannah, where they rested for two days while the wagons were loaded with provisions. They crossed the river into South Carolina on 4 February.[3] The march was off to a successful beginning in spite of the constant rain and flooded roads. The long Union columns made steady progress as the men chopped down trees and laid them in corduroy fashion on the muddy roads. There were several skirmishes, but the Confederates were easily driven off. The burning continued and the men watched huge columns of smoke rise from burning buildings and even from the pine forests themselves.

While the Union army marched forward, General Joseph Wheeler's Confederate cavalry and other small detachments of infantry did their best to fight a delaying action while Beauregard tried to discern Sherman's target and concentrate his forces there.

The Cedar Falls Reserves marched 19 miles on 1 February. The weather had been pleasant but clouds gathered as the men made night camp. The next day, the clouds darkened the sky and promised rain. The Reserves were sent out ahead of the column as advance skirmishers. They could hear musket fire ahead as they advanced into the thick, wet underbrush. Private Myron L. Tracy became separated from the rest of the Cedar Falls skirmishers and was captured. The ragged Confederates immediately stripped their prisoner of all his clothing except his drawers, socks, and undershirt. That night the promised rain came, freezing cold on the near naked man. Tracy's guards took shelter and fell asleep. He then managed to slip away and hide in a thicket of underbrush, shivering in the cold. He lay there all the night and most of the next day, listening to the skirmishing between the two sides. He crawled out toward evening, hoping that his captors had been driven off. He could still hear gunfire to the front and carefully made his way toward the sound. He saw a company of blue-coated cavalry trot by and he ran out to meet them. They were Confederates, Wheeler's men dressed in captured Yankee uniforms. Even their horse trappings were Union made. Tracy was once more a prisoner. He was taken to Augusta and from there to the horrible pen at Andersonville, where he remained until late March.[4]

While Tracy was hiding in the wet underbrush, the Reserves were once more on the skirmish line. The soldiers advanced carefully, carrying their Springfields as if they were hunting birds back in Iowa, ready to fire at the enemy or drop to the earth and act on the defensive if they ran into serious trouble. As they advanced, Private Ephraim Smelser was shot and killed. Smelser had been one of the original members of the company, and on 3 February 1865, he became the last of the Reserves to be killed in combat.[5]

The Carolinas campaign was more fortunate for another Cedar Falls soldier, Edward Shields of the Pioneer Greys, who had been a prisoner in Andersonville since the Meridian campaign. Shields had been transferred to a prison at Wilmington shortly before General Schofield began his campaign against the city. It was obvious that the city could not be held, and orders were given to transfer the prisoners to Goldsboro. There was much confusion as the Confederates prepared to evacuate the city, and Shields saw his opportunity to escape. He grabbed a leaky bucket and joined a detail of prisoners assigned to carry water, but instead of staying with them, he simply walked away. His ragged blue uniform was little different from the clothes worn by the enemy, and he was able to walk by without notice. He kept moving at a sober pace until he saw an elderly black woman. As he walked by, he hurriedly asked if she had seen any Yankee soldiers. The woman told him to go to a particular house, where he would find friends. Shields did as he was directed. When he came to the house, he walked in and presented himself to the woman who lived there, a Mrs. Leslie. She hid and fed the escapee for several days while the last Confederate troops left town. When Schofield took possession of the city, Shields reported to his headquarters and was finally sent home to Cedar Falls.[6]

By mid-February, it had become very clear that Sherman's intended target was Columbia. The Confederates in the city hurriedly gathered what provisions could be transported and prepared to hold the place as long as possible. The Congaree River, formed where the Saluda and Broad rivers joined about half a mile northwest of the city, offered a natural defense. The flooded river's current was swift, its banks were high, and the surrounding bottomlands were thick swamps covered by several feet of icy water. A strong rear guard of Confederate infantry and cavalry was ready to fight as long as necessary for the main body to withdraw.

The Reserves advanced on the city on 15 February, another rainy day. Enemy skirmishers were driven to the Congaree, where a strong defensive line had been prepared. The Union troops made a flank movement through the waist-deep water of a 300-yard swamp, and the enemy was forced to leave its works and retreat across a creek. General Sherman was on shore, nervously watching his soldiers. The Cedar Falls troops could see him, off by himself, pacing up and down, smoking a cigar. Generals Howard, Logan, and Woods were also on hand, observing as their skirmishers made it to a low, open field. The Union troops could see Confederates across the field, and it looked like an open field battle would be fought, but darkness fell before the men could be deployed.[7]

The enemy retreated the next day, and the Union troops marched across the Congaree to the Columbia side, burning the bridges behind them. The weather was clear, and the men could see the city as it was shelled by Union cannon. At 4:00 P.M., they crossed a pontoon bridge at the junction of the Saluda and Broad rivers. The Broad River was all that still stood between them and the city. That night the Reserves, as part of the advance, were ordered to cross under cover of darkness. Confederate campfires were visible, and the Reserves could even hear the enemy pickets call to one another. The Union troops feared that they would be shot as they tried to cross the swiftly moving stream or that the enemy would simply wait until they had crossed and then capture them on the other side.

The Reserves' brigade had the assignment of laying a pontoon bridge across the river. The engineers could lay the bridge, but the problem was how to get the first footing on the other side. At 2:00 A.M., the first line still had not been put across, and volunteers were called for. Several men from the Reserves volunteered to carry a rope across. Private Wellington Prouty was one of the first to wade into the rushing water, and one hour later the rope was across. Two pontoon boats were lashed together to make a large raft, which was used to ferry a load of 160 men across; among them were the rest of the Reserves.[8]

Once on the other side, the men discovered that they were actually on a large island. The real shore still lay to their front, across a 30-foot bog flooded over by several feet of water. Rather than remain stuck on the island, the men held their rifles and cartridge boxes over their heads and waded in, using logs, brush, and anything else that could support them as footing. Confederate troops on the opposite shore had discovered what was going on and began firing at the men in the swamp. The first ones across threw themselves behind the steep bank and started to dig in. More and more troops were ferried across to the island, 60 at a time, and these men splashed across the bog as well. After four regiments had made it across, a charge was ordered. The Union troops attacked, and the enemy retreated into the city. The full brigade was across by then, advancing through the swamp and up the banks toward the hill where the city was located. The men were halted in front of the city. As they were being put into battle formation, they could see a carriage coming toward them.[9]

The carriage contained Mayor T. J. Goodwyn and three Columbia aldermen. A white flag was attached to the buggy. Goodwyn had been ordered by General Wade Hampton, the richest planter in the Old South, whose large plantation was nearby and who now commanded the Confederate forces in the area, to surrender Columbia in the hopes that the city might be spared. While Goodwyn was riding to meet Colonel

George Stone of the 25th Iowa, now in command of the 3d Brigade, Hampton was trying to save what he could from the city. What could not be carried away was to be destroyed. All cotton stored in the city, thousands of bales, was to be carried outside of town and burned. Hundreds of the large bales had been carried from warehouses to the streets for faster loading, but the wagons never arrived, and the bales were still there when the city fell.

After accepting the surrender, Colonel Stone ordered his troops into the city. The Cedar Falls Reserves were among the first inside. Some men from the 31st grabbed the regiment's national flag and raced toward the statehouse. Members of the 15th Iowa took down the large, 20-by-36-foot South Carolina flag that had flown over the first secession convention, and the men from the 31st Iowa raised their flag on the building itself. It was the first Union flag to fly on that staff in more than four years.[10]

As the 15th Corps reached the outskirts of the city, they were met by about 30 thin, ragged men—former prisoners of war. A prison camp for Union officers, Camp Sorgum, was located several miles northwest of town. Five days before Sherman arrived, the prisoners had been hurriedly transported to Charlotte. During the confusion, about 30 men had managed to hide themselves and were missed in the final search. When they heard of the surrender, they came out of hiding to joyously greet their liberators.[11]

Sherman had promised Mayor Goodwyn that his men would remain under control, but such a promise was more easily made than kept. Thousands of jubilant, angry soldiers were not easily contained. The 31st Iowa was named provost guard and Lieutenant Colonel Jenkins was named provost marshal, but the provosts did more celebrating than policing.[12]

The Union soldiers were received like conquering heroes. Liberated slaves by the hundreds lined the streets and cheered their arrival. Citizens who feared for their safety and their homes offered the troops food and liquor. John Rath described what happened:

> All the citizens opened their doors to the Soldiers wherever a Soldier would go by a house the would call him in to take dinner and I dont know of any one that ever Refused I myself took three dinners. . . . several fires got started but soon put out by the firemen, but the town was doomed to be burned all the releast prisners swore they would set the town afire there was a heavy Northwest wind all day and as soon as it got dark fires could be seen in every direction north of town, and in less than no time it looked as though it Rained fire from heaven Women and children could be seen Runing from one place to another to protect them from the fire Everything was wild with excitement Soldiers could

be seen everywheres with plunder of every description allso hundred of them drunk of liquor that the got of Citizens thinking that that would safe them, at 10 oclock pm oure brigade was releaved from duty by the first and we marched to camp 1 mile out of town while the fire was at its highest pitch.[13]

All parts of the city were hit by the arsonists. Drunken soldiers ran from building to building carrying rags that had been soaked in turpentine. Some soldiers used their bayonets to stab holes in the fire hoses that other soldiers were using trying to stop the flames. The cotton bales in the streets had ripped open and the wind blew the tinderlike cotton everywhere. Sherman himself came out of his quarters to help fight the flames, as did division commander Charles R. Woods. Their efforts proved all but ineffective; by morning most of the city lay in smoldering ruins.

The Pioneer Greys entered Columbia about 4:00 in the afternoon and joined in the fray. One of the men reflected on the city and its fate:

Columbia, when our troops first took possession of it, was, without exception, the prettiest place I have seen in the South. It was situated, however, in a rebellious country and had been one of the favorite resorts of rebels, and still more to its discredit there was located here one of those hell-holes known as Southern prisons. The later, of all others, went to seal its fate.[14]

The army remained at Columbia for two more days. The Pioneer Greys were put to work tearing up the Columbia-to-Charleston railroad. After wrecking about 20 miles of the line, they were ordered to march on 20 February. The Cedar Falls Reserves were among those assigned to burn the last of the cotton that had escaped the fire, some 8,000 bales, and were placed in the rear of the column when the soldiers marched out. The Reserves, from their position at the end of the line of march, could see the piteous army of refugees, both black and white, who left the charred ruins of their homes to follow the troops.

The Pioneer Greys were in the advance of the column when it left Columbia. Two days later, Private Martin Adams, a veteran who had been wounded at Shiloh in 1862, at Jackson in 1863, and at Atlanta the previous July, was shot and killed by a hidden Confederate while on forage detail. Martin has the sad distinction of being the last of the Pioneer Greys to be killed—less than four months short of four years after he and the rest of the volunteer company had donned their hometown uniforms and boarded the train for Dubuque.[15]

The march became hard, cold, and wet work once more as Sherman headed for his rendezvous with Schofield at Goldsboro. The town of Cheraw was captured on 3 March, and three days later the troops crossed into North Carolina. The final leg of the march was from Cheraw to Fayetteville, and from there to Goldsboro. Sherman also received a piece of interesting news: his old adversary, Joseph E. Johnston, had replaced Beauregard as commander of the Confederate forces in the Carolinas.

The troops left Fayetteville on the morning of 15 March. They traveled in three columns: Slocum on the left, moving toward Bentonville; Howard on the extreme right; and Logan between the two. With Joe Johnston in command of the enemy troops, Sherman moved cautiously, fearing that the old soldier would be able to mass his troops and smash one of the Union wings before the others could come to its aid. The march through North Carolina was marked by Johnston's strong defensive positions and well-timed retreats. There was fighting at Kinston between Johnston and Schofield's troops as the Union general moved toward Goldsboro, and at Averasboro and Bentonville as Johnston tried to hit Sherman's columns separately. Johnston failed to destroy either of Sherman's columns, but Sherman failed to rush enough troops to the battles to destroy Johnston's army before his wily opponent managed to get away. Sherman arrived at Goldsboro on 22 March. His men were ragged and many were dressed in captured civilian clothes. Many, having worn out their shoes in the march, were now barefoot.

The army was united with Schofield's force and both settled into camp, taking advantage of the chance to rest and be resupplied. Sherman left the army in its Goldsboro camp and hurried north for a meeting with President Lincoln and his old friend General Grant. The three met aboard the presidential steamer *River Queen*, anchored near Richmond on the James River, to map out the final strategy of the war. Grant was to finish off Lee's army and capture Richmond, while Sherman was to march on Raleigh and smash Johnston's army along the way. Sherman then returned to Goldsboro on 9 April, ready to begin the new campaign. That same day, he received word that Richmond had been captured on 3 April and that President Jefferson Davis and the Confederate cabinet were on the run. There was more news yet to come. General Lee had met with Grant at Appomattox Court House and had surrendered his Army of Northern Virginia on 9 April.

The Cedar Falls telegraph operator, railroad agent J. B. Cavanaugh, was the first to receive the news of Lee's surrender. The brief message had been sent by the Secretary of War, Edwin Stanton, at 9:00 P.M. on Sunday, 9 April, to General John A. Dix at New York; from there it was relayed to Dubuque. It was sent to Cedar Falls the next morning. The message was short and clear:

> This Department has just received official report of the surrender, this day, of General Lee and his army to Lieutenant-General Grant, on

the terms proposed by General Grant. Details will be given as speedily as possible.

Edwin M. Stanton
Secretary of War[16]

The message was received at 9:00 A.M., and within the hour the news had spread across town. The stores were closed and the owners and clerks joined the gathering crowd on Main Street. Children escaped from the schoolhouse on Fifth Street, and women carrying their young ones left their houses and hurried downtown. People shouted and cheered, and the saloons did a brisk morning business. Two flags were hung between the Carter House Hotel and the Overman Building, and dozens more were hung in windows, on porches, and in storefronts. The old town cannon was hauled out, loaded, and fired so that the farmers living within range of the booming sound could saddle up and ride into town to see what was up.[17]

Henry and George Perkins flew into action, determined not only to spread the news but also to lead the celebration. A real celebration needed fireworks, and George shouted to his brother that he would write the needed extra edition if Henry would take care of the rest. Henry Perkins all but ran from the office, carrying his copy of the telegram. He raised close to $75 within half an hour and was able to wire Dubuque to send $50 worth of fireworks by the day's express; there was money left for any other needed expenses.[18]

George Perkins and his printer's apprentice quickly put together a one-page broadside which served as the extra. Its headline read "Victory," and its subheadings read "Lee and His Whole Army Captured," "Fling Out Your Banners," and "Bad Luck on the Man Who Is Sober Tonight!" Delivery boys were put to work distributing the handbills. The boys hurried through the streets shouting the news. They ran out of papers and were forced to return to the *Gazette* office for a second printing. Men on horseback took yet a third printing and galloped north to Janesville and Waverly, west to New Hartford, and south to Hudson.[19]

While the handbills were being printed and distributed, the celebration continued. A group of older boys climbed to the schoolhouse belfry and lowered the 150-pound bell to the ground. They then mounted the bell on a one-horse wagon, raised a flag on the wagon, and drove through town cheering and ringing the bell. One of the boys also rang a large dinner bell, and soon every child who could lay hands on a cowbell or sleighbell was in the streets adding to the joyous din. Some other people took a large, heavy cart used for hauling logs to the sawmill and created an ox-drawn float. The float carried the effigies of Jefferson

Davis and General Lee. Both had been symbolically lynched, and Davis's likeness was dragging behind the cart in the mud. Lee was accorded a minimum of respect: his effigy hung just out of the muddy street. Driving the wagon was a black man who worked for the Overman family. The man was known as "Old Bunk," and his contribution to the float was to allow a sign bearing the word "Contraband" to be hung around his neck. A crowd of young boys followed "Old Bunk," jeering at him and shouting racial slurs. A small, very dirty and ragged child sat on the wagon's axletree carrying a sign which read "Poor White Trash of the South."[20]

Lieutenant Peter Melendy put on his blue militia uniform and called the Governor's Guards to their armory. The Guard's bandboys struck up a marching tune and the column stepped out. Hundreds of people fell in step with the militia company as it paraded to Overman Hall. It was barely 10:00 A.M., and the hall was packed with happy, cheering citizens. Zimri Streeter, now an unofficial veteran of Sherman's army, presided over the victory meeting. Streeter called for cheers for Lincoln and for all of those who had supported the cause for so long. Peter Melendy took the stage and tearfully called this a day of celebration. The popular speaker, Reverend Eberhart, was called for; he made an enthusiastic speech and soon had the hall ringing with song as he led the crowd in gospel and patriotic tunes.[21]

While the meeting in Overman Hall continued, the streets of Cedar Falls were fast filling up as farmers drove their wagons into town, bringing their families along to join the festivities. There were more than 3,000 people in town by nightfall. The crowd was a mixed group: veterans in their uniforms, farmers and their families dressed in their Sunday best, local business people, and the hard-working women of the aid societies. There were happy children playing and chasing each other through the crowd, and soon the sky was lit with roman candles, skyrockets, and pinwheels. It was the largest display the town had yet sponsored.[22]

When the fireworks ended, the crowd moved one block south to where a huge bonfire had been prepared.[23] When the fire died down, the celebration returned to Overman Hall, where Streeter and Eberhart continued to call for speeches and lead the crowd in song.[24]

George Perkins wrote an editorial for that week's full edition of the *Gazette* expressing his pride in the services of the Iowa soldiers, the pain of the long war, and the longing of those at home who were anxious to have their loved ones back:

> God forgive us that we have had so little sympathy for the stricken ones—that we so hardened our hearts amidst the havoc of the shot and the shell, and the horrors of the hospital.

Soon the heroes of many fights will be marching home! How many long-waiting, anxious hearts, beat wildly joyous last Monday in contemplation of the happy day.

The Union is not only saved, but regenerated, too. Surely now we may sing,

"The land of the free,
And the home of the brave!"

"Redeemed, regenerated and disenthralled!" The Proud Republic stands to-day before God and man.[25]

The Pioneer Greys and the Cedar Falls Reserves were camped at a place called Pineville, just short of Raleigh, when they received word of Lee's surrender. The camps came alive with excitement. Fires burned high and hundreds of impromptu salutes were fired. Many deserters from Johnston's army came into camp and gave themselves up; they were hungry men dressed in the tattered remains of their uniforms, men who would rather go home than be among the last killed in a lost cause. The army moved out the next day and made camp that night just outside of Raleigh. Joseph Johnston evacuated the town without a fight, and on 14 April Sherman, Howard, Logan, and Woods formally reviewed their troops as they marched through the shady streets of Raleigh.

The people of Cedar Falls were hardly settled back into their daily lives after the great surrender celebration when they were hit with more news. President Abraham Lincoln had been assassinated.

Crowds gathered once more on the new plank sidewalks of Main Street, but no one was cheering this time. The Perkins brothers rushed another extra into print, and once again the newsboys ran through the streets. The extra confirmed the terrible news and announced that there would be a special service that Sunday, Easter Sunday, at the Presbyterian Church.[26]

The walls, pews, altar, and pulpit of the church were draped in black crepe and muslin. There were pictures of Lincoln on the walls; also, draped in black above the pictures were several flags in a V formation. There were more flags on the communion table and pulpit, their staffs furled in black. The first to arrive were the choir members and pastors from the town's other churches: Baptist, Episcopal, Methodist, Universalist, and Congregational. The front pews were reserved for the Governor's Guards. The rest of the church was filled to capacity, and a large, silent crowd outside filled the entire block. Veterans were dressed in their uniforms and had black armbands on their left sleeves, as did most of the male civilians, while many women wore black shawls.

The people had become familiar with military funerals over the last four years, but this one had a special, solemn tone to it. Those in the streets were the first to hear the muffled drums and fifes of the Governor's Guards as they slowly marched from their armory past the church to the Commons on Ninth Street, where three volleys were fired in honor of the slain president. The company then formed a column and marched back to the church. When they reached the door, the men took off their hats and marched to the front pews. A detail marched to the front, carrying their muskets, and formed a half-circle in front of the pulpit. The rest stacked arms and took their reserved places.

Methodist minister R. Norton began the service with a reading from the Bible and then turned the program over to the combined choir. After several minutes of solemn music, Reverend Eberhart took the pulpit. The fiery orator began by reading the latest news that had come over the wire. He spoke in a low voice, praising the dead president and the Union cause, but his voice became louder and more forceful as he continued. He became angrier as he spoke and condemned all those who had fought on the Southern side as being equally guilty of the crime, they and their copperhead sympathizers in the North. He declared that Lincoln had completed his divine mission by saving the Union, and his death was proof that a righteous God demanded a change from his policy of leniency. He demanded, in the name of Heaven, that justice to the guilty not be sacrificed to mercy.

The violent anguish from the pulpit was frequently interrupted by applause and shouts of approval. Some people said later that perhaps Eberhart's remarks were too harsh. Most, however, agreed that he spoke for the town and also as a father whose son had been in Andersonville and who was still in North Carolina with Sherman. An editorial in the *Gazette* said this: "Some have intimated that his remarks were too severe; but we believe he spoke the honest convictions of the people of this community, who are firmly of the opinion that nothing can be too severe for the demons of this hell-born rebellion or for their apologists and proselytes in the North."[27]

One Cedar Falls leader was away from home when he heard about Lincoln's death. Two days after the celebration of Lee's surrender, Peter Melendy had left town to meet with other members of the state fair board at Burlington, where they hoped to complete preparations for the September fair. Melendy stopped at Iowa City on Monday, 15 April. While there, he had an opportunity to meet with his old friends, Judge N. H. Brainerd and the former governor, Samuel J. Kirkwood. The three men were at the Iowa City post office discussing Lee's surrender and the preparations for the fall fair when they were interrupted by an excited man who had heard a rumor that the president had been killed.

The news spread rapidly. Soon there were hundreds of people in the streets, all asking if it was true: was Lincoln really dead? Iowa City did not have a telegraph, so a rider was quickly sent to Muscatine to find out the truth. Melendy was horrified, and being too impatient to wait for the rider's return, took the afternoon train to Muscatine. When he stepped from the train, he saw that the flags were at half-mast and the buildings were draped in black. The rumor was true. He was heartsick and, like Reverend Eberhart, bitterly angry. He then left town for the rural comfort of his friend Suel Foster's large farm. The farm was near the Mississippi, and Melendy found much solace in the sight of the hills overlooking the river and Foster's well-kept fruit orchards.[28]

While visiting Foster, Melendy took time to write a letter to Henry Perkins in Cedar Falls. The letter expressed the pain of a man who felt that both he and the nation had lost a dear friend. It also expressed the same unforgiving anger Eberhart had shown in his Cedar Falls address:

> But a few short months ago I took the great good man by the hand at the White House, and when I remember the warm reception he gave me, as well as the entire Iowa delegation to the national Convention at Baltimore, the thought would arise, Can it be possible that he is dead? It seems but yesterday that he stood there in all of his manliness and great goodness, with high hopes of his country's future.
>
> Would to God that the hot wrath of the people might swing every man that rejoices in this calamity. Revenge is my motto.[29]

Melendy was given the honor of representing Cedar Falls at the service for Abraham Lincoln held in Chicago on 1 and 2 May, when the funeral train carrying Lincoln's body was to stop there on its way to Lincoln's home in Springfield. The service was a huge, elaborate affair with thousands of people attending. The morning had been cloudy and it looked as though it might rain, but as the funeral train pulled into the Chicago station, the sun had shone through. The scene impressed the romantic farmer; it was as if the heavens too had joined in the service:

> The morning promised unfavorable weather. It was cloudy until about 8 A.M., when the sun shone out in all its beauty, throwing a rich mellow glow upon the beautiful scenery in and around the sacred spot; there to the east the placid waters of Lake Michigan lay unruffled. Oh, what a sublime scene. The waters have come to join the requiem. The placid deep chants the dirge in the low beating ripple. Strange sadness touches all that behold the beautiful scene—something whispered in silvery tones and seemed to say, "Passing away! passing away!" The tolling bell, the sad and mournful salute of the minute gun, all tell the wonderful and sublime occasion.[30]

General William Sherman was just boarding a car to take him to a place called Durham's Station, where he and Joseph Johnston were to meet and discuss terms of surrender, when he was stopped by a messenger carrying a telegram—the announcement of Lincoln's assassination. If Eberhart and Melendy expressed an angry rage at the murder of their leader, Sherman's soldiers had the ability to put those feelings into action. Sherman feared that if the men heard the news before he had arranged for Johnston's surrender, they would turn the city of Raleigh into another Columbia.

A cease-fire was arranged on 14 April, and Sherman issued strict orders forbidding acts of revenge or violence. His soldiers learned of the assassination four days later. John Rath wrote that "everybody morns his loss and swears Vengence to the Rebs."[31] Sherman's orders and strict camp discipline prevented serious trouble as he negotiated with Johnston.

When Lee surrendered his army to Grant, the terms were quite simple. It was not an unconditional surrender, but virtually so. Mounted men were permitted to keep their horses, and the officers could keep their sidearms. There was to be a formal surrender of all other arms and of the army's battle flags, but beyond that, the men were to return home. Political matters would be decided in Washington. Sherman and Johnston went much further. They made a peace that allowed the soldiers to keep their weapons and deposit them in their state arsenals. They even negotiated items beyond military matters, including the right of the existing Southern legislatures to remain in power and the constitutional status of the seceded states. They had, in effect, negotiated a national peace treaty.

Sherman had greatly exceeded his authority in making such an agreement. The new president, Andrew Johnson, called a cabinet meeting to discuss the terms, and it was unanimously decided that they must be rejected. Grant was sent to Raleigh to inform both Sherman and Johnston that the terms of surrender had to be the same as those offered to Lee. Secretary of War Stanton considered Sherman's generous terms a political power grab and even hinted that Sherman had been bribed by Southern money and the promise of postwar support by Northern copperheads. Sherman never forgave Stanton for the insult.

The army was ordered to make one more march—through North Carolina, into Virginia, and then to Washington, D.C.—where they were to participate in the Grand Review of the victorious Union troops.

The Army of the Potomac and Sherman's army were both encamped around the capital by 20 May. The double encampment was more of an uneasy truce than a victory celebration. Sherman's westerners had always resented the soldiers in the East, the hated "Potomacs" who had always received the very best equipment and who were the darlings of the New York press but who could not whip Lee until a western general, Grant, came to lead them. Conditions were not helped by newspaper reports of the peace terms offered to Johnston. These reports sided with Secretary Stanton and accused Sherman of disloyalty. Sherman's rough troopers considered such stories to be more examples of how both they and their general had been mistreated by the press and the government. It had taken the Army of the Potomac four years to advance the 100 miles from the capital to Richmond. During that time, the western troops had stormed through almost every state in the Confederacy. The victory was due to them, not to the "paper collars" in the East.

The westerners' boast that they had actually won the war was deeply resented by soldiers who had watched their friends die by the thousands at such places as Antietam, Gettysburg, Spotsylvania, and Cold Harbor. The victory celebration was marred by fistfights and brawls between members of the two victorious armies. The situation was eased a bit by having Sherman's men camp on the Virginia side of the Potomac. The real showdown would come on 23 and 24 May, during the Grand Review, when the soldiers' appearance and performance would be judged by everyone in the capital.

The Army of the Potomac was the first to march down Pennsylvania Avenue and pass in review before President Johnson, General Grant, and the members of the Cabinet. The flags lining the route were at full staff for the first time since Lincoln's assassination, and all the crepe had been removed from the public buildings; this was a day of celebration. General George G. Meade led the way, riding proudly at the head of the two-mile-long column. When he reached the stand in front of the White House, he wheeled his horse and saluted President Johnson, General Grant, and the other dignitaries assembled there. He then dismounted, took his place on the platform, and watched his men march past. He was very pleased with what he saw. The men had received new uniforms, and all the brass and steel was brightly polished and gleamed in the May sun. The ranks were straight and the men kept the regulation twenty-two-inch step perfectly. The parade stretched as far as one could see. Beyond the two miles of infantry were seven miles of cavalry, not to mention the artillery with hundreds of guns and the Engineer Corps with its equipment. It was the grandest display ever seen in the capital city. Sherman, thinking that his own troops might be hard-pressed to follow such a military spectacle, remarked to Meade that he feared "my poor tatter-demalion corps will make a poor appearance tomorrow when contrasted with yours."[32]

Sherman need not have feared. Midwestern pride and a powerful sense of their own accomplishments would make up for the men's appearance.

He was at the head of the column the next morning, mounted on his handsome bay and looking straight ahead. At 9:00 A.M., a cannon boomed and the parade began. When he finally turned his head, Sherman was very pleased with what he saw. The column was tight. The men, who enjoyed such a fierce reputation as undisciplined bummers, were keeping to the step, the long, swaggering step of the West, a kind of rolling gate that made the whole column sway with the regularity of a pendulum. Following each corps was another parade, this one made up of its black Pioneers and camp followers, refugees from slavery, who rode or led heavily laden mules or walked next to the army supply wagons. The massive crowd cheered them all.

"Raider" described the review:

> Outsiders say that Sherman's Army reviewed very favorably; and all express themselves very surprised at the appearance and bearing of the soldiers in our army, so much so, that the Rappatomacs feel the least bit jealous, as in fact they may, for men whose judgement may be relied upon said that our army done the best marching ever witnessed in Washington. What I could see of the marching was splendid, and I believe it can only be equalled not bettered.
>
> The 3d Brigade (ours) of the 1st Division, 15th A.C., was pointed out to the President by General Logan as it passed, and, "Columbia" was heard.—The President, Grant, Sherman, and several ladies laughed heartily. What they were laughing at I can only guess and you may want to guess as well as I, I'll not bet that I guess right, altho' I don't think I'll come far from it. My opinion is that they were glad that we did not suffer with the cold while in Columbia, as they knew we had a warm fire there; or perhaps they were so pleased because we had so soon become soldiers after being bummers.[33]

There were 15 regiments from Iowa in the Grand Review. Four of them—the 2d, 9th, 16th, and 31st—contained soldiers from Cedar Falls and other towns in Black Hawk County. There were more than 30 members of the Cedar Falls Reserves with the 31st. Ten of the original Pioneer Greys marched with the 2d Iowa; they had come as far as any in the long column, from the death of their first member at the battle of Blue Mills, Missouri, to their last death outside of Columbia, South Carolina. And soon, after four years of bloody warfare, the soldiers from Cedar Falls, Iowa, were coming home.

EPILOGUE

T he Cedar Falls troops did not all muster out at once and arrive home in one victorious parade. They remained in their different regiments for varying lengths of time, depending on when they had been mustered into service. The soldiers who had been sworn in before 1 October 1862 were classified as veterans, mustered out while still in Washington, and sent directly to Iowa. The nonveterans of the Army of the Tennessee were sent to Louisville, Kentucky, to await a later discharge.

The soldiers were anxious to return home, and the Cedar Falls Reserves were resentful of the rule, for it classified them as nonveterans. The muster date for the 31st Iowa was 12 October 1862, less than two weeks short of the time required for veteran's status. The injustice caused "Raider" to send the *Gazette* one of the most bitter letters he had written:

> We enlisted and organized our companies, varying in date, from the 11th to the 28th of August, 1862. The then Colonel of the regiment, who was appointed through political inotives [*sic*], received his commission on the 10th of September, but did not appear for muster until about the 10th of October. Now, after having fought our way from Arkansas Post to Bentonville, and marched from Helena, Arkansas, to the Sea at Savannah, and from there to Washington, we are very cooly told that because our Colonel was attending to political matters, and thus delayed our muster nearly one month, we must stay in the service until October 13th, 1865, as it was no fault of the Government.
>
> Again, we have some sixteen members of our regiment; who are to be immediately mustered out, simply because their time expires before the 1st of October, 1865—having enlisted, or were drafted, for one year. Let us see the justice of this matter, and I take one of our own company as a sample: He enlisted some time in September, 1864; has been with the regiment and carried a musket 58 days, has never seen an armed rebel, and yet he pockets $350 bounty from the County, which the old members who pay taxes there help to pay; gets also, as I

162

understand, $200 from the town of Cedar Falls, $100 bounty from the Government, and tomorrow receives $128 pay proper.[1]

The injustice was corrected through a special order from the War Department. The newest recruits were transferred to the 17th Iowa Infantry, and the veteran members of the regiment, which included 50 members of the Reserves, were mustered out on 21 June 1865.[2]

They turned over their weapons and equipment in Davenport, Iowa, on 1 July and received their discharge papers and last pay. They were no longer soldiers.[3]

Twenty members of the Reserves took the steamboat *S.B. Muscatine* to Dubuque. When they arrived, they discovered that a terrific summer storm had damaged a section of the railroad to Cedar Falls. Rather than stay and wait for repairs to be made, the men hired five livery teams and started for home by wagon. They had a rough trip. The roads were muddy and the streams flooded, but they caught up to the repair train at Raymond on 4 July and exchanged the wagons and teams for railroad tickets.[4]

No one in Cedar Falls had organized an official Fourth of July celebration, but that did not seem to matter. The Union victory, pleasant weather, and prospect of the soldiers' return once the railroad repairs were completed gave the day a festive atmosphere. The town Commons and city square were filled with people enjoying the summer day with friends, families, and picnic lunches. The repair train carrying the 20 Reserves arrived just before sunset; the surprise arrival of the veterans added the perfect touch to the holiday. After the sun went down, there was a display of fireworks. The rest of the Reserves, who had come by train from Davenport by way of Cedar Rapids, arrived after midnight. The holiday crowd was still out in force, and the men were greeted at the station by flags, cheers, and the tearful embraces of their loved ones.[5]

The Pioneer Greys had to wait in Louisville until 12 July before they were discharged; the last 10 members arrived home on 21 and 22 July. There were large crowds at the depot, and the Ladies' Soldiers' Aid Society organized a welcome-home dance for all the veterans.[6]

The four years of civil war had, in many respects, been boom years for the city of Cedar Falls. The war had all but halted railroad development in the West, and with the tracks west halted at the Cedar and the tracks going north proceeding at a snail's pace, Cedar Falls had become the key city in the Cedar Valley. Most goods going in and out of the valley during the war had been, naturally, funneled through Cedar Falls. There were also thousands of settlers who were heading west, spurred on by the free land offered in the Homestead Bill of 1862. Most rode the train to Cedar Falls and, once there, reoutfitted for a wagon journey.

163

Both the size and population of Cedar Falls doubled between 1861 and 1865. There were six mills on the river and many thriving businesses downtown. It seemed that Peter Melendy's dream of the town's becoming a Cincinnati on the Cedar would become reality.[7]

Such was not the case. The postwar years were times of economic boom and bust cycles, most of them linked to the great surge of postwar railroad building. Battles between communities courting the favor of the railroads became as bitter and heated as those in the past over which town would be the county seat. The railroad terminus, which had been at Cedar Falls during the war, went, like the county seat in 1855, to the city of Waterloo in 1866. The railroads brought other industries, and Waterloo, not Cedar Falls, became the postwar industrial city of the Cedar Valley. Waterloo, over the years, became home not only for the present-day Illinois Central Railroad but also for the giant Rath Pork Packing Plant, established in 1891, and in the 20th century, for the John Deere Tractor Works.

The war had settled the political issue of the supremacy of the federal government, but it had loosed many more, such as the future status of black people and Reconstruction in the defeated South. Postwar politics were almost as turbulent and bitter as prewar politics had been. Postwar politics in Iowa and across the nation were dominated by battles over Reconstruction issues. George Perkins, who, along with his brother Henry, had closed the *Cedar Falls Gazette* in 1866 and moved to Sioux City (where they founded the *Sioux City Journal*), remained active in Iowa politics. Henry Perkins died shortly after the war, but George became one of Iowa's most respected publishers and a recognized leader of the conservative wing of the Republican Party of Iowa.[8]

Peter Melendy, Cedar Falls's best-known political organizer, also remained active in politics, serving on the Republican Party Central Committee and, from 1865 through 1866, as a federal marshal. Melendy's political enemies used his war record as a political weapon. While Melendy had probably done more for the war effort as a home-town organizer than he could have as a musket-carrying soldier, he had still chosen to remain at home with his frail wife, who would die in 1866, and their two children. Melendy and other leading Republicans who had not gone to the war were taunted as "stay-at-homes," businessmen who supported the war and made money from it while others suffered on the march and died in battle.[9]

Melendy's contributions to both the war effort and the city of Cedar Falls had always been of the behind-the-scenes, organizational variety. He seldom sought public office, though he eventually served as mayor of Cedar Falls for six years. He preferred instead to work one-on-one as a businessman and citizen. One of his favorite projects became a Cedar Falls institutional landmark and made the town a center of education— first the Iowa State Normal School, then the Iowa State Teacher's College, and today the University of Northern Iowa. All three institutions were built upon foundations going back to the Civil War and Peter Melendy.

The people of Iowa recognized the tragic need for an institution to house and educate the children who had been orphaned by the war. The first such orphanage was established in Van Buren County in 1864. The facilities there soon proved to be inadequate, and a commission met at Marshalltown in 1865 to select a different site. Peter Melendy served as the delegate from Cedar Falls, and through his efforts the town was chosen as the site of one of three new orphanages.

The orphanage was first located in the former American Hotel, across the street from the school on Fifth and Main streets. The hotel had been refurbished through private contributions, many of them from veterans, and was opened in October 1865. There were 96 children living there by the end of the year, and within two years the number had increased to 220. It became obvious that a larger building was needed. Melendy and his friend, state senator J. B. Powers, convinced the citizens of Cedar Falls to aid the project by funding the purchase of 40 acres of land just southwest of town. Powers shepherded a bill through the Iowa General Assembly that appropriated $25,000 for the building and the staff needed to maintain it. One of the points Melendy used to sell the idea to the people of Cedar Falls was the concept of an ongoing project. When the generation of Civil War orphans had grown, the building and grounds could be converted to a normal school, which would be a long-term asset to both the town and the state. The new building was finished and occupied in 1869 and for seven years was home to several hundred orphans.

The Civil War orphans had either grown or been placed in new homes by 1875, and their orphanage became Central Hall, the first classroom, administration building, and residence hall of the new Iowa State Normal School. The old building was located just southwest of the new school's auditorium, which still stands and remains in use. The building was used by both the normal school and Iowa State Teacher's College until 1965, when it was destroyed by fire. There is nothing left of the original structure, but the land purchased for the orphanage is today the central part of the campus of the University of Northern Iowa.[10]

The university is the most visible legacy the town has of the war, but there are others. About seven miles west of town, a mile west of the small town of Benson, Iowa, on State Highway 57, is a small red granite monument. The monument marks the birthplace of James H. Brownell, the first of the Pioneer Greys to die in battle. The flag that the Ladies of Cedar Falls gave to the Cedar Falls Reserves is on display at the Grout Museum in Waterloo, and the Cedar Falls Historical Society has a fine collection of photos and artifacts. Greenwood Cemetery has a statue of a Civil War soldier that was put there by Captain Robert Speer and other veterans.

Monuments and relics are lifeless things, but Cedar Falls has one living link with its history, a flowing connection with the past—the river. There are houses on the bluffs now, and the cedar groves on the northeast side are gone, but the water still flows and crashes over a small dam near the downtown area. Someone looking at the river today can easily imagine the area in William Sturgis's day. Sturgis could see ahead to a time of mills and waterwheels and a thriving town on the Cedar. People today can look back to the same image. There is a new highway bridge near the old railroad bridge, just off First and Main streets. Someone looking from Main Street across the bridge toward Dubuque can easily imagine the excitement the people of the settlement felt as they stood near the same spot and saw the smoke from the first railroad engine. The river gave the town its life, and the railroad determined its future. The tracks took the produce from the Cedar Valley to the rest of the world. They also took the men of the valley to war.

NOTES

CHAPTER 1

1. Albert M. Lea, *The Book That Gave Iowa Its Name: Notes on the Wisconsin Territory: Particularly with Reference to the Iowa District, or Black Hawk Purchase* (Iowa City: State Historical Society of Iowa, 1935), 2.

2. John C. Hartman, ed., *History of Black Hawk County Iowa and Its People*, vol. 1 (Chicago: S. J. Clarke Publishing Co., 1915), 48, 159.

3. Ibid., 38; Peter Melendy, *Historical Record of Cedar Falls, the Garden City of Iowa* (Cedar Falls, Iowa: Peter Melendy, 1893), 7.

4. Melendy, *Historical Record*, 79.

5. Glenda Riley, *Cities on the Cedar* (Parkersburg, Iowa: Mid Prairie Books, 1988), 12.

6. Luella M. Wright, *Peter Melendy: The Mind and the Soil* (Iowa City: State Historical Society of Iowa, 1943), 94–95.

7. Hartman, 61.

8. U.S. Census Office, Eighth Census, 1860 (Washington, D.C.: National Archives and Records Service, 1967), roll 312 Iowa Black Hawk to Bremer Counties; Riley, 16.

9. Wright, *Melendy*, 43–44, 109.

10. Ibid., 109.

11. Roger Leavitt, *When Cedar Falls Was Young* (Cedar Falls, Iowa: Record Press, 1928), 10; *Historical and Biographical Record of Black Hawk County, Iowa*, vol. 2 (Chicago: Interstate Publishing Co., 1886), 270.

12. *Historical and Biographical Record*, vol. 2, 233.

13. 1860 Census.

14. William Boehmler, "Chronology of Wm Boehmler," TS, n.d., "Military Affairs," ser. 14, file 1, Archives of the Cedar Falls Historical Society, Cedar Falls, Iowa.

15. Charles Rath, *A Love Story* (Unpublished manuscript, property of Jean Parker, Waterloo, Iowa).

16. Melendy, *Historical Record*, 122; Leavitt, 13; Hartman, 366.

17. Hartman, 366.

18. Hartman, 162.

19. *Cedar Falls Gazette* (hereafter *Gazette*), 12 April 1861.

20. Ibid.

C H A P T E R   2

1. 1860 Census.

2. Leland L. Sage, *A History of Iowa* (Ames, Iowa: Iowa State University Press, 1974), 129.

3. Ibid., 136.

4. Wright, *Melendy*, 38-39.

5. Ibid., 250.

6. *Gazette*, 16 March 1860.

7. *Gazette*, 22 June 1860.

8. *Gazette*, 25 May 1860.

9. *Gazette*, 7 September 1860.

10. *Webster's Guide to American History* (Springfield, Mass.: G & C Merriam Co., 1971), 220.

11. Wright, *Melendy*, 258.

12. John E. Briggs, "The Enlistment of Iowa Troops During the Civil War," *Iowa Journal of History and Politics* 15 (July 1917): 328.

13. *Gazette*, 18 January 1861.

14. *Gazette*, 8 March 1861.

15. Briggs, 334; *Gazette*, 7 June 1861.

16. *Gazette*, 7 June 1861.

17. Wright, *Melendy*, 45–46.

18. *Gazette*, 8 March 1861.

19. Jacob A. Swisher, *Iowa in Times of War* (Iowa City: State Historical Society of Iowa, 1943), 77.

20. *Gazette*, 19 April 1861.

21. Ibid.

22. Ibid.

23. Luella M. Wright, "The Pioneer Greys," *Palimpsest* 22 (January 1941): 10.

24. *Gazette*, 31 May 1861.

25. Briggs, 343.

26. Wright, "The Pioneer Greys," 14.

27. *Gazette*, 31 May 1861.

28. Wright, "The Pioneer Greys," 16.

29. *Gazette*, 7 June 1861.

30. Ibid.

31. Briggs, 334.

32. *Dubuque Times*, 8 June 1861.

33. *Gazette*, 7 June 1861.

34. Sgt. John T. Boggs, K Company, 3d Iowa Infantry. *Gazette*, 7 February 1862.

CHAPTER 3

1. Swisher, 133.

2. Lieutenant S. D. Thompson, *Recollections With the Third Iowa Regiment* (Cincinnati: By the author, 1864), 19. Held in Special Collections, Donald O. Rod Library, University of Northern Iowa, Cedar Falls.

3. Mark M. Boatner, *The Civil War Dictionary* (New York: David McKay Co., 1959), 612.

4. *Roster and Record of Iowa Soldiers in the War of the Rebellion*, vol. 1 (Iowa General Assembly, 1910), 296.

5. Swisher, 115; Thompson, 20.

6. Boatner, 624.

7. Thompson, 30.

8. William E. Parrish, *Turbulent Partnership: Missouri and the Union 1861-1865* (Columbia: University of Missouri Press, 1963), 9.

9. Ibid., 15.

10. Ibid., 24.

11. *Keokuk Gate City*, 29 June 1861; Swisher, 119; Thompson, 30.

12. Thompson, 30.

13. Ibid., 31.

14. *Gazette*, 26 July 1861.

15. Ibid.

16. Thompson, 39.

17. Captain A. A. Stuart, 17th Iowa Infantry, *Iowa Colonels and Regiments: Being a History of Iowa Regiments in the War of the Rebellion* (Des Moines, Iowa: Mills and Co., 1865), 82; *Roster and Record*, vol. 1, 283.

18. Letter from John Scott to Governor S. J. Kirkwood, 25 June 1861, *Records of the Third Iowa Volunteer Infantry*, Adjutant General's Records, Record Group No. 3, "Correspondence," Iowa State Historical Society, Des Moines, Iowa.

19. *Gazette*, 26 July 1861; Thompson, 49–50.

20. *Gazette*, 26 July 1861.

21. Thompson, 49–50.

22. *Gazette*, 26 July 1861.

23. Thompson, 52.

24. *Gazette*, 26 July 1861.

25. *Roster and Record*, vol. 1, 396.

26. *Gazette*, 26 July 1862; Thompson, 58–59.

27. *Gazette*, 26 July 1862.

28. Thompson, 71.

29. Lurton D. Ingersoll, *Iowa and the Rebellion* (Dubuque, Iowa: J. B. Lippincott and Co., 1866), 54–55; *Cedar Falls Gazette*, 6 September 1861.

30. Ingersoll, 54.

31. *Gazette*, 20 September 1861; Ingersoll, 54.

32. Boatner, 658–659.

33. *Gazette*, 20 September 1861.

34. *Gazette*, 16 August 1861; 6 September 1861.

35. Boatner, 932–34.

36. Ibid., 935.

37. Charles P. Brown, "The Battle of Blue Mills Landing," *Annals of Iowa* 14, no. 3 (April 1924): 289.

38. Thompson, 129.

39. Ibid., 132.

40. *Gazette*, 18 October 1861.

41. Brown, 293.

42. Ibid., 292.

43. Thompson, 138.

44. *Gazette*, 27 September 1861.

45. *Gazette*, 25 October 1861.

46. *Gazette*, 4 October 1861.

CHAPTER 4

1. Briggs, 351.

2. *Gazette*, 19 July 1861.

3. *Gazette*, 26 July 1861; 9 August 1861.

4. *Gazette*, 2 August 1861; 16 August 1861; 23 August 1861.

5. *Gazette*, 13 September 1861; 27 September 1861.

6. Earl S. Fullbrook, "Relief Work in Iowa During the Civil War," *Iowa Journal of History and Politics* 16 (April 1918): 166; Ruth A. Gallaher, "Annie Turner Wittenmyer," *Iowa Journal of History and Politics* 29 (October 1931): 529.

7. *Gazette*, 25 April 1862.

8. *Gazette*, 9 August 1861.

9. *Gazette*, 17 January 1862.

10. H. W. Lathrop, *The Life and Times of Samuel J. Kirkwood: Iowa's War Governor* (Iowa City: State Historical Society of Iowa and by the author, 1893), 190.

11. James M. McPherson, *Battle Cry of Freedom* (New York: Oxford University Press, 1988), 483.

12. *Gazette*, 27 September 1861.

13. *Gazette*, 25 October 1861.

14. Dan Elbert Clark, *Samuel Jordan Kirkwood* (Iowa City: N.p., 1917), 205.

15. *Gazette*, 6 September 1861.

16. *Gazette*, 11 October 1861.

17. *Gazette*, 6 December 1861; 2 August 1861.

18. Wright, *Peter Melendy*, 110.

19. *Gazette*, 20 December 1861.

20. *Gazette*, 2 August 1861.

C H A P T E R   5

1. Agatha Young, *The Women and the Crisis* (New York: McDowell, Obolensky, 1959), 142–44.

2. Boatner, 397.

3. Ibid., 628.

4. *Gazette*, 25 October 1861.

5. *Gazette*, 13 December 1861.

6. Ibid.

7. *Gazette*, 6 December 1861; 3 January 1862; 28 February 1862.

8. *Gazette*, 28 February 1862.

9. Thompson, 188.

10. Boatner, 757.

11. *Gazette*, 11 April 1862.

12. Boatner, 754.

13. Shelby Foote, *The Civil War: A Narrative*, vol. 1 (New York: Random House, 1952), 331.

14. Thompson, 210.

15. Foote, 331.

16. Thompson, 210; *Official Records of the Union and Confederate Armies in the War of the Rebellion*, ser. 1, vol. 10, pt. 1, 203.

17. Mildred Throne, "Iowans and the Civil War," *Palimpsest* 50 (February 1969): 87.

18. *Gazette*, 25 April 1862.

19. Ibid.

20. Boatner, 757.

21. Throne, 95.

22. *Roster and Record*, vol. 1, 288.

23. *Gazette*, 18 April 1862.

24. *Gazette*, 25 April 1862.

C H A P T E R   6

1. *Gazette*, 2 May 1862.

2. *Gazette*, 13 June 1862.

3. Throne, 99.

4. Throne, 102.

5. *Roster and Record*, vol. 1, 290.

6. *Gazette*, 17 October 1862.

7. Briggs, 354.

8. Ibid., 358.

9. *Gazette*, 25 July 1862.

10. Ibid.

11. Briggs, 376–77.

12. "Report of General Hurlbut" and "Report of Colonel Isaac C. Pugh," *Official Records*, series 1, vol. 10, pt. 1, 205, 212.

13. *Gazette*, 23 May 1862.

14. Nelson G. Williams, "Letter to Governor Kirkwood," 13 August 1862, *Records of the Third Iowa Volunteer Infantry*, Adjutant General's Record, record group no. 3, "Correspondence," Iowa State Historical Society, Des Moines, Iowa.

15. *Gazette*, 18 July 1862.

16. *Gazette*, 15 August 1862.

17. *Gazette*, 26 September 1862.

18. *Gazette*, 31 October 1862.

19. *Gazette*, 24 October 1862.

20. Hartman, 169.

21. *Gazette*, 1 August 1862; 19 September 1862.

22. Hartman, 169.

23. *Gazette*, 12 September 1862.

24. *Gazette*, 18 August 1862.

25. *Gazette*, 31 May 1861.

26. Leavitt, 22–23; Rath, 1.

27. *Gazette*, 18 August 1862.

28. *Historical and Biographical Record*, vol. 2, 233, 270.

29. 1860 *Census*.

30. *Gazette*, 15 August 1862.

31. Ibid.

32. *Gazette*, 12 September 1862.

33. *Gazette*, 19 September 1862.

34. *Gazette*, 26 September 1862.

35. Ibid.

36. Rath, 2.

37. *Roster and Record*, vol. 5, 1581.

38. Stuart, 467.

39. Wylie E. Burke, "Letter to his brother in Pennsylvania," 5 November 1862, "Letters to his family while he served in 31st Iowa Infantry, Co-K," Manuscript Room, cabinet 2, State Historical Society of Iowa, Iowa City, Iowa.

40. Burke; *Gazette*, 7 November 1862.

41. Ibid.

42. Burke, "Letter to Mother," 17 November 1862.

CHAPTER 7

1. Bruce Catton, *Grant Moves South*, (Boston: Little, Brown and Co., 1960), 326.

2. John Rownd, "Letter to Parents," 30 April 1862, AMs, "Collected Letters of John and George Rownd," box 10A, series 3, Archives of the Cedar Falls Historical Society, Cedar Falls, Iowa.

3. George W. Rownd, "Letter to Parents," 30 April 1862, AMs, "Collected Letters of John and George Rownd," box 10A, series 3, Archives of the Cedar Falls Historical Society, Cedar Falls, Iowa.

4. John Rownd, "Letter to Parents," 8 Dec. 1862.

5. *Gazette*, 26 December 1862.

6. Samuel Carter III, *The Final Fortress: The Campaign for Vicksburg 1862–1863*, (New York: St. Martin's Press, 1980), 102–103.

7. *Gazette*, 23 January 1863.

8. Boatner, 25.

9. Ibid.

10. "Report of General A. Hovey," *Official Records*, ser. 1, vol. 17, pt. 1, 765–67.

11. Ibid.

12. Catton, 374.

13. Joseph Needham, "The Civil War as a Personal Experience" (M.A. thesis, University of Northern Iowa, 1981), vol. 2, 329.

14. *Gazette*, 6 March 1863.

15. *Gazette*, 10 April 1863.

16. *Gazette*, 13 March 1863.

17. *Gazette*, 6 March 1863.

18. *Gazette*, 26 December 1862.

19. *Gazette*, 16 January 1863.

20. *Gazette*, 3 January 1863.

21. Hartman, 129.

22. *Gazette*, 5 June 1863; 16 October 1863; 23 October 1863; Luella M. Wright, "A 'Tater Patch For Soldiers,'" *Palimpsest* 22 (1941): 240–46.

CHAPTER 8

1. George W. Rownd, "Letter to Parents," 11 September 1863.

2. *Gazette*, 12 June 1863.

3. Frederick Jacob, "Letter to Family," 16 April 1863.

4. H. W. Lathrop, *The Life and Times of Samuel J. Kirkwood: Iowa's War Governor* (Iowa City: State Historical Society of Iowa and by the author, 1893), 258–59.

5. *Gazette*, 3 July 1863.

6. *Gazette*, 6 March 1863.

7. *Gazette*, 8 May 1863.

8. Hubert H. Wubben, *Civil War Iowa and the Copperhead Movement*, (Ames: Iowa State University Press, 1980), 114.

9. *Gazette*, 13 March 1863.

10. *Dubuque Herald*, quoted in the *Gazette*, 20 March 1863.

11.*Gazette*, 20 May 1863.

12. Ibid.

13. *Dubuque Times*, quoted in the *Gazette*, 12 June 1863.

14. *Gazette*, 17 July 1863; Wright, *Peter Melendy*, 259.

15. Throne, 107.

16. Boatner, 876.

17. Throne, 107.

18. *Gazette*, 5 June 1863.

19. *Gazette*, 22 May 1863.

20. Carter, 214.

21. S. H. M. Byers, *Iowa in Wartime*, (Des Moines, Iowa: W. D. Condit and Co., 1888), 225.

22. Boatner, 876; Carter, 229.

23. J. K. P. Thompson, *Report of the Commission to Locate the Position of Iowa Troops in the Siege of Vicksburg*, (Des Moines, Iowa: State Printer, 1901), 22.

24. *Gazette*, 19 June 1963.

25. Soloman B. Humbert, "A Brief History of Our Part Taken in the U.S. Army, Against the Rebellion," TS; Records of the 31st Iowa Volunteer Infantry, "Miscellaneous Personnel," file H-881, folder 1, Iowa State Historical Society, Des Moines, Iowa.

26. *Gazette*, 3 July 1863.

27. *Gazette*, 10 July 1863.

28. *Roster and Record,* vol. 5, 291; Byers, 235.

29. Throne, 109.

CHAPTER 9

1. *Gazette*, 12 February 1864.

2. Ibid.

3. *Gazette*, 8 January 1863.

4. *Gazette*, 31 July 1863.

5. *Gazette*, 13 November 1863.

6. Wright, *Peter Melendy*, 204–6.

7. Ibid., 261–62.

8. Wubben, 143, 211.

9. *Gazette*, 16 October 1863.

10. Boatner, 152.

11. James Lee McDonough, *Chattanooga: Death Grip on the Confederacy* (Knoxville: University of Tennessee Press, 1984), 49.

12. *Gazette*, 23 October 1863.

13. Foote, *The Civil War*, vol. 2, 842.

14. *Gazette*, 22 January 1864.

15. Needham, 338–39.

16. Ibid., 339.

17. Charles Rath, 1.

18. *Official Records*, ser. 1, vol. 3, pt. 2, 86.

19. Briggs, 363.

20. Wubben, 130; Briggs, 363.

21. Briggs, 362.

22. *Gazette*, 22 January 1864.

23. *Gazette*, 11 December 1863; 18 December 1863; 25 December 1863.

24. *Gazette*, 8 January 1864.

25. *Davenport Gazette*, quoted in the *Gazette*, 5 February 1864.

26. Ibid.

27. *Roster and Record*, vol. 5, 1595.

28. *Gazette*, 15 January 1864.

29. *Gazette*, 8 January 18

CHAPTER 10

1. Briggs, 367.

2. Ibid.

3. Ibid., 368.

4. *Gazette*, 25 December 1863.

5. Briggs, 367–68.

6. Boatner, 543.

7. *Roster and Record*, vol. 1, 293.

8. *Gazette*, 25 March 1864.

9. *Roster and Record*, vol. 1, 292.

10. *Gazette*, 8 April 1864.

11. Ibid.

12. Boatner, 689; Byers, 548.

13. *Gazette*, 24 June 1864.

14. "Receipt for Arms and Equipage, 9 May 1864, signed by Colonel Aaron Brown," *Records of the Third Iowa Volunteer Infantry*, Adjutant General's Records, record group no. 5, "Records and Alterations," Iowa State Historical Society, Des Moines, Iowa.

15. James Lee McDonough and James Pickett Jones, *War So Terrible: Sherman and Atlanta* (New York: W. W. Norton & Co., 1987), 35.

16. *Gazette*, 6 May 1864.

17. Needham, 344; Humbert, 6; McDonough and Jones, 109.

18. McDonough and Jones, 115; Stuart, 467, 474; Needham, 344.

19. *Gazette*, 27 May 1864; Needham, 344.

20. *Gazette*, 10 June 1864; 24 June 1864.

21. *Gazette*, 3 June 1864; 10 June 1864; 29 July 1864.

22. *Gazette*, 27 May 1864.

23. *Gazette*, 1 July 1864; 8 July 1864.

24. *Gazette*, 17 June 1864; Wright, *Peter Melendy*, 262–65.

25. Wright, *Peter Melendy*, 262–65.

26. *Gazette*, 12 August 1864; Humbert, 10.

27. Humbert, 10; Needham, 347.

28. *Gazette*, 12 August 1864.

29. McDonough and Jones, 193.

30. *Gazette*, 12 August 1864; Humbert, 11; Burke, "Letters to Brother," 23 July 1864.

31. *Gazette*, 5 August 1864; 19 August 1864.

32. McDonough and Jones, 228–29.

33. Ingersoll, 73.

34. *Gazette*, 5 August 1864; 19 August 1864.

35. *Official Records*, ser. 1, vol. 30, pt. 3, 753.

36. *Battle Flag Committee Report to the 24th General Assembly of the State of Iowa* (Des Moines, Iowa: J. P. Conway, State Printer, 1896), 77.

37. Gue, *A History of Iowa*, vol. 2 (New York: Century History Co.), 144.

38. Boehmler, 1.

39. Humbert, 12.

40. Throne, 121.

41. McDonough and Jones, 313.

CHAPTER 11

1. Willam T. Sherman, *Personal Memoirs*, vol. 2 (New York: Charles L. Webster and Co., 1891), 152.

2. John McElroy, *This Was Andersonville,* ed. Roy Meredith, (New York: Fairfax Press, 1979) 98–99.

3. Benjamin F. Gue, "Iowans at Andersonville," *Palimpsest*, 42, no. 6 (June 1961): 227–33.

4. *Gazette*, 30 September 1864.

5. Briggs, 391.

6. *Gazette*, 2 September 1864; 23 September 1864.

7. *Gazette*e, 7 October 1864.

8. *Gazette*, 13 January 1865.

9. Briggs, 392; *Gazette*, 27 January 1865.

10. *Gazette*, 27 February 1865.

11. *Gazette*, 30 September 1864.

12. Sage, 169; *Gazette*, 11 November 1864.

13. *Gazette*, 18 November 1864.

14. *Gazette*, 6 January 1865.

15. Foote, vol. 3, 646.

16. *Gazette*, 6 January 1865; Boehmler, 5.

17. Richard Wheeler, *Sherman's March* (New York: Thomas Y. Crowell, 1978), 126–37.

18. *Gazette*, 13 January 1865.

19. Ibid.

20. Ibid.

CHAPTER 12

1. Needham, 360.

2. Ibid., 383.

3. *Gazette*, 28 April 1865.

4. Ibid.

5. *Gazette*, 14 April 1865.

6. *Gazette*, 28 April 1865.

7. Needham, 362.

8. *Gazette*, 14 April 1865; 5 May 1865.

9. Ibid.

10. Ibid.; Charles Ballard, "South Carolina Wants Iowa to Return Civil War Flag," *Des Moines Register*, 8 February 1989.

11. Marian B. Lucas, *Sherman and the Burning of Columbia* (College Station: Texas A & M University Press, 1976) 56–57.

12. Lucas, 83.

13. Needham, 389.

14. *Gazette*, 28 April 1865.

15. Ibid.

16. *Gazette*, 7 April 1865.

17. Luella M. Wright, "Victory and Mourning," *Palimpsest* 21, no. 4 (April 1940): 101–10; *Gazette*, 14 April 1865.

18. Wright, "Victory and Mourning," 101–10.

19. Ibid.

20. Ibid.

21. Ibid.

22. Ibid.

23. Ibid.

24. Ibid.

25. *Gazette*, 14 April 1865.

26. Wright, "Victory and Mourning," 111–21; *Gazette*, 21 April 1865.

27. Wright, "Victory and Mourning," 122–32; *Gazette*, 21 April 1865.

28. Wright, "Victory and Mourning," 122–32.

29. *Gazette*, 21 April 1865.

30. *Gazette*, 5 May 1865.

31. Needham, 371.

32. Foote, vol. 2, 1015.

33. *Gazette*, 8 June 1865.

EPILOGUE

1. *Gazette*, 9 June 1865.

2. Humbert, 26.

3. Ibid.

4. Ibid., 27.

5. *Gazette*, 7 July 1865.

6. *Gazette*, 28 July 1865.

7. *Gazette*, 17 February 1865.

8. Brigham Johnson, *Iowa: Its History and Its Foremost Citizens,* vol. 3 (Chicago: S. J. Clarke Publishing Co., 1915), 625.

9. Wright, *Peter Melendy*, 272–89.

10. Ibid., 112–14.

REFERENCES

Ballard, Charles. "South Carolina Wants Iowa to Return Civil War Flag." *Des Moines Register*, 8 February 1989.

Battle Flag Committee Report to the 24th General Assembly of the State of Iowa. Des Moines, Iowa: J. P. Conway, State Printer, 1896.

Bergmann, Leola N. "The Negro in Iowa." *Iowa Journal of History and Politics* 44 (January 1948): 3–89.

Boatner, Mark M. *The Civil War Dictionary.* New York: David McKay Co., 1959.

Boehmler, William. "Chronology of Wm Boehmler." TS. N.d. "Military Affairs," ser. 14, file 1. Archives of the Cedar Falls Historical Society , Cedar Falls, Iowa.

Boston, Ray. "General Matthew Mark Trumble: Respectable Radical." *Journal of the Illinois Historical Society* 66 (Summer 1973): 159–76.

Briggs, John E. "The Enlistment of Iowa Troops During the Civil War." *Iowa Journal of History and Politics* 15 (July 1917): 323–92.

Brown, Charles P. "The Battle of Blue Mills Landing." *Annals of Iowa* 14, no. 3 (April 1924): 287–294.

Burke, Wylie E. "Letters to his Family While he Served in 31st Iowa Infantry, Co-K." Manuscript Room, cabinet 2, State Historical Society of Iowa, Iowa City, Iowa.

Byers, S. H. M. *Iowa in Wartime.* Des Moines, Iowa: W. W. Condit and Co., 1888.

Carter, Samuel, III. *The Final Fortress: The Campaign for Vicksburg 1862–1863.* New York: St. Martin's Press, 1980.

Catton, Bruce. *Grant Moves South.* Boston: Little, Brown and Co., 1960.

Cedar Falls Gazette, 1860–1865. Pub. Henry and George Perkins.

Clark, Dan Elbert. *Samuel Jordan Kirkwood.* Iowa City: N.p., 1917.

Cole, Cyrus. *A History of the People of Iowa.* Cedar Rapids, Iowa: Torch Press, 1921.

Davenport Daily Democrat and News, 2 November 1862.

Foote, Shelby. *The Civil War: A Narrative.* 3 vols. New York: Random House, 1958.

Fullbrook, Earl S. "Relief Work in Iowa During the Civil War." *Iowa Journal of History and Politics* 16 (April 1918): 155–274.

Gallaher, Ruth A. "Annie Turner Wittenmyer." *Iowa Journal of History and Politics* 29 (October 1931): 518–69.

Grant, U. S. *Personal Memoirs*. New York: Charles L. Webster Co., 1885.

Gue, Benjamin F. *A History of Iowa*. New York: Century History Co., 1903.

——."Iowans at Andersonville," *Palimpsest* 42, no. 6 (June 1961): 211–81.

Hartman, John C., ed. *History of Black Hawk County Iowa and Its People*. Vol. 1. Chicago: S. J. Clarke Publishing Co., 1915.

Historical and Biographical Record of Black Hawk County, Iowa. 2 vols. Chicago: Interstate Publishing Co., 1886.

Humbert, Soloman B. "A Brief History of Our Part Taken in the U.S. Army, Against the Rebellion." TMs Records of the 31st Iowa Volunteer Infantry. "Miscellaneous Personnel," file H–881. Iowa State Historical Society, Des Moines, Iowa, 1.

Ingersoll, Lurton D. *Iowa and the Rebellion*. Dubuque, Iowa: J. B. Lippincott and Co., 1866.

Jacob, Frederick. "Collected Letters of Frederick Jacob." Transcribed by Larry J. O'Connor. Letters courtesy of the Robert Kline and Ramona Ruth O'Connor families, Waterloo, Iowa.

Johnson, Brigham. *Iowa: Its History and Its Foremost Citizens*. 3 vols. Chicago: S. J. Clarke Publishing Co., 1915.

Keokuk Gate City, 29 June 1861.

Lathrop, H. W. *The Life and Times of Samuel J. Kirkwood: Iowa's War Governor*. Iowa City: State Historical Society of Iowa and by the author, 1893.

Lea, Albert M. *The Book That Gave Iowa Its Name: Notes on the Wisconsin Territory: Particularly with Reference to the Iowa District, or Black Hawk Purchase*. Iowa City: State Historical Society of Iowa, 1935.

Leavitt, Roger. *When Cedar Falls Was Young*. Cedar Falls, Iowa: Record Press, 1928.

Lucas, Marian B. *Sherman and the Burning of Columbia*. College Station: Texas A & M University Press, 1976.

McDonough, James Lee. *Chattanooga: Death Grip on the Confederacy*. Knoxville: University of Tennessee Press, 1984.

McDonough, James Lee, and James Pickett Jones. *War So Terrible: Sherman and Atlanta*. New York: W. W. Norton & Co., 1987.

McElroy, John. *This Was Andersonville*. Ed. Roy Meredith. New York: Fairfax Press, 1979.

McPherson, James M. *Battle Cry of Freedom*. New York: Oxford University Press, 1988.

Melendy, Peter. *Historical Record of Cedar Falls, the Garden City of Iowa*. Cedar Falls, Iowa: Peter Melendy, 1893.

——."Zimri Streeter—'Old Black Hawk,'" *Annals of Iowa*, ser. 3, vol. 1 (August 1894): 412–15.

Needham, Joseph. "The Civil War as a Personal Experience." 2 vols. M.A. thesis, University of Northern Iowa, 1981.

Official Records of the Union and Confederate Armies in the War of the Rebellion. Washington, 1880–1901. 128 vols.

Parrish, William E. *Turbulent Partnership: Missouri and the Union 1861–1865*. Columbia: University of Missouri Press, 1963.

Pelzer, Louis. "The Negro and Slavery in Early Iowa." *Iowa Journal of History and Politics* 11 (1904): 471–84.

Rath, Charles. *A Love Story*. TS. No date. Property of Jean Parker, Waterloo, Iowa.

Records of the Third Iowa Volunteer Infantry, Adjutant General's Records, Record group no. 3, "Correspondence," and no. 5, "Records and Alterations." Iowa State Historical Society, Des Moines, Iowa.

Riley, Glenda. *Cities on the Cedar*. Parkersburg, Iowa: Mid Prairie Books, 1988.

Roster and Record of Iowa Soldiers in the War of the Rebellion. 6 vols. Iowa General Assembly, 1910.

Rownd, George and John Rownd. "Collected Letters of John and George Rownd." Box 10A, series 3. Archives of the Cedar Falls Historical Society, Cedar Falls, Iowa.

Sage, Leland L. *A History of Iowa*. Ames: Iowa State University Press, 1974.

Sherman, William T. *Personal Memoirs*. 2 vols. New York: Charles L. Webster and Co., 1891.

Stuart, Captain A. A. 17th Iowa Infantry, *Iowa Colonels and Regiments: Being a History of Iowa Regiments in the War of the Rebellion*. Des Moines, Iowa: Mills and Co., 1865.

Swisher, Jacob A. *Iowa in Times of War*. Iowa City: State Historical Society of Iowa, 1943.

Thompson, J. K. P. *Report of the Commission to Locate the Position of Iowa Troops in the Siege of Vicksburg*. Des Moines,Iowa: State Printer, 1901.

Thompson, Lieutenant S. D. *Recollections With the Third Iowa Regiment*. Cincinnati: By the author, 1864.

Throne, Mildred. "Iowans and the Civil War." *Palimpsest* 50 (1969): 65–145.

U.S. Census Office. Eighth Census, 1860. Washington, National Archives and Records Service, 1967. Roll 312 Iowa Black Hawk to Bremer Counties.

Webster's Guide to American History. Massachusetts: G. & C. Merriam Co., 1971.

Wheeler, Richard. *Sherman's March*. New York: Thomas Y. Crowell, 1978.

Wright, Luella M. *Peter Melendy: The Mind and the Soil*. Iowa City: State Historical Society of Iowa, 1943.

——. "The Pioneer Greys." *Palimpsest* 22 (January 1941): 1–32.

——. "A 'Tater Patch For Soldiers.'" *Palimpsest* 22 (August 1941): 240–46.

——. "Victory and Mourning." *Palimpsest* 21, no. 4, (April 1940): 101–32.

Wubben, Hubert H. *Civil War Iowa and the Copperhead Movement*. Ames: Iowa State University Press, 1980.

Young, Agatha. *The Women and the Crisis*. New York: McDowell, Obolensky, 1959.

INDEX

Abernathy, Jacob, 131
Acworth, Georgia, 123, 126, 134
Adams, Catherine Sturgis, 3
Adams, Erasmus, 4, 15
Adams, Martin, 59, 102, 130, 152
Adams, S.P., 16
Alabama, 62, 119, 134, 143, 145
Allan, Moses, 116, 136
Allatoona, Georgia, 134
Allensworth, Elias, 118
Allison, William B., 125
American Party, 13
Andersonville, Georgia, 135, 136, 138,
    141, 148, 149, 157
Antietam Creek, Maryland, 128, 160
Appomattox Court House, Virginia, 153
Arkansas, 47, 58, 60, 118
Arkansas Post, Arkansas, 83, 84, 162
Arkansas River, 83, 84
Army of Georgia, 140
Army of Northern Virginia, 63, 111, 153
Army of the Cumberland, 106, 107, 108,
    110, 111, 120, 127, 128, 136, 145
Army of the Mississippi, 83, 84
Army of the Ohio, 50, 58, 61, 107, 120,
    126
Army of the Potomac, 46, 63, 101, 107,
    111, 120, 125, 145, 159, 160
Army of the Tennessee, 60, 61, 84, 107,
    116, 118, 120, 126, 128, 132, 137
Army of Virginia, 61
Atlanta, Georgia, 62, 112, 118, 119,
    123, 124, 126, 128, 130, 131, 132,
    133, 134, 136, 138, 139, 143, 152
Augusta, Georgia, 147, 148
Averasboro, North Carolina, 53

Baker, James, 131
Bald Hill, 130, 131, 139
Ball, J.J., 21
Baltimore, Maryland, 125, 138, 158
Bank, Hilary W., 13
Banks, Nathaniel, 116, 117
Barnum, A.D., 44
Barrick, John T., 4
Battle above the Clouds, 110
"Battle Hymn of the Republic," 139
Bawn, George, 123
Beaufort, South Carolina, 147
Beauregard, P.G.T., 51, 52, 58, 60, 61,
    145, 147, 148, 153
Bell, John, 18
Benson, Iowa, 165
Benton Barracks, 49, 71, 72, 80
Bentonville, North Carolina, 153, 162
Berry, Samuel, 21
Bethel, Missouri, 34
Big Black River, 96
Big Kennesee Mountain, 123, 126, 127,
    128, 134, 135
Bill Henderson (steamship), 70
Black Hawk County, 4, 6, 7, 9, 18, 43,
    64, 70, 71, 86, 105, 106, 112, 113,
    138, 161
Black Hawk County Republican
    Convention, 43
Blair, Frank (Francis) P., Jr., 27, 107,
    118, 126, 130
Blakeslee, Nelson, 122, 124
Blaseberg, Charles, 131
Blinn, John, 102
Blue Mills Ferry, Missouri, 36, 38, 47,
    49, 51, 64, 70, 105, 116, 131, 161

Boehmler, Barbara Schoffner, 8, 40
Boehmler, Charles, 40, 117, 131, 132, 136
Boehmler, Edward, 117, 131, 132, 136, 140, 141
Boehmler, George H., 7, 8, 13, 43
Boehmler, Jacob, 117, 131, 132
Boehmler, William, 132
Boggs, J.T., 56, 57
Boss, W.B., 124
Bowen, Jessie, 20
Bradley, Orlando, 86
Bragg, Braxton, 61, 62
Brainerd, Judge N.H., 157
Breckinridge, John C., 15, 18
Bremer County, 16
Briggs, Wallace, 59
Broad River, 149, 150
Brown, A.F., 10, 15
Brown, Aaron, 102
Brown, Alfred E., 10
Brown, Atherton, 59
Brown, Edwin, 8, 9, 10, 13, 15, 44, 69, 86
Brownell, James, 38, 166
Brown's Ferry, Tennessee, 108
Buell, Don Carlos, 50, 58, 60
Bull Run, 46, 63
Burke, James W., 122, 124
Burlington, Iowa, 39, 157
Burnside, Ambrose, 63
Butler, George, 113
Butler Center, 16
Butler County, 16, 22, 25

Cain, Martin, 102
Cameron, John R., 9
Cameron, Mary, 9
Cameron, Simon, 19
Camp Ellsworth, 25
Camp Franklin, 70
Camp Herron, 70
Camp Jackson, 27
Camp Kirkwood, 26
Camp McClellan, 113
Camp Sorgum, 151
Cape Giraradeau, Missouri, 96
Carey, A.H., 137
Carpenter, H.H., 10, 124
Carpenter, T.B., 124
Carrol, Anna, 46

Carter, Frederick J., 118
Carter House Hotel, 19, 20, 21, 93, 116, 117, 154
Castle, Leonard, 131
Cedar Falls, Iowa, 4, 6, 7, 8, 9, 10, 12, 13, 15, 16, 18, 19, 20, 21, 23, 24, 25, 39, 40, 41, 43, 44, 45, 49, 59, 64, 65, 66, 67, 68, 69, 70, 71, 80, 86, 87, 88, 90, 91, 93, 94, 95, 101, 103, 104, 105, 106, 110, 112, 113, 115, 117, 118, 119, 123, 124, 125, 127, 130, 137, 138, 139, 143, 148, 149, 153, 155, 156, 157, 158, 161, 162, 163, 164, 165, 166
Cedar Falls Banner, 6, 7, 8
Cedar Falls Brass Band, 16, 17, 20, 22, 101, 116, 125
Cedar Falls Gazette, 8, 11, 15, 19, 20, 28, 41, 44, 64, 66, 67, 69, 87, 91, 103, 104, 113, 137, 155, 157, 162, 164
Cedar Falls Glee Club, 125
Cedar Falls Historical Society, 166
Cedar Falls Lincoln and Hamlin Club, 16
Cedar Falls Republican Club, 16
Cedar Falls Reserves, 68, 69, 70, 71, 80, 81, 82, 84, 86, 87, 90, 96, 98, 99, 101, 104, 107, 108, 110, 111, 114, 117, 118, 119, 120, 122, 123, 124, 126, 127, 128, 130, 132, 136, 137, 140, 147, 148, 149, 150, 151, 152, 156, 161, 162, 163, 166
Cedar Falls Unionists, 93, 94, 95
Cedar Rapids, Iowa, 8, 103
Cedar River, 3, 44, 163, 164, 166
Cedar Valley, 3, 4, 23, 33, 44, 45, 67, 87, 103, 163, 164, 166
Chambers, Alexander, 25
Champion Hill, Mississippi, 95, 98
Charles, Lewis, 118
Charles City, Iowa, 16, 20, 69
Charleston, South Carolina, 11, 12, 147
Charlotte, North Carolina, 151
Chase, Salmon P., 125
Chattahoochie River, 128
Chattanooga, Tennessee, 61, 62, 106, 107, 108, 110, 111, 112, 119, 124, 127, 134, 135, 136
Cherow, North Carolina, 152, 153
Chicago, Illinois, 137, 158
Chickamauga, Georgia, 106, 110, 111,

134

Chickasaw Bluffs, Mississippi, 82, 84, 104

Chickasaw County, 39

Chief Black Hawk, 3

Chillicothe, Missouri, 28, 29, 33, 34

Cincinnati, Ohio, 6, 125, 164

Cleburne, Patrick, 130, 131

Clough, John, 123

Cold Harbor, Virginia, 160

Cold Water, Mississippi, 81, 85

Columbia, South Carolina, 147, 149, 150, 152, 159, 161

Columbus, Ohio, 82

Congaree River, 149, 150

Constitutional Union Party, 18

Continental (steamboat), 72, 80

Cool, Daniel M., 35, 38, 64, 65

Cooper, Horace T., 40, 111, 122

Cooper, Jesse, 131

Corinth, Mississippi, 51, 58, 60, 61, 62, 85, 100

Corse, John M., 134, 137

Crescent City (steamboat), 96, 98

Culver, Bryon, 87, 106, 137

Culver, Ed, 85, 86, 104

Cumberland River, 46

Curtis, Samuel R., 18, 47

Dallas, Georgia, 123

Dalton, Georgia, 119, 120

Daniels, James, 131

Davenport, Ross W., 38

Davenport, Iowa, 19, 70, 107, 113, 114, 118, 163

Davis, Jefferson, 101, 128, 153, 155

Decatur, Georgia, 130

Department of Texas, 113

Department of the West, 36

Des Moines, Iowa, 7, 8, 16, 93, 138

Dix, Dorothea, 42

Dix, John A., 153

Dixie, 24, 124

Dodge, Grenville, 130

Douglas, Stephen A., 13, 15, 17, 18

Dow, Clayton, 118

Drummond, Tom, 16, 17

Dubuque, Iowa, 8, 10, 16, 18, 23, 25, 30, 34, 35, 39, 44, 69, 70, 93, 94, 103, 104, 117, 124, 152, 153, 154, 163, 166

Dubuque and Pacific Railroad, 9

Dubuque and Sioux City Railroad, 9, 10, 70

Dubuque Herald, 15, 23, 66, 93, 94

Dubuque Times, 94

Dug Gap, 120

Durham's Station, North Carolina, 158

Dutton, Minerva, 13

Dutton, William, 13

Eberhart, A.G., 116, 155, 157, 158, 159

Eberhart, George, 117, 136

Edwards, A., 136

Edwards, Thomas, 29, 30, 34, 35

Elkhorn Tavern, Arkansas, 47, 51, 68, 69, 104

Emancipation Proclamation, 67, 90, 91, 141

Enfield rifle, 26, 71, 72, 123

Eyestone, Ames, 111

Farragut, David, 61

Fayetteville, North Carolina, 153

Fellows, Spencer, 111

Fifield, H.B., 117

5th Iowa Congressional District, 64, 68

Fitkin, Francis F., 130

Fletcher, C.H., 39

Florence, South Carolina, 136

Florida, Missouri, 30

Floyd County, 69

Forrest, Bedford, 82, 134, 135

Fort Dodge, 4

Fort Donelson, 46, 47, 51, 59, 60, 85, 100, 105, 107

Fort Henry, 46, 47, 59

Fort Hindman, Arkansas, 83, 84

Fort McAllister, 141

Fort Pillow, 60

Fort Sumter, 11, 12, 19, 20

Foster, Suel, 158

Franklin, Tennessee, 143

Fredericksburg, Virginia, 63

Free Soil Party, 13

Fremont, John C., 13, 15, 36

Gelpeke, Herman, 10

Georgia, 112, 123, 126, 127, 135, 136, 137, 139, 140, 143, 145, 147

Gettysburg, Pennsylvania, 101, 103, 128, 160
Goldsboro, South Carolina, 145, 149, 152, 153
Goodwyn, T.J., 150, 151
Gorhum, Ellsworth, 102
Grand Review of Union troops, 159, 160, 161
Grant, Ulysses S., 46, 47, 49, 51, 52, 53, 56, 58, 60, 61, 79, 80, 81, 82, 83, 84, 85, 88, 89, 95, 96, 98, 99, 100, 101, 104, 107, 108, 111, 112, 114, 118, 119, 124, 125, 134, 135, 137, 145, 153, 154, 159, 160, 161
Graves, A.J., 7
Green, Martin, 34, 36
Greenville, Mississippi, 98
Grenada, Mississippi, 82
Griggs, Luther, 49
Grimes, James W., 15, 125, 126
Grinnell, Josiah B., 125
Griswaldville, Georgia, 140
Groom, Edward, 131
Grove, Samuel, 102, 103
Grundy County, 38

Hager's Woods, Missouri, 32, 33, 34
Haines Bluff, Mississippi, 98
Halleck, Henry, 60, 61, 79, 80, 83, 84
Hamlin, Hannibal, 15, 16
Hammill, William, 59
Hampton, Wade, 150, 151
Hannibal, Missouri, 26, 28, 29, 30
Hannibal and St. Joseph Railroad, 28, 30
Hardee, William, 143
Harris, Thomas, 30, 36
Hartman, John, 124
Hatchie River, 62, 116
Hayden, M.M., 44
Hazen, William, 141
Heldt, Albert, 126
Helena, Arkansas, 72, 79, 80, 81, 85, 104, 162
"Hell Hole," 123
Herman, Mrs. R., 41
Hodnett, John, 94, 95
Holly Springs, Mississippi, 81, 82
Hood, John Bell, 126, 128, 130, 131, 132, 133, 134, 135, 136, 143, 145
Hooker, Joseph "Fighting Joe," 107,

108, 110
Hornet's Nest, 52, 58, 59
Horticultural Hall, 21, 116, 137
Hovey, Alvin, 80, 84
Howard, Oliver Otis, 107, 132, 137, 147, 149, 153, 156
Hoyt, Earl, 131, 136, 143, 144
Hubbard, Asahel W., 125
Hudson, Iowa, 154
Humbert, Soloman, 99
Hurlbut, Stephen, 34, 35, 50, 51, 52, 53, 54, 56, 62, 64, 65, 96
Hutchins, Stilson, 93, 94, 95
Hutchinson's Island, Georgia, 141

Illinois, 7, 13, 30, 46, 49, 79, 80, 101, 118, 135
Illinois Central Railroad, 164
Illinois military units
  14th Illinois, 96
  16th Illinois, 30, 34, 36, 38
  39th Illinois, 132
  41st Illinois, 54, 64
Indiana, 115
Inman, Mary, 138, 139
Inman House Hotel, 138
Iowa, 3, 7, 8, 12, 13, 15, 18, 19, 20, 21, 28, 30, 33, 40, 43, 50, 54, 58, 62, 63, 68, 81, 88, 92, 93, 96, 102, 103, 105, 111, 112, 113, 115, 125, 126, 131, 134, 136, 137, 138
Iowa City, 3, 4, 19, 114
Iowa General Assembly, 6, 7, 41, 165
Iowa military units
  1st Iowa, 25, 26, 69
  1st Iowa (African Descent), 112
  1st Iowa Battery, 39, 67, 80, 81, 104
  2d Iowa, 25, 26, 136, 137, 140, 171
  3d Iowa, 25, 26, 28, 29, 30, 32, 33, 34, 35, 36, 38, 47, 49, 51, 53, 54, 58, 62, 65, 69, 80, 93, 96, 99, 100, 102, 105, 107, 112, 113, 115, 116, 117, 118, 130, 131, 132, 136
  3d Iowa Battery, 40, 117
  3d Iowa Veteran Battalion, 115, 126, 131
  4th Iowa, 98, 107, 139
  4th Iowa Cavalry, 113
  6th Iowa, 54, 139
  6th Iowa Cavalry, 68
  7th Iowa Cavalry, 113

8th Iowa, 58, 62
9th Iowa, 80, 98, 99, 107, 117, 139, 161
9th Iowa Cavalry, 112
10th Iowa, 62
11th Iowa, 54
12th Iowa, 58, 59, 62, 98
13th Iowa, 54
14th Iowa, 58, 62
16th Iowa, 62, 161
17th Iowa, 62, 163
21st Iowa, 68
25th Iowa, 107, 151
26th Iowa, 98, 107
30th Iowa, 98, 99, 107, 139
31st Iowa, 71, 80, 84, 99, 107, 113, 137, 151, 161, 162
32d Iowa, 68, 69, 118
37th Iowa (Greybeards), 68
Butler County Union Guards, 22, 25, 37, 117
Cedar Falls Governor's Guards, 106, 112, 138, 155, 156, 157
Cedar Falls Reserves. See Cedar Falls Reserves
Chickasaw County Lincoln Guards, 39
Dubuque Washington Guards, 23, 25
Governor's Greys, 19, 104, 125
Iowa Brigade, 107, 110, 111, 119, 122
Iowa Home Guard Militia, 104
Iowa State Militia, 104
Pioneer Greys. See Pioneer Greys
Iowa Republican Party, 43
Iowa Sanitary Commission, 40, 42, 88
Iowa State Fair, 105
Iowa State Normal School, 165
Iowa State Teacher's College, 165
Iuka, Mississippi, 62

Jackson, Claiborne F., 27
Jackson, Mississippi, 79, 85, 95, 98, 101, 102, 103, 116, 131, 152
Janesville, Iowa, 154
Jefferson, Eugene, 59
Jefferson City, Missouri, 27
Jenkins, Jeremiah, 71, 99, 122, 151
"John Brown's Body," 139
John Deere Tractor Works, 164
Johnson, Andrew, 138, 159, 160
Johnston, Albert Sidney, 50, 51, 52, 56, 57, 58
Johnston, Joseph E., 95, 96, 100, 101, 102, 118, 119, 120, 122, 123, 126, 127, 128, 153, 156, 158, 159, 160
Jones, Calvin, 38, 59

Kansas, 13, 17, 35
Kansas City, 36
Kansas military unit: 2d Kansas, 34, 35
Kansas Territory, 13
Kasson, John A., 16, 17
Keokuk, Iowa, 18, 21, 22, 23, 24, 25, 29, 39, 40
Key City (steamboat), 23, 25
Kilpatrick, Judson, 147
King, Henry, 131
Kirksville, Missouri, 34, 35
Kirkwood, Samuel J., 18, 19, 20, 21, 29, 41, 42, 43, 44, 65, 91, 104, 105, 106, 157
Knights of the Golden Circle, 92
Kolb's Farm, 127

Ladd, Lathrop, 104
Ladies' Aid Society, 40, 87
Ladies of Cedar Falls, 17, 70
Ladies' Soldiers' Aid Society, 163, 166
Ladies' Union League of Cedar Falls, 105
Ladies' Union League of Iowa, 104
La Porte City, Iowa, 71
Lauman, Jacob, 65, 96, 101
Lea, Albert, 3
Lee, Robert E., 63, 101, 111, 118, 120, 128, 145, 153, 155, 156, 157, 159
Leslie, Mrs., 149
Leversee, Austin, 102
Lexington, Missouri, 36
Liberty, Missouri, 36, 38
Lincoln, Abraham, 15, 16, 17, 18, 20, 27, 39, 43, 46, 61, 62, 63, 66, 67, 68, 79, 80, 91, 106, 107, 115, 117, 126, 135, 137, 138, 139, 141, 153, 156, 157, 158, 159, 160
Lincoln and Hamlin Club, 16
Lincoln and Johnson Club, 138
Linn County, 71, 122
Little Kennesaw Mountain, 123, 126, 127
Little Round Top, 128

Logan, John "Black Jack," 118, 120, 128, 131, 147, 149, 156, 161
Lookout Mountain, 108, 110
Lost Mountain, 123
Louisiana, 91
Louisiana Purchase, 3, 12
Louisville, Kentucky, 162, 163
Lovell, Carrie, 104
"The Low Backed Cat," 110
Loyal Leagues, 105
Lyon, Nathaniel, 27, 35, 36, 47

Mabie, Daniel, 131, 136
McClellan, George B., 46, 62, 63, 138, 139
McClernand, John, 50, 53, 54, 79, 80, 81, 82, 83
McClure, William H., 40, 68
McPherson, James B., 120, 122, 127, 130, 132
Maggart, James M., 131
Mahoney, Dennis, 66, 67, 93
Maquoketa, Iowa, 71
Marion, Francis "Swamp Fox," 143
Marshalltown, Iowa, 165
Massachusetts, 7, 8, 19
Massengale, Laura J., 131
Matamora Heights, 62, 116
Meade, George G., 101, 160
Melendy, Charles, 106
Melendy, Etta, 106
Melendy, John, 15, 125
Melendy, Martha, 7, 106
Melendy, Peter, 6, 7, 8, 9, 10, 15, 19, 21, 39, 44, 45, 67, 86, 93, 94, 95, 104, 105, 116, 125, 126, 138, 139, 155, 157, 158, 159, 164, 165
Memphis, Tennessee, 60, 79, 81, 82, 84, 85, 96
Meridian, Tennessee, 115, 116, 136, 149
Merrill, John, 49
Mexican War, 7, 8, 12, 29, 34, 46
Mexico, Missouri, 49
Michigan military unit: 18th Michigan, 113
Military Division of the Mississippi, 107
Military units. See each state
Mill Creek Gap, 119, 120
Milledgeville, Georgia, 135
Millen, Georgia, 135
Milliken's Bend, 83, 85, 91, 92, 98

Millrace Bridge (Race Bridge), 9, 22, 44, 116
Mills, Joseph, 123
Missionary Ridge, 108, 110, 111, 127
Mississippi, 98, 102, 116, 124
Mississippi River, 3, 13, 23, 25, 26, 39, 46, 58, 60, 61, 79, 82, 84, 98, 100, 101, 103, 107
Missouri, 12, 26, 27, 28, 29, 34, 35, 36, 38, 41, 47, 49, 118
Missouri Compromise, 12, 13, 26
Missouri military units
  3d Missouri, 84
  12th Missouri, 99
  German-Missouri Artillery Battery, 36, 37
  Hannibal Home Guards, 30
  Missouri Home Guards, 34, 36
  Missouri Mounted Home Guards, 36
  Missouri State Militia, 27
Missouri River, 36
Mobile, Alabama, 62
Monroe, Lousiana, 85
Monroe Station, Missouri, 30, 32, 33, 34, 35, 41
Morgan, George, 83
Moscow, Tennessee, 96
Moulten, Charles, 59
Moury, George W., 58
Mullarkey, Andrew, 6, 13, 44, 68
Mullarky, Charles, 20, 21, 22, 69
Muscatine, Iowa, 158

Nashville, Tennessee, 50, 119, 143
Nashville and Chattanooga Railroad, 119
Natchez, Mississippi, 107
National Enrollment Act, 112
Nebraska, 96
Nebraska military unit: 1st Nebraska, 96
Neosho, Missouri, 27
New Carthage, Louisiana, 89
New Hartford, Iowa, 16, 154
New Hope Church, Georgia, 123
New Orleans, Louisiana, 61, 79
Newton's Station, Mississippi, 89
New York, 6, 8, 153, 159
Nickajack Creek, 127
North Carolina, 145, 149, 153, 157, 159
Northeast Iowa Sanitary Fair, 124
North Missouri Railroad, 49

Northrup, James, 69
Northwest Democrat, 66, 93
Norton, R., 157

"Occasional" (pen name), 38, 47
Ogeechee River, 141
Ohio, 6, 7, 51, 101, 115
Ohio Company, 7
Ohio military units
  39th Ohio, 36
  53d Ohio, 51
  Cincinnati Harrison Guards, 19
Ohio River, 46
"Old Black Hawk." *See* Streeter, Zimri
"Old Bunk," 155
Oostanaula River, 119, 122
Orcutt, Darius, 111
Ord, Edward, 63
Osterhaus, Peter J., 107, 108, 111
Overman, Dempsey, 4, 9, 13, 16, 88, 155
Overman, John, 4, 6, 9, 13, 104, 155
Overman Block, 6
Overman Building, 6, 10, 16, 17, 19, 20,
  106, 116, 117, 154
Overman Hall, 17, 21, 22, 68, 155
Overman Mill, 4
Overman Park, 125

Palmer, William H., 127
Paris, Missouri, 34
Parmeter, John, 123
Payton, William, 131
Peace Democracts, 43, 66, 67, 92, 105,
  138
Peachtree Creek, 128, 130
Pea Ridge, Arkansas, 47, 51, 68, 69, 104
Pemberton, John C., 95, 96, 98, 99,
  100, 101
Peninsular Campaign, 63
Pennsylvania, 103
Perkins, George, 7, 8, 11, 15, 18, 21,
  42, 67, 69, 86, 94, 104, 125, 154,
  155, 156, 164
Perkins, Henry, 8, 11, 15, 18, 21, 42,
  43, 66, 67, 68, 91, 93, 94, 106, 113,
  125, 136, 138, 154, 156, 158, 164
Perry, Harlow, 123
Perryville, Kentucky, 62
Philpot, Charles P., 136, 138
Philpot, George, 7, 138, 139

Philpot, George, Jr., 138
Philpot, John, 138
Pine Knob, 126
Pine Mountain, 123
Pineville, North Carolina, 156
Pioneer Greys, 19, 20, 21, 22, 23, 24,
  25, 26, 28, 29, 30, 35, 37, 38, 39,
  40, 42, 43, 47, 49, 50, 51, 53, 54,
  56, 58, 60, 61, 62, 64, 68, 69, 96,
  98, 99, 101, 102, 103, 107, 114, 115,
  116, 117, 118, 126, 127, 130, 131,
  136, 137, 138, 139, 140, 143, 148,
  149, 152, 156, 161, 163, 166
Pittsburg Landing, Tennessee. *See* Shiloh
  Church, Tennessee
Pleasant Hill, Louisiana, 118
Pope, John, 34, 35, 36, 60, 61, 63
Porter, David, 84, 88, 89
Port Gibson, Mississippi, 95, 98
Port Hudson, Louisiana, 79, 100
Port Royal Sound, 147
Powers, Jennie, 9, 40
Powers, Joseph B., 9, 10, 70, 165
Prentice, Benjamin, 50, 53, 54, 56, 58,
  59, 62
Price, Sterling, 36, 61, 62
Prouty, Wellington M., 123, 132, 150
Pugh, Isaac C., 54, 64, 101
Pulver, Gilbert, 59

Quincy, Illinois, 38, 47, 49

Raccoon Mountain, 108
Race Bridge, 9, 22, 44, 116
Radical Republicans, 43
"Raider," (pen name), 161, 162
Raleigh, North Carolina, 153, 156, 159
Rambach, Michael, 59
Rath, George, 8, 70, 111
Rath, John, 8, 69, 70, 85, 110, 111, 122,
  147, 151, 159
Rath Pork Packing Plant, 164
Raymond, Iowa, 163
Raymond, Mississippi, 85, 95, 98
Red River, 116, 117, 118
Relief Society, 86, 87
Republican Club, 15, 16
Resaca, Georgia, 120, 122, 123, 134
Richardson, James, 84
Richmond, Virginia, 63, 103, 118, 124,

Richmond, Virginia, (*continued*) 128, 145, 153, 160
Rider, Van Ransalaer, 59
River Queen, 153
Rocky Face, 119, 120
"Root Hog or Die," 110
Rosecrans, William, 106, 107
Rosen, Henry, 131, 136
Ross, Joseph, 59
Rossville, Tennessee, 110
Rossville Gap, 108
Rosswell Road, 111
Rothemal, George, 131
Rownd, Ann Lawvey, 7
Rownd, Caroline Brown, 7, 104
Rownd, Charles, 90
Rownd, Eliza, 7
Rownd, George, 39, 69, 80, 81, 90, 104
Rownd, James Q., 7, 8, 39, 69, 104
Rownd, John, 69, 80, 81
Rownd, Samuel, 7, 8, 44, 69
Rownd, Samuel, Jr., 69
Roy, Rob, 21

S. B. Muscatine, 163
"St. Charles," 62, 96, 99
St. John, O.O., 113
St. Louis, Missouri, 27, 35, 49, 71, 80, 96
Salisbury, Thomas, 20, 21, 69, 111, 137
Saluda River, 149, 150
Savannah, Georgia, 135, 137, 141, 143, 144, 145, 148, 162
Savannah, Tennessee, 50, 52, 58
Savannah River, 141, 147, 148
Schofield, John M., 126, 127, 132, 145, 149, 152, 153
Scott, John, 29, 30, 34, 36, 37, 38, 69, 70, 118
Secord, George, 10
Seick, F., 136
Sessions, Daniel, 69
Sessions, Elmira, 8, 40
Sessions, Fitzroy, 8, 15, 16, 19, 22, 23, 30, 32, 37, 40, 49, 53, 54, 57, 64, 65, 66, 93, 94, 104, 106, 116, 124, 125
Sessions, William, 7, 8, 10, 15, 16, 21, 43, 68, 69, 104, 138
Sharpsburg, Maryland, 128, 160
Shelbina, Missouri, 34, 35, 49, 52, 56

Shell Rock River, 3
Sherman, William T., 50, 51,52, 53, 54, 80, 82, 83, 84, 98, 101, 102, 107, 108, 110, 111, 112, 115, 116, 118, 119, 120, 122, 123, 124, 126, 127, 128, 130, 132, 133, 134, 135, 136, 137, 138, 139, 140, 141, 143, 144, 145, 147, 148, 149, 151, 152, 153, 155, 156, 157, 158, 159, 160, 161
Shields, Edward, 116, 136, 149
Shiloh Church, Tennessee, 49, 50, 51, 52, 56, 58, 59, 60, 61, 62, 64, 65, 79, 85, 100, 104, 105, 116, 152
Sioux City, Iowa, 164
Sioux City Journal, 164
Sister's Ferry, Georgia, 148
6th Iowa Congressional District, 64, 68, 125, 137
Slocum, Henry W., 137, 147, 153
Smelser, Ephraim, 148
Smith, John B., 18, 19, 20, 22, 25, 29, 30, 37, 41, 49, 53, 57, 68, 96
Smith, John T., 130
Smyth, William, 71, 81, 122
Snake Creek Gap, Georgia, 119, 120, 123, 134
Soldiers' Aid Society, 40, 87, 88
Sons of '76, 92
South Carolina, 145, 147, 148, 149, 151
Speer, Robert P., 69, 70, 82, 91, 92, 99, 107, 110, 112, 119, 126, 127, 166
Spotsylvania, Virginia, 160
Springfield, Illinois, 158
Springfield, Missouri, 36
Springfield musket, 26, 49, 53
Springfield rifle, 118, 131, 140, 144, 148
Stanton, Edwin M., 107, 153, 154, 159, 160
Steele, Frederick, 80
Stimming, Theodore, 69, 70, 81, 122
Stitler, Dave, 17
Stone, William, 29, 37, 49, 53, 54, 57, 58, 105, 106, 115, 139, 151
Streeter, Lucinda Dean, 7
Streeter, Zimri ("Old Black Hawk"), 6, 7, 15, 16, 22, 68, 116, 125, 139, 143, 155
Sturgis, Dorothy Kidder, 3
Sturgis, Samuel D., 36
Sturgis, William, 3, 4, 166
Sturgis Falls. *See* Cedar Falls
Sucker State (steamship), 71

Taggart, Samuel, 59
"Tater Patch" (pen name), 88
Taylor, Byron E., 38
Taylor, William A., 131
Taylor's Ridge, 120
Tennessee, 11, 33, 46
Tennessee military unit: 59th Tennessee, 100
Tennessee River, 46, 49, 50, 51, 52
Texas, 117, 118
Texas military unit: 24th Texas Cavalry (dismounted), 131
Thayer, Edward, 137
Thomas, George ("Rock of Chickamauga"), 106, 107, 110, 119, 120, 128, 136, 143, 145
Thyne, Francis, 102
Tigress, 52
Tirrell, John, 123
Townsend, Edward, 69
Tracy, Myron L., 148
Troutner, John F., 102
Trumbull, Matthew M., 22, 23, 25, 37, 57, 58, 62, 93, 112
Tunnel Hill, 108, 110
Tuttle, James M., 105, 106, 138
Tyrell, Francis, 59

"Udonoho" (pen name), 28, 32, 35, 49
Union Committee of Public Safety, 27
Union League of Cedar Falls, 93, 94, 95
Union Leagues, 93, 104
U.S. Army Nursing Corps, 42
U.S. Sanitary Commission, 40, 42, 125
U.S. War Department, 27
University of Northern Iowa, 165
U.S.S. *Pontiac,* 147
Utica, Missouri, 29

Van Buren County, 165
Vandever, William, 18, 19, 39, 40
Van Dorne, Earl, 58, 60, 61, 82
Van Saun, G.B., 10
Vicksburg, Mississippi, 61, 72, 79, 80, 82, 83, 84, 85, 87, 88, 89, 91, 95, 96, 98, 99, 100, 101, 102, 103, 104, 105, 107, 116, 122, 124, 132
Vining's Station, Georgia, 128
Vinton, Iowa, 16
Virginia, 46, 63, 120, 159, 160

Walkup, George, 95
Walkup, Thomas, 68, 106, 125
Wallace, Lew, 50, 53
Wallace, William H., 50, 53
War Democrats, 43, 92, 105
War Department of Iowa, 63
War of 1812, 22, 125
Waterbury, 87
Waterloo, Iowa, 6, 7, 8, 22, 23, 40, 43, 71, 93, 113, 164, 166
Waterloo Courier, 44
Waterloo Republican Club, 16
Watson, George, 59
Watson, James, 123
Waverly, Iowa, 20, 22, 154
Wayne, John, 59, 104, 106, 112
Wells, Erastus, 86
West, Cyrus, 33
Western and Atlantic Railroad, 119
Western Sanitary Commission, 40
West Point, 29, 30, 33, 34, 46, 61
West Union, Iowa, 92
Wheeler, Joseph, 134, 135, 148
Whig Party, 13, 15
Wilder, W., 136
Wilderness, 120
William Jewel College, 38
Williams, Henry E., 132
Williams, Nelson G., 29, 30, 35, 49, 52, 53, 54, 58, 65, 70
Williamson, James A., 107
Willoughby, Iowa, 16
Wilmington, North Carolina, 145, 149
Wilson's Creek, Missouri, 36, 51, 69
Wisconsin, 115
Wisconsin Territory, 3
Wittenmyer, Annie, 40, 88
Wood, Walter W., 38
Woods, Charles R., 149, 152, 156
Woodsville, Alabama, 119
Woolcott, Norman, 59

Yazoo River, 82
Young's Point, Mississippi, 84, 85
Young Womens' Soldiers' Aid Society, 41, 87